Bush II, Obama, and Decline of U.S. Hegemony in the Western Hemisphere

MW00816692

Bush II, Obama, and the Decline of U.S. Hegemony in the Western Hemisphere applies competing definitions and conceptions of hegemony to various foreign policy initiatives and events during the administrations of George W. Bush and Barack H. Obama to test whether they manifest a decline in traditional United States dominance and leadership in the Western Hemisphere. In particular, the book examines the continued relevancy of the inter-American system, the failure to establish a Free Trade Area of the Americas (FTAA), and the stillborn Energy and Climate Partnership of the Americas (ECPA). It also discusses the implications of the People's Republic of China becoming a major trading partner and important source of financing and investment capital throughout Latin America and the Caribbean. The book provides critical reviews of Plan Colombia, the Mérida Initiative, Pathways to Prosperity in the Americas, the Central American Regional Security Initiative (CARSI), the Caribbean Basin Security Initiative (CBSI), *100,000 Strong in the Americas*, and the restoration of normal U.S. diplomatic relations with Cuba. There are extensive analyses, unusual for a work in English, of the *Alianza Bolivariana para los Pueblos de Nuestra América* (ALBA), *Comunidad de Estados Latinoamericanos y Caribeños* (CELAC), and *Unión de Naciones Suramericanas* (UNASUR).

Thomas Andrew O'Keefe has been the President of Mercosur Consulting Group, Ltd. since 1993 and currently teaches at Stanford University. A dual U.S.–Chilean national, he has degrees from Columbia University, Villanova University's School of Law, and the University of Oxford. The author of numerous books and articles on Latin America and the Caribbean, he chaired the Western Hemisphere Area Studies program at the U.S. State Department's Foreign Service Institute between 2011 and 2016.

Bush II, Obama, and the Decline of U.S. Hegemony in the Western Hemisphere

Thomas Andrew O'Keefe

Routledge
Taylor & Francis Group

NEW YORK AND LONDON

First published 2018
by Routledge
711 Third Avenue, New York, NY 10017

and by Routledge
2 Park Square, Milton Park, Abingdon, Oxon, OX14 4RN

Routledge is an imprint of the Taylor & Francis Group, an informa business

© 2018 Taylor & Francis

Library of Congress Cataloging-in-Publication Data
Names: O'Keefe, Thomas Andrew, 1961- author.
Title: Bush II, Obama, and the decline of U.S. hegemony in the Western
Hemisphere / Thomas Andrew O'Keefe.
Description: New York, NY: Routledge, 2018. | Includes bibliographical
references and index.
Identifiers: LCCN 2017044286 | ISBN 9781138080850 (hbk) |
ISBN 9781138080867 (pbk) | ISBN 9781351624299 (epub) |
ISBN 9781351624282 (mobipocket/kindle) | ISBN 9781315113197 (ebk)
Subjects: LCSH: United States–Foreign relations–Latin America. |
Latin America–Foreign relations–United States. | United States–
Foreign relations–Caribbean Area. | Caribbean Area–Foreign relations–
United States. | United States–Foreign relations–Canada. | Canada–Foreign
relations–United States. | Free Trade Area of the Americas (Organization) |
Energy and Climate Partnership of the Americas (Organization) |
United States–Foreign relations–2001–2009. | United States–Foreign
relations–2009–2017.
Classification: LCC F1418.O39 2018 | DDC 327.7308–dc23
LC record available at https://lccn.loc.gov/20170442

ISBN: 978-1-138-08085-0 (hbk)
ISBN: 978-1-138-08086-7 (pbk)
ISBN: 978-1-315-11319-7 (ebk)

Typeset in Times New Roman
by Sunrise Setting Ltd, Brixham, UK

In memory of my father Thomas Augustus O'Keefe (1933–2000) and my mother Rosa Maria Valenzuela Ferrari (1929–2010).

Contents

Acknowledgments

I deeply appreciate the encouragement that my colleagues and friends Annette Hester, Robin King, Barbara Kotschwar, and Carol Wise have extended to me over the years in our mutual quest to create a more economically integrated Western Hemisphere rooted in equity, as well as the intellectual support of decades from Cathy Schneider in deepening my understanding of Latin American politics. I am indebted to Jane Kamide as well, whose retirement offered me the opportunity to get an inside view of how U.S. foreign policy is formulated and implemented while serving as Chair of the Western Hemisphere Area Studies program at the U.S. State Department's Foreign Service Institute between 2011 and 2016. I am also grateful to Stanford University and the trust it has put in me since 2007 to educate its students, and the access it gave me to its rich archival and book collections as well as its data banks and electronic resources, which facilitated writing this book. I especially want to thank the following Stanford University faculty and staff: Rodolfo Dirzo, Herbert Klein, Ivan Jaksic, Adrienne Jamieson, Julie Kennedy, Lynn Orr, Ken Schultz, Stephen Stedman, Megan Gorman, and Elizabeth Sáenz-Ackermann. Finally, I would be remiss if I did not acknowledge the anonymous reviewer at the Middle Atlantic Council of Latin American Studies (MACLAS) journal, *Latin American Essays*, who faulted an article I had submitted for publication some years ago for not including a discussion of the different theories of hegemony. Although this omission did not prevent the article from being published, it did serve as the catalyst for me to eventually write this book to remedy that oversight.

1 What Is Hegemony and When Has the United States of America Been a Hegemon?

Introduction

The genesis for this book is the flurry of discussions in the media and academic circles on the purported decline of U.S. hegemony in the Western Hemisphere that coincided with the start of the twenty-first century. These assertions blossomed following the September 2001 terrorist attacks in the United States, as the administration of George W. Bush concentrated its attention on eliminating Al Qaeda and other extremist Islamist cells in Afghanistan, the Middle East, and Somalia. There was a widespread sentiment that because of this new focus, the United States was "ignoring" Latin America and the Caribbean. This period also coincided with the election of leftist governments in many Latin American countries that frequently adopted policy positions that were blatantly hostile to the agenda long promoted by Washington, DC. Unlike the response that might have been seen in the past, the United States now seemed to acquiesce to the new status quo in the Americas. This book tests the thesis of whether there has indeed been a decline in the hegemony traditionally exercised by the United States in the Western Hemisphere since at least the end of the nineteenth century.

At the outset, it is important to underscore that this book is about hegemony and not about power *per se*. Although the United States emerged as the sole superpower after the end of the Cold War, with cumulative economic, military, and other capabilities, preponderant capabilities across the board do not guarantee effective influence in any given arena.[1] For one thing, American dominance in the international security arena no longer translates into effective leverage in the international economic arena, as the United States faces rising economic challengers with their own agendas and with greater discretion in international economic policy.[2] Accordingly, this book focuses on those international relations theories where the concept of hegemony is a key component for explaining United States foreign policy and actions. It also addresses the conception of hegemony as developed by the Italian sociologist and neo-Marxist Antonio Gramsci. Furthermore, this book does not attempt to wade into the lively debate within the international relations field over which conception of hegemony is more valid, or to propose yet another theory of international relations, for that matter. Instead, its goal is less ambitious. It utilizes existing definitions and notions of hegemony to answer the question of whether its exercise by the United States in Latin America and the Caribbean objectively declined under the administrations of George W. Bush and Barack H. Obama.

It is also important to emphasize the distinction between imperialism and hegemony. The fact that both terms are often used interchangeably to describe the United States' behavior in the Western Hemisphere leads to much confusion, even in academic circles. Although the precise definition of imperialism may be as contested as that of hegemony, imperialism reflects a geopolitical arrangement whereby one state extends its dominion—frequently through use of force—over populations beyond its borders that are culturally and ethnically distinct from its own.[3] While an imperial power attempts to control both the internal and external affairs of a client state, a hegemon respects a subaltern's domestic sovereignty but impinges on its autonomy to conduct an independent foreign policy.[4] Without a doubt, the forcible annexation of the Kingdom of Hawaii in 1898 against the clear wishes of its monarch and of the overwhelming majority of its indigenous population provides an egregious example of U.S. imperialism. A similar case can be made for the U.S. annexation of Puerto Rico and the Philippines, where, following the defeat of Spanish forces in 1898, the U.S. refused to recognize, and in the Filipino case ruthlessly crushed, a vibrant independence movement. On the other hand, labeling as imperialistic the U.S. invasions and subsequent occupations of Haiti, the Dominican Republic, and Nicaragua in the earlier part of the twentieth century would be debatable, given that there was never an expressed intention by U.S. government officials to hold on to these countries indefinitely. In fact, the delays in restoring sovereignty often came about because U.S. efforts to implement "reforms" and make a hasty exit were complicated by the fierce armed resistance to American occupation that arose.

This work utilizes four case studies to test whether there has indeed been a decline in U.S. hegemony in the Western Hemisphere since the January 2001 inauguration of George W. Bush. These include the inter-American system centered on the Organization of American States, the Free Trade Area of the Americas, the Energy and Climate Partnership of the Americas, and the expanding role of China as a major trade and investment rival to the United States in Latin America and the Caribbean. In addition, the book also examines other illustrative foreign policy initiatives under Bush and Obama to support or debunk the notion that there has been a decline in U.S. hegemony. In particular, the book examines: (1) Plan Colombia; (2) the Mérida Initiative; (3) the Central American Regional Security Initiative (including the subsequent Alliance for Prosperity of the Northern Triangle of Central America); (4) the Caribbean Basin Security Initiative; (5) Pathways to Prosperity; (6) *100,000 Strong in the Americas*; and (7) the re-establishment of normal diplomatic relations between the United States and Cuba.

The Theoretical Underpinnings of Hegemony

Though the concept may be traced all the way back to ancient Greece, the term "hegemony" first emerged as a conceptual and theoretical tool in the mid-twentieth century as a consequence of the dissemination of the work of Italian revolutionary and neo-Marxist sociologist Antonio Gramsci.[5] In ancient Greece, the term "hegemon" meant the leader of a voluntary military alliance of various city-states, either permanent or temporary, created in order to respond to a particular military threat. This description evokes an interstate system wherein a given state exercises power and leadership over an alliance of reciprocally consenting states.[6] In practice, however, the Greeks also recognized that such an alliance could lead to a situation in which a state attained preeminent military and political leadership and thereby transformed itself into an imperial power.[7] The Ancient Greeks also associated the concept of hegemony with the notion of a guiding or governing principle or idea.[8] Accordingly, Athens—as the generator and organizer of moral, intellectual, cultural, and educational ideas—was viewed as the logical and natural hegemonic leader of all ancient Greece.[9]

In current international relations theory and analysis, while the concept of hegemony lacks settled definition, its terms of debate have revolved largely around two principal meanings: domination and leadership.[10] Domination refers to the dominance of one state over others, or a nation's standing within a hierarchical order of great powers, and is usually measured by the aggregate resources possessed by a single actor across a wide range of material capabilities—including military and economic—as well as the degree of concentration of these resources in terms of their international distribution.[11] By contrast, leadership derives from the capabilities underlying the claim or from what others see in the hegemon in terms of perceived attributes.[12]

Classical realism is based on the simple assumption that states are led by human beings who have a "will to power" hardwired into them at birth.[13] John Mearsheimer, who labels himself an "offensive realist," believes that the international system forces great powers to maximize their relative power because that is the optimal way to maximize their survival.[14] Mearsheimer admits that such an outlook leads to a gloomy assessment of international relations because no state is likely to achieve global hegemony, and therefore the world is condemned to perpetual great-power competition.[15]

Realism is based on three key assumptions:

(1) the most important actors in world politics are territorially organized entities (i.e., states);
(2) state behavior can be explained rationally (i.e., states are guided by the logic of the "national interest") and is influenced mainly by their external characteristics;
(3) states seek power and calculate their interests in terms of protecting, if not maximizing, power, relative to the nature of the international system they face: anarchy.[16]

The central aspects of the international system, which in turn cause states to fear one another, are the absence of a central authority that sits above states and can protect them from each other, the fact that states always have some offensive military capability, and the fact that states can never be certain about other states' intentions.[17]

Realism argues that the key interest of states is not individual well-being: rather, it is survival.[18] Accordingly, the overriding goal of each state is to maximize its share of world power, which means gaining power at the expense of other states, and thereby to achieve hegemony and become the only great power in the system.[19] Power, traditionally understood as resources or capabilities, has been used as an indicator for the strength of actors, and consequently the capacity to affect or control outcomes.[20] Even though a realist such as Mearsheimer would acknowledge that states, on occasion, may cooperate with each other, at root they have conflicting interests.[21]

Realism, or *realpolitik*, dominated U.S. foreign policy during World War II and the Cold War. It is most associated with exponents such as John H. Herz, George F. Kennan, Walter Lippmann, Hans J. Morgenthau, and Henry Kissinger. Following the end of the Cold War, realism lost credibility due to its inability to explain and predict international developments such as the demise of the Soviet Union and the subsequent wave of democratization and adoption of market-based economic policies that swept the planet.

Kenneth Waltz is a neo-realist who focused on the structure of the international system and the balance of power in order to get around realism's limitations in explaining why states are not in a position of constant warfare as each tries to protect or maximize power. Neo-realists, rather than viewing power as an end in itself, see it as a useful means for achieving their ultimate concern: security.[22] Security "is understood as one state's position relative to other states' positions, and as being a function of one state's aggregate capabilities *vis-à-vis* others."[23] For Waltz, understanding the structure of an international system facilitates explaining patterns of behavior, since states determine their interests and strategies based on calculations about their own positions in the system.[24] "Structure is invisible, a purely theoretical construction" and "has to do with the fundamental organization of the system: anarchy or hierarchy and the distribution of capabilities across the units."[25]

Similar to realists, neo-realists reduce hegemony to the single dimension of dominance.[26] While neo-realists incorporate the realist concept of an anarchic world, they believe states behave defensively in response to that reality to maintain rather than upset the balance of power, so that preserving power, rather than increasing it, is the main goal of states.[27] Accordingly, neo-realists accept that states will enter into alliances or mutual defense pacts directed against a serious and imminent threat to their security. For neo-realists, a concentration of power is unnatural and any imbalance of power will, at some point, inevitably be restored.[28] Accordingly, while neo-realism may have become irrelevant for explaining the unipolar world that emerged following the collapse of the Soviet Union in 1989, Waltz was confident this phenomenon would not last long—hegemony, he said, inevitably leads to balance, as "the response of other countries to one among them seeking or gaining preponderant power is to balance against it."[29]

Dissatisfaction with realist and neo-realist explanations led to other theories that, while retaining the realist core notion of states operating in an anarchic world, provided new conceptions of hegemony. The most influential of these was hegemonic stability theory, or HST. HST was premised on two major propositions: (1) order in world politics is typically created by a single dominant power or hegemon; (2) the maintenance of that order requires continued hegemony.[30] For proponents of HST, hegemony is defined as a situation in which one state is powerful enough to maintain the essential rules governing interstate relations, and is willing to do so because it disproportionately benefits from such an international order.[31] The essential role of the hegemon is to assume the costs of providing certain key public goods that establish and maintain international order in a system in which other actors lack either the resources or capabilities to do so.[32] "[S]uch public goods may include stability, openness, property rights, monitoring and other transaction costs, establishing and enforcing rules for free trade, providing and underpinning a stable international currency regime, promoting the overall economic growth of the system, crisis prevention and the like."[33]

Robert Gilpin, a major proponent of HST from a political economy perspective, acknowledged that while a hegemon may have created a liberal international economy, for example, primarily to promote its own interests as well as political and security interests, it also had to entice, if not overtly coerce, other states to obey the rules and regimes governing international economic activities.[34] Ideally,

> a genuinely hegemonic actor, in pursuing its own interests, should be rationally led to pursue the interests of the system as a whole, or else the hegemon turns in on itself and becomes not only systemically destructive but also self-destructive—to the extent that its own self-interests are bound up in the maintenance of the wider system.[35]

Liberals challenge realism's underlying pessimistic premise that the world is doomed to see endless battles for dominance and supremacy among states. Instead, liberals envisage alternatives to power politics based on conceptions of harmony of interest or of morality.[36] At the risk of oversimplification, liberals— or an idealist subset, in any event—embrace a world-view based, *inter alia*, on the belief that human nature is essentially altruistic. People are, therefore, capable of mutual aid and collaboration, and the outbreak of war can be avoided by eradicating the anarchic conditions that encourage it, through collective or multilateral action.[37] Liberals regard individual human beings as the primary international actors. Although liberals may view states as the most important collective actors in our present era, states consist of pluralistic actors whose interests and policies are determined by bargaining among groups and elections.[38] In addition, liberals view the interests of states as multiple and changing, and both self-interested and other-regarding.[39]

Liberal internationalists have shared the view that institutions and rules established between states facilitate and reinforce cooperation and collective problem solving.[40] One strand of liberal international theory—republican liberalism—argues that republics are more peacefully inclined than despotisms, as leaders are answerable to an electorate and, therefore, less likely to resort to war; another—commercial liberalism—argues that commerce leads necessarily to peace, as war can be very disruptive of trade and bad for business.[41] Given that autonomy is a core liberal value, and democracy is the form of government that (to date, at least) best allows people to develop their individual capacities, liberals view the universal adoption of representative democracy as a primordial end goal.[42]

International liberalism, particularly in its early twentieth-century form, implied juridical equality among states.[43] In its purest, classical guise, the liberal tradition also stands for non-interventionism.[44] Accordingly, many variants of liberal international relations theory consider the notion of hegemony as anathema to the ideal international order.[45] Liberals tend to assume that powerful states will act with restraint in the exercise of their power and find ways to credibly convey commitments to other states.[46] Liberals who do accept the existence of a hegemon do so in the context of an institutionalized practice of leadership legitimated by the international community, thereby evoking one ancient Greek understanding of hegemony. Under such a conceptualization, the "hegemon is in principle first among equals" and is a power "without whom no final decision on crucial issues can be reached within the system, whose task and responsibility it is to see that necessary decisions are reached."[47] Accordingly, hegemony exists solely to manage and maintain some degree of order and decision-making capacity within a system of dispersed authority, and can be shared and exercised in common through the establishment of partnerships.[48]

International regime theory, or what its main proponent, Robert Keohane, described as "neoliberal institutionalism," appeared after Europe and Japan began challenging the post-World War II political and economic leadership of the United States. "[T]he political purpose of regime theory was, at least in part, to reassure Americans and others that a liberal international order would survive America's economic decline and the severe economic problems of the 1970s."[49] Keohane felt that hegemony alone was insufficient to create a stable international economic order in which cooperation flourished. Instead, Keohane argued that international regimes are a necessary feature of the world economy and are required to facilitate efficient operation of the international economy.[50] Regimes are defined by explicit rules usually agreed to by governments at international conferences and often associated with formal international organizations, such as the rules governing international commerce set by the World Trade Organization.[51] Keohane acknowledged that a particular regime may have initially been created because of the pressures of a self-centered hegemon, and that hegemonic powers have capabilities to maintain international regimes they favor, utilizing coercion to enforce adherence to rules.[52] However, the most important point for Keohane is that an effective international regime takes on a life of its own over time, and, when states experience the success of an international regime, they learn to change their own behavior and even to redefine their national interests.[53] Keohane largely restricted his view to economic hegemony and invoked military power as germane only insofar as it is necessary to prevent others from denying the hegemon access to major areas in which it is economically active.[54] In a tacit acknowledgment of Gramsci, Keohane accepted the value of ideology for the continuance of international political economic regimes.[55]

Class struggle lies at the heart of Marxist interpretations of world politics. Adherents of Gramsci would argue that hegemony is a relation of domination by a social class not through force, but rather by its exercise of political and ideological leadership that obtains the consent of subaltern classes.[56] In particular, hegemony refers to the ability of a dominant class to exercise power by winning the consent of those it subjugates, as an alternative to the use of coercion.[57] "In a hegemonic order, the dominant power makes certain concessions or compromises to secure the acquisition of lesser powers to an order that can be expressed in terms of general interest."[58] To build the basis of an alternative state and society upon the leadership of the working class, it was necessary to establish a counter-hegemony within an established bourgeois hegemony, while resisting the pressures and temptations to relapse into pursuit of incremental gains for subaltern groups.[59] Although Gramsci used the concept of hegemony to analyze the relation of forces within a given society, many international relations scholars have extrapolated and applied his analysis to the international context.

Although many Marxists downplay the role of the nation-state, they share with realists the view that power is crucial and world systems are dominated by hegemonic powers wielding both economic and military resources.[60] In the international context, hegemony rests on the subjective awareness by elites in secondary states that they are benefiting from the status quo, as well as on the willingness of the hegemon to sacrifice tangible short-term benefits for intangible long-term gains.[61] Ideology is key to facilitating hegemony globally, just as it is at the national level. "[I]n Gramsci, the strength of ideology does not lie so much in the obscuring of truth (although that element is still present) but is located in the capacity of a set of ideas and consciousness to tie together divergent interests into a singular hegemonic interpretative horizon."[62] In the Gramscian tradition, hegemony is not "American" *per se*, but is rather the domination of a transnational capitalist class—even if currently rooted in the agency of the U.S. government and/or American elites—that, through inclusive strategies, enables cross-class coalition building and incorporates subaltern groups into the dominant consensus.[63]

Robert Cox's contribution to the development of a neo-Gramscian theory of international relations is his emphasis on the role of international institutions in sustaining hegemony. "International institutions and rules are generally initiated by the state which establishes the hegemony" and "help define policy guidelines for states" as well as "reflect orientations favorable to the dominant social and economic forces."[64] "[I]n the same way state and civil society organizations within national social formations may diffuse certain ideological values and notions, international institutions propagate certain conceptions as to what is legitimate and acceptable in a way that is consistent with the interests of the hegemonic state" and in a manner that "can be flexible and adapt to incorporate subordinate states into the hegemonic world order."[65]

Variegated Hierarchy

David Lake proposes that a system of variegated hierarchy describes the traditional position of the United States in the Western Hemisphere more accurately than the concept of hegemony. According to Lake, international relations is better explained by acknowledging the existence of relations based on dominant and voluntarily subordinate nations (i.e., hierarchy) rather than unrealistic notions of indivisible and equal sovereign states, each surviving in an anarchic world as best they can. He notes that throughout much of the twentieth century, the United States has been at the apex of an international economic and security pyramid that has encompassed many states in Latin America and the Caribbean. For Lake, hierarchy is premised on the level of authority—a form of power—exercised by a dominant nation over subordinate countries. A dominant nation's authority to command is conferred by subordinate countries who strategically give up some of their sovereignty in exchange for the provision of public goods such as security or economic stability. A dominant nation can lose its authority, and therefore its legitimacy, if it acts opportunistically by failing to adhere to its own rules and exploits subordinate nations.[66] On the other hand, "nothing in a relational conception of authority implies that hierarchy is 'fair' or equitable or that fairness is a requirement for legitimacy."[67] All that is required is that the subordinate nations be marginally better off under hierarchy than in the anarchic state of nature they would otherwise inhabit.[68] "Under hierarchy, political struggle shifts from raw interests to debates over rules and rights, which in turn embody or reflect questions of interests."[69] International hierarchy rejects the notion of pure coercion on the part of the dominant power derived from differences in material capabilities to get subalterns to comply. When subordinates transgress against the agreed-upon rules, however, dominant states can impose discipline.

The United States of America as a "Global" Hegemon

By the latter part of the nineteenth century, the United States (along with Germany) was challenging the industrial might of Great Britain and contesting its domination of global markets. At same time, the United States began asserting its hegemony over Latin America, which leading expansionists saw as confirmation that the United States was becoming a world power.[70] When and if the United States actually became a global hegemon, and how long that hegemony persisted, is the subject of much debate among the different schools of international relations theory. Many adherents of unipolarity would argue that the end of the Cold War meant the United States, as the world's sole superpower, became a global hegemon by default. Realists such as John Mearsheimer, on the other hand, point out there has never been a global hegemon, and there is not likely to be one any time soon, except in the unlikely event that one state achieves clear-cut nuclear superiority.[71]

Undoubtedly, one explanation for the difficulty in ascertaining dates for the reign of U.S. hegemony—whether global or more limited in scope—is the conflation of the concepts of primacy and hegemony. "Too often, the United States is described as the current hegemon, when nothing is intended beyond its enjoyment of degrees of material primacy."[72] Accordingly, writers who tally up U.S. military capabilities, extol the role of the U.S. dollar as the global reserve currency of choice, and proclaim U.S. technological prowess and innovation that has allowed it to concentrate much of the world's wealth are really focused on U.S. primacy.[73] This distinction is significant because, as Stephen Walt emphasizes, primacy falls well short of global hegemony, which means that major powers must continue to worry about security issues and take steps to guarantee it, either alone or in concert with others.[74]

Realists (including neo-realists) and adherents of hegemonic stability theory claim that the United States began exercising global hegemony—at least outside the Communist bloc of nations—in the years after World War II.[75] For Robert Gilpin, an adherent of hegemonic stability theory, the dollar's key role in the international monetary system held the post-World War II American alliance system and the world economy together, and became a cornerstone of the global economic and political position of the United States. The latter gave the U.S. hegemonic capacity to finance its fiscal and external deficits and made it possible to continue its hegemonic military role.[76] Moreover, the U.S. was willing to make sacrifices consistent with a hegemonic role, including toleration of European and Japanese protectionism, which was deemed crucial for European and Japanese recovery after the devastation of World War II.[77] G. John Ikenberry argues that the United States gradually became the hegemonic organizer and manager of a Western liberal order built around multilateralism, alliance partnership, strategic restraint, cooperative security, and institutionalized and rule-based relationships.[78]

How long U.S. "global" hegemony lasted, if indeed it has ended, is a matter of contention among international relations theorists. Realists are more likely to argue that the United States remains a hegemon, even if that hegemony is not global in scope and there are increasing signals that its days are numbered. Advocates of unipolarity, many of whom (but not all) are realists, also argue about the increasingly uncertain future of U.S. global hegemony.[79] Adherents of hegemonic stability theory and international regime theory would point to

the 1971 collapse of the Bretton Woods arrangement, after the Nixon administration decided to take the United States off the gold standard, as the beginning
of the decline of U.S. hegemony.[80] Among those liberals that even acknowledge
the existence of a hegemon, global hegemony by the United States entered into
a period of decline with the Bush administration's decision to bypass the United
Nations Security Council, having been unable to secure a simple nine-vote
majority, and unilaterally invade Iraq in 2003.[81] Furthermore, the international
financial turmoil of 2008–9 discredited the American model of capitalism and
diminished the weight of the United States in the global economy in favor of
East Asia. In addition, the United States is increasingly isolated from those
very institutions, such as the UN and the World Trade Organization, which it
spawned to support its vision of an international liberal order, thereby deinsti-
tutionalizing its own hegemony.[82]

Gramsci's conception of hegemony, which is not linked to a particular
nation-state but instead to transnational elites, provides the strongest support
for arguing that the hegemony of sociopolitical and economic ideology long
espoused by the United States remains intact. In that sense, globalization
encapsulates the global hegemonic power wielded by the planet's economic elites
irrespective of nationality.[83] This is evident even in countries such as China and
Russia, where, despite continuing challenges to U.S. unipolarity and promotion
of representative democracy, both countries remain firmly in the capitalist fold.

The United States of America as a Regional Hegemon

While different schools of international relations theory may offer conflicting
interpretations as to whether the United States of America was and remains a
global hegemon, there is widespread consensus regarding its role as hegemon in
the Western Hemisphere from the latter part of the nineteenth and throughout
the twentieth century. This does not mean that governments as well as domestic
companies, organizations, and individuals throughout Latin America and the
Caribbean were unable to promote their own interests during this time period.
There are examples of Latin American leaders achieving substantial degrees of
autonomy and even influencing U.S. policy at times.[84] One would be that of
Rafael Leonidas Trujillo in the Dominican Republic, who, after ordering a mas-
sacre of thousands of Haitians in 1937 that brought severe condemnation from
the United States, eventually regained Washington, DC's favor by admitting
Jewish refugees fleeing Nazi persecution in Europe and Spanish Republicans
defeated by Franco. He also became a generous contributor to the campaigns of
key U.S. Congressmen. Another example is the October 1971 vote in the UN
General Assembly, when seven countries from Latin America and the Caribbean
(Chile, Cuba, Ecuador, Guyana, Mexico, Peru, and Trinidad and Tobago) defied
the United States and voted to give China's seat in the UN to the Communists in
Beijing over the Kuomintang Party government based in Taiwan. Overall,
though, the United States remained the dominant presence in the Americas, its
cultural, economic, military, and political influence pervasive. Rarely was U.S.

leadership directly challenged. When it was, the consequences could be dire and the alternative inevitably proved to be unsustainable and short-lived. The one notable exception was Cuba, which managed to escape from the American fold and successfully establish a counter-hegemonic narrative.

According to the realist John Mearsheimer, American foreign policy in the nineteenth century had one overarching goal: achieving hegemony in the Western Hemisphere. The United States established this regional hegemony by relentlessly pursuing two closely linked policies: (1) expanding across North America and building the most powerful state in the Western Hemisphere through a policy of "Manifest Destiny"; (2) minimizing the influence of the United Kingdom and the other great powers in the Americas through rigid enforcement of the Monroe Doctrine.[85] Manifest Destiny was an ideology based on an assumption that the society and political system of the United States were exceptional and uniquely virtuous compared to others, that its Anglo-Saxon racial stock was naturally superior to other ethnic groups, and that it was divinely predestined to increase its stature, prestige, and territory.[86] For its part, the Monroe Doctrine was a declaration made in 1823 by President James Monroe, during an annual address to Congress, that those nations in the Western Hemisphere that had already achieved independence were now off-limits for future European colonization. Furthermore, the United States would view any recolonization effort as a threat to its own security.

The first successful example of the United States exercising its hegemony in the Americas came in 1895, under the guise of enforcing the Monroe Doctrine. The United States intervened in a long-simmering dispute between Venezuela and the United Kingdom over the demarcation of the western border of British Guiana. The administration of Grover Cleveland convinced London to submit the matter to binding arbitration. There were two important repercussions from this intervention: the end of a regular British naval presence in South America, and the decision by London to forgo long-standing plans to build a canal across the Central American isthmus. In this way, London effectively recognized that the Western Hemisphere lay within the U.S. sphere of influence. Oft-cited explanations for why the British acquiesced to this new reality included the impressive size of the U.S. naval fleet by the end of the nineteenth century and the need to ensure the Americans remained neutral in the event of any war in Europe with another rising naval power, Germany.

At the conclusion of the Spanish–American War of 1898, the United States acquired Puerto Rico, and Cuba became a U.S. protectorate under military occupation. Although Cuba eventually achieved its independence in 1902, the Platt Amendment gave the United States the right to intervene in Cuba in order to preserve the country's independence; protect the lives, property, and individual liberty of its citizens; and make sure Cuba paid debts owed to the Americans.[87] The Platt Amendment also required Cuba to sell or lease territory to the United States for use as coaling or naval stations. This provision served as the legal foundation for the lease Cuba gave the United States for its military base at Guantanamo Bay, which it retains to this day (despite Cuban opposition).

The United States provided support for a rebellion in the Colombian province of Panama in 1903 that led to Panamanian independence. Soon thereafter, U.S. Secretary of State John Hay and Panama's newly minted Ambassador to Washington, DC, a Frenchman by the name of Philippe Bunau-Varilla who had been involved in previous failed projects to build a trans-Panama canal, signed a treaty. The accord gave the United States sovereignty over a ten-mile-wide strip of land, within which to build a canal that the United States would administer in perpetuity. The United States also acquired the right to intervene militarily in Panama to maintain order and defend the canal. Although Panama received some monetary compensation for loss of its territory, it had no right to share in the revenues collected from canal tolls.

In his annual address to Congress in 1904, President Theodore Roosevelt issued his interpretation of the Monroe Doctrine, known as the Roosevelt Corollary. Roosevelt warned that

> chronic wrongdoing, or an impotence which results in a general loosening of the ties of civilized society, may . . . ultimately require intervention by some civilized society, and in the Western Hemisphere the adherence of the United States to the Monroe Doctrine may force the United States . . . to the exercise of an international police power.[88]

If a nation wished to preserve its freedom or independence, it had to act responsibly. If not, the United States would intervene in any Latin American country that proved unable or unwilling to respect the rule of law and violated the rights of the United States or a foreign nation outside the Western Hemisphere. Interestingly, Roosevelt did make a distinction among Latin American nations, explicitly excluding Argentina, Brazil, and Chile from the dictates of the Roosevelt Corollary.[89] In fact, after his presidency, Roosevelt confirmed that he viewed Argentina, Brazil, and Chile as junior partners that could be guarantors of the Monroe Doctrine and enforce the corollary named after him.[90]

The period between 1904 and 1933 is generally associated with putting into practice the Roosevelt Corollary. In what was often denominated "dollar diplomacy," the United States invaded and temporarily occupied countries throughout the Caribbean Basin to enforce loan contracts taken out with U.S.-based banks or European lenders if there was a risk of extra-hemispheric intervention. This period also coincided with a significant expansion of U.S. investment in and trade with Latin America, hence internal political stability became an important consideration as well. The three countries in which the United States intervened for the longest period in an attempt to instill fiscal and political discipline—the Dominican Republic, Haiti, and Nicaragua—are also the countries that suffered from decades of misrule by brutal dictators after the U.S. Marines finally left.

Even before he was elected President of the United States, Franklin Delano Roosevelt had published an article in *Foreign Affairs* magazine in 1928 calling for an end to U.S. intervention in the internal affairs of its southern neighbors and stating that "[i]f order should collapse in any of them, restoration should be the joint task of the several American states."[91] In his inaugural address in March 1933, now-President Roosevelt stated that he would dedicate the United States "to the policy of the Good Neighbor—the neighbor who resolutely respects himself and, because he does so, respects the rights of others—the neighbor who respects his obligations and respects the sanctity of his agreements in and with a world of neighbors."[92] One month later, at a speech before the Pan-American Union, Roosevelt specifically extended the concept of the good neighbor to U.S. relations with Latin America. Abrogation of the Platt Amendment followed (although the United States retained control of the naval base at Guantanamo). In 1936, some of the most egregious provisions in the 1903 Hay–Bunau-Varilla Treaty with Panama were modified, thereby ending the United States' ability to intervene unilaterally in that country's internal affairs. Remarkably, the U.S. government did not make a major issue of the Bolivian nationalization of a U.S. oil company in 1937, nor of the Mexican nationalization of the petroleum sector in 1938.[93]

By 1947, a huge breach had developed among the former World War II allies, with the United States spearheading a new coalition opposed to the Soviet Union's alleged expansionist efforts to establish Communist satellites throughout the world. Reviving the Monroe Doctrine and elements of the Roosevelt Corollary, the United States spent the next 40 or so years of the Cold War undermining democracy and propping up brutal military dictatorships in the name of keeping Communism out of the Western Hemisphere. The only respite came under the one-term, late 1970s administration of President Jimmy Carter, who made respect for human rights a centerpiece of U.S. foreign policy in the Americas. Among the most egregious of the interventions by other leaders was President Dwight D. Eisenhower's authorization for the Central Intelligence Agency (CIA) to work with disgruntled members of the Guatemalan military to overthrow Jacobo Arbenz's reformist government in 1954, based on unfounded allegations that he was a Communist sympathizer. Arbenz's removal from office ushered in decades of civil war and massacres of civilians in Guatemala that reached fever pitch under the dictatorship of General Efraín Ríos Montt in the early 1980s.[94]

One country in the Western Hemisphere that managed to escape the United States' grip was Cuba, following the 1959 revolution that brought Fidel Castro to power. By the early 1960s, in a direct challenge to U.S. hegemony, Castro had begun courting closer economic and military ties with the Russians while expropriating many U.S. businesses. The eventual alliance that developed between Cuba and the Soviet Union challenged the Monroe Doctrine by offering entry into the Western Hemisphere to a nuclear-armed, extra-continental U.S. adversary that Washington, DC had been trying to keep out for more than a decade.[95] The Cubans paid a huge price for their defiance, however, enduring trade and political embargoes by their hemispheric neighbors (which only Canada and Mexico ignored). Although this economic and diplomatic isolation had begun to crumble by the late 1970s, the United States did not re-establish diplomatic relations with Havana until long after the Cold War had ended. The U.S. trade embargo against Cuba (albeit with numerous exceptions) remains in place.

In 1964, the CIA helped foment race riots in what was then British Guiana in an effort to prevent Cheddi Jagan and his People's Progressive Party from winning the elections scheduled for December of that year. The Johnson administration was concerned that Jagan would establish a Communist beachhead in South America once independence from Great Britain had been obtained (even though Guyana was isolated from its continental neighbors by impenetrable rainforests and the absence of any road links). The U.S. also funneled covert financial support to Linden Forbes Burnham's Afro-Guyanese dominated People's National Congress Party. Burnham (with support from another political party) became prime minister in the post 1964 elections, inaugurating a long period of corruption and mismanagement that turned post-independence Guyana into an economic basket case. It also led to a mass exodus of its citizens, so that most Guyanese today reside outside their own country.

President Lyndon Johnson ordered the U.S. Marines into the Dominican Republic in April 1965, following a popular uprising to overthrow a military government that, in turn, had overthrown the democratically elected government of Juan Bosch in September 1963. Although the action was ostensibly to protect the lives of American citizens, the real concern was the allegedly Communist and pro-Castro sympathies of some Bosch supporters. The U.S. Marines effectively suppressed the popular uprising and remained in the country until new elections in 1966. Joaquín Balaguer, a loyalist of the long-time Dominican dictator and erstwhile U.S. ally Rafael Leonidas Trujillo, won those elections. Balaguer remained in power until 1978 through numerous re-elections marred by fraud and state-sanctioned violence against political opponents. After a brief period out of actual office (although he remained the true power in the country), Balaguer returned to the presidency in 1986; he was re-elected in 1990 and again in 1994, amid accusations of widespread electoral fraud. The Clinton administration eventually pressured Balaguer, by this time in his nineties and blind, to withdraw from Dominican politics and permit new elections in 1996.

In anticipation of the 1964 presidential election in Chile, the CIA funneled millions of dollars into the country to ensure that the Christian Democratic Party's candidate, Eduardo Frei Montalva, would defeat the Socialist Party's candidate, Salvador Allende.[96] Frei won with 57 percent of the vote, and Chile became a major beneficiary of U.S. aid in an effort to make it a showcase of non-Marxist reform in Latin America. In the 1970 presidential election, Salvador Allende, heading a Popular Unity coalition of political parties, won a plurality, with 36.2 percent of the vote. Under the rules of the Chilean Constitution at the time, when no candidate had obtained an outright majority, Congress was required to choose the president from between the two candidates who had received the most votes. The CIA attempted to prevent Allende's selection by offering bribes to wavering Christian Democratic Party members in the Chilean Congress to vote for the second-place finisher, Jorge Alessandri. It also engaged the services of a neo-fascist group to capture the head of the Chilean armed forces, General René Schneider, in order to blame the kidnapping on extreme leftists and thereby provoke a major political crisis that might lead to Alessandri's confirmation as president. Both tactics failed miserably: insulted Congressmen voted to confirm Allende, and General Schneider was killed after he opened fire on his would-be kidnappers.

Unable to prevent Allende's inauguration, the Nixon White House launched a covert operation to make Chile's economy "scream" by funding strikes (including the crucial trucking sector that sparked massive food shortages), organizing international boycotts of Chilean copper (responsible for some 70 percent of Chile's foreign exchange earnings at the time), and withholding loan approval by multilateral agencies. In addition, the CIA subsidized the right-wing press to engage in widespread fearmongering. When the March 1973 midterm legislative elections did not produce the required votes in the Chilean Congress for the president's impeachment, that same right-wing press began calling for Allende's overthrow. Eventually, the CIA's covert operations, coupled with the Allende government's ineptitude shown in its pursuit of policies that culminated in hyperinflation and massive economic chaos, succeeded in convincing the Chilean military to overthrow Allende on September 11, 1973. The iron-fisted dictatorship that followed remained in power until 1990, through the widespread use of disappearances and torture of opponents. The successive coalition governments that followed included many of the same political parties and figures that had participated in Allende's Popular Unity government.

A popular insurrection led by the Sandinista National Liberation Front (FSLN) toppled the Somoza family dictatorship in Nicaragua in July 1979. President Jimmy Carter quickly recognized the new government. Upon Ronald Reagan's arrival at the White House in 1981, relations with Managua rapidly deteriorated, and the U.S. eventually began funding and training guerilla groups based primarily in Honduras, and to a lesser degree in Costa Rica, in an attempt to overthrow the Nicaraguan government by force. When the Democratic-controlled U.S. Congress cut off all funding for these guerilla groups, known as counter-revolutionaries or Contras, the White House turned to illicit sales of U.S. weapons to Iran—leading to the Iran–Contra scandal. In 1986, the International Court of Justice (ICJ) in The Hague found that the CIA had mined Nicaraguan harbors in violation of international law, and ordered the U.S. to pay Nicaragua compensation. The Reagan administration ignored the ICJ's ruling, having already withdrawn recognition of the ICJ's compulsory jurisdiction on all matters related to Central America after Nicaragua filed its case in 1984. Although the Contra war failed militarily, it inflicted great pain on Nicaragua, destroying its economy and causing some 30,000 deaths.[97] The FSLN candidate, Daniel Ortega, who had won the 1984 elections that the Reagan administration condemned as illegitimate, left office peacefully after he was defeated in the 1990 elections. The ultimate irony is that Daniel Ortega eventually came back to power in 2007. In a sign of the decline in U.S. hegemony, to date Ortega remains in the Nicaraguan presidency, despite ample evidence of his using his role for personal enrichment and numerous violations of the basic rules of democratic governance.

A coup in El Salvador in October 1979 brought a group of reformist military officers to power. It soon became apparent that they had lost control of the situation, as death squads funded by El Salvador's wealthy elite, opposed to any changes in the country's highly inequitable status quo, began targeting members of the new government. The inability to enact any type of meaningful reform soon detonated a 12-year civil war, with the leftist Farabundo Marti National Liberation Front (FMLN) and the more moderate *Frente Democrático Revolucionario* (FDR) on one side, and the various military and civilian governments that had emerged over the years and were supported by the United States on the other. The Reagan administration frequently invoked the Monroe Doctrine to justify its participation in the Salvadoran civil war, asserting it was waging a proxy war against international Communism. By the time the United Nations brokered a peace deal in 1992, some 75,000 people (primarily civilians) had been killed, one million Salvadorans had fled their country, and the nation's economy lay in ruins. For its part, the United States had spent US$6 billion in one of its longest Cold War military assistance efforts.[98] In yet another irony of history, the FMLN eventually came to power peacefully when Mauricio Funes was elected to the Salvadoran presidency in January 2009 (after the FMLN had previously won the mayoralties of a number of Salvadoran cities, including the capital San Salvador). In the 2014 elections, the FMLN retained the Salvadoran presidency under Salvador Sánchez Cerén, a former guerilla fighter in the civil war.

President Ronald Reagan sent some 6,000 U.S. troops to the tiny island nation of Grenada in October 1983, ostensibly to protect the lives of American medical students and restore stability following an internal power struggle between rival factions of the country's socialist government. The U.S. was also concerned about the presence of Cuban construction workers building a new airport on the island. The fact that a British construction firm, Plessey Ltd., was a key player in the airport project is one reason Reagan's close ally, Margaret Thatcher, opposed the action (his not having consulted her prior to the invasion of a member of the British Commonwealth was another). Further north in the Caribbean, following the end of the Duvalier family dictatorship in 1986, the United States often found itself helpless to influence political events in Haiti. After the problems the United States confronted in the country in the earlier part of the twentieth century, Haiti continues to provide a poignant example of the fact that a hegemon cannot always steer matters in a direction it would like, or impose its will on a subaltern.

In December 1989, President George H.W. Bush ordered the invasion of Panama by U.S. troops to remove that country's dictator, General Manuel Antonio Noriega, from power. A former CIA informant, Noriega had allowed the U.S. to place a Contra training camp in Panama in the mid-1980s and served an important role in smuggling guns to the Contras fighting to overthrow the Nicaraguan government. Noriega also had been known to have a long-standing involvement in drug trafficking, but "[a]s long as the United States considered defeat of the Sandinista government in Nicaragua a priority,

Noriega was somewhat insulated from criticism over his governing style and drug smuggling."[99] The drawing down of the Contra war in Nicaragua meant, however, that Noriega was now expendable. After he annulled the results of the May 1989 presidential elections in Panama, the Bush administration used unilateral economic sanctions and OAS mediation efforts to try to force Noriega out of power, but he only became more defiant. Within weeks of the U.S. invasion of his country, Noriega left the Papal Nuncio's residence (where he had sought refuge) and gave himself up to the Americans, who promptly sent him to the United States to stand trial for drug trafficking. He eventually was convicted of racketeering, money laundering, and a variety of narcotics-related crimes by a federal court in Miami, and sentenced to 40 years in Federal prison. This sentence was subsequently reduced to 30 years in 1999 because the judge argued that Noriega deserved credit for helping the United States pursue its interests in Central America while he was in power.[100] Noriega's successor was Guillermo Endara, the victor of the annulled election of May 1989, who was administered the oath of office in the Canal Zone by the U.S. military command within hours of the U.S. invasion. The invasion itself caused the deaths of hundreds of Panamanian civilians, and destroyed the homes of thousands of others.

The conclusion of the Cold War, which coincided with the last years of the George H.W. Bush administration, did not end U.S. hegemony in the Western Hemisphere. What did change, however, was the United States' obsession—heavily influenced by realism—with the need to confront and root out Communism, which had frequently caused it to sacrifice the promotion of democracy and self-determination in favor of its own national security concerns, whether real or imagined. At the same time, the painful economic crises of the 1980s and the collapse of the socialist model as a viable alternative meant that the vast majority of countries in Latin America and the Caribbean were now receptive to pursuing the liberal economic model long prescribed by the United States. Facilitating acceptance of these free market-oriented policies, which included reducing fiscal deficits and controlling inflation, was the fact that Chile offered a model of success (thanks to many years of trial and error and the huge social cost paid by Chileans as this experiment was pursued under a brutal military dictatorship). Accordingly, the long tradition of unilateral military interventions and support for repressive dictators that often characterized U.S. hegemony in the Americas came to an end with the 1990s. Henceforth, when intervention did come in the Western Hemisphere, it would be through the United States acting in concert with its fellow American republics in support of preserving democratic governance.

Notes

1 Michael Mastanduno, "System Maker and Privilege Taker: US Power and the International Political Economy," in *International Relations Theory and the Consequences of Unipolarity*, ed. G. John Ikenberry et al. (New York: Cambridge University Press, 2011), 142.

2 Michael Mastanduno, "System Maker and Privilege Taker: US Power and the International Political Economy," in *International Relations Theory and the Consequences of Unipolarity*, ed. G. John Ikenberry et al. (New York: Cambridge University Press, 2011), 142. The high levels of public debt held by Japanese and Chinese investors in the form of U.S. treasury notes diminish the United States' ability to derive influence from its relatively preponderant economic capabilities. Daniel Deudney, "Unipolarity and Nuclear Weapons," in *International Relations Theory and the Consequences of Unipolarity*, ed. G. John Ikenberry et al. (New York: Cambridge University Press, 2011), 293–4.

3 Mark Eric Williams, *Understanding U.S.–Latin American Relations* (New York: Routledge, 2012), 78–9.

4 Carlos Gustavo Poggio Teixeira, *Brazil, the United States, and the South American Subsystem* (Lanham, MD: Lexington Books, 2012), 8. A widely cited consensus definition of empire emphasizes the political control exercised by the dominant metropole over both the internal and external policies of the subordinate. David A. Lake, *Hierarchy in International Relations* (Ithaca, NY: Cornell University Press, 2009), 37.

5 Benedetto Fontana, "State and Society: The Concept of Hegemony in Gramsci," in *Hegemony and Power*, ed. Mark Haugaard et al. (Lanham, MD: Lexington Books, 2006), 23.

6 Benedetto Fontana, "State and Society: The Concept of Hegemony in Gramsci," in *Hegemony and Power*, ed. Mark Haugaard et al. (Lanham, MD: Lexington Books, 2006), 24.

7 Benedetto Fontana, "State and Society: The Concept of Hegemony in Gramsci," in *Hegemony and Power*, ed. Mark Haugaard et al. (Lanham, MD: Lexington Books, 2006), 25. An example would be "the Delian League, originally established as a consensual alliance of free states under the hegemony of Athens as a means to repel the Persian threat against the common interests of the members, gradually turned into an Athenian Empire, in which allies were transformed into dependent subjects." Ibid at 24.

8 Benedetto Fontana, "State and Society: The Concept of Hegemony in Gramsci," in *Hegemony and Power*, ed. Mark Haugaard et al. (Lanham, MD: Lexington Books, 2006), 25–6.

9 Benedetto Fontana, "State and Society: The Concept of Hegemony in Gramsci," in *Hegemony and Power*, ed. Mark Haugaard et al. (Lanham, MD: Lexington Books, 2006), 25.

10 Ian Clark, *Hegemony in International Society* (Oxford: Oxford University Press, 2011), 18.

11 Ian Clark, *Hegemony in International Society* (Oxford: Oxford University Press, 2011), 18.

12 Ian Clark, *Hegemony in International Society* (Oxford: Oxford University Press, 2011), 19.

13 John J. Mearsheimer, *The Tragedy of Great Power Politics* (New York: W.W. Norton & Co., 2001), 19.

14 John J. Mearsheimer, *The Tragedy of Great Power Politics* (New York: W.W. Norton & Co., 2001), 21.

15 John J. Mearsheimer, *The Tragedy of Great Power Politics* (New York: W.W. Norton & Co., 2001), 2.

16 See Robert O. Keohane, *International Institutions and State Power* (Boulder, CO: Westview Press, 1989), 38–9 and John J. Mearsheimer, *The Tragedy of Great Power Politics* (New York: W.W. Norton & Co., 2001), 17.

17 John J. Mearsheimer, *The Tragedy of Great Power Politics* (New York: W.W. Norton & Co., 2001), 3.

18 Joseph M. Grieco, "Anarchy and the Limits of Cooperation: A Realist Critique of the Newest Liberal Institutionalism," in *Controversies in International Relations*

Theory: Realism and the Neoliberal Challenge, ed. Charles W. Kegley, Jr. (New York: St. Martin's Press, 1995), 160.

19 John J. Mearsheimer, *The Tragedy of Great Power Politics* (New York: W.W. Norton & Co., 2001), 2. See also Joseph M. Grieco, "Anarchy and the Limits of Cooperation: A Realist Critique of the Newest Liberal Institutionalism," in *Controversies in International Relations Theory: Realism and the Neoliberal Challenge*, ed. Charles W. Kegley (New York: St. Martin's Press, 1995), 161. "[T]he fundamental goal of states in any relationship is to prevent others from achieving advances in their relative capabilities."

20 Stefano Guzzini, *Power, Realism and Constructivism* (New York: Routledge, 2013), 114. Such an interpretation, according to Guzzini, requires that power be measurable.

21 John J. Mearsheimer, *The Tragedy of Great Power Politics* (New York: W.W. Norton & Co., 2001), 18.

22 Kenneth N. Waltz, "Realist Thought and Neorealist Theory," in *Controversies in International Relations Theory: Realism and the Neoliberal Challenge*, ed. Charles W. Kegley, Jr. (New York: St. Martin's Press, 1995), 79–80.

23 Birthe Hansen, "Dynamics of the Unipolar World Order," in *The New World Order: Contrasting Theories*, ed. Birthe Hansen et al. (New York: St. Martin's Press, 2000), 115. A state's capabilities include "size of population, and territory, resource endowment, economic capability, military strength, political stability, and competence." Kenneth N. Waltz, *Theory of International Politics* (New York: Random House, 1979), 131.

24 Robert O. Keohane, *International Institutions and State Power* (Boulder, CO: Westview Press, 1989), 41.

25 Bertel Heurlin, "Virtual War and Virtual Peace," in *The New World Order: Contrasting Theories*, ed. Birthe Hansen et al. (New York: St. Martin's Press, 2000), 171. "Increase in a state's relative capabilities implies that its position improves with more security being the byproduct (and vice versa)." Ibid at 115.

26 Robert W. Cox, "Social Forces, States and World Orders: Beyond International Relations Theory," in *Neorealism and Its Critics*, ed. Robert O. Keohane (New York: Columbia University Press, 1986), 246.

27 John J. Mearsheimer, *The Tragedy of Great Power Politics* (New York: W.W. Norton & Co., 2001), 21. "Balance-of-power politics prevail wherever two, and only two requirements, are met: that the order be anarchic and that it be populated by units wishing to survive." Kenneth N. Waltz, *Theory of International Politics* (New York: Random House, 1979), 121. "The first concern of states is not to maximize power but to maintain their positions in the system." Ibid at 126.

28 Kenneth N. Waltz, *Theory of International Politics* (New York: Random House, 1979), 128. See also Kenneth N. Waltz, *Realism and International Politics* (New York: Routledge, 2008), 213. One major limitation of the neo-realist theory is that it cannot predict when that balancing will occur. For Waltz, U.S. unipolarity is not durable because "dominant powers take on too many tasks beyond their own borders, thus weakening themselves in the long run" and "even if a dominant power behaves with moderation, restraint, and forbearance, weaker states will worry about its future behavior." Kenneth N. Waltz, *Realism and International Politics* (New York: Routledge, 2008), 214.

29 Kenneth N. Waltz, "Intimations of Multipolarity," in *The New World Order: Contrasting Theories*, ed. Birthe Hansen et al. (New York: St. Martin's Press, 2000), 14. "The American aspiration to freeze historical development by working to keep the world unipolar is doomed [as] the task will exceed America's economic, military and political resources; and the very effort to maintain a hegemonic position is the surest way to undermine it." Ibid at 15.

30 Robert O. Keohane, *After Hegemony* (Princeton, NJ: Princeton University Press, 1984), 31.

31 Robert O. Keohane, *After Hegemony* (Princeton, NJ: Princeton University Press, 1984), 34–5.

32 Philip G. Cerny, "Dilemmas of Operationalizing Hegemony," in *Hegemony and Power*, ed. Mark Haugaard et al. (Lanham, MD: Lexington Books, 2006), 68.

33 Philip G. Cerny, "Dilemmas of Operationalizing Hegemony," in *Hegemony and Power*, ed. Mark Haugaard et al. (Lanham, MD: Lexington Books, 2006), 69. "These goods may be provided either by the hegemon itself, if its resources and will are sufficient, or through the hegemon's support for cooperative institutions and practices, including international regimes, 'global governance,' or various forms of multilateral governance and webs of bilateral and 'minilateral' agreements." Ibid.

34 Robert Gilpin, *Global Political Economy: Understanding the International Economic Order* (Princeton, NJ: Princeton University Press, 2001), 99–100.

35 Philip G. Cerny, "Dilemmas of Operationalizing Hegemony," in *Hegemony and Power*, ed. Mark Haugaard et al. (Lanham, MD: Lexington Books, 2006), 69.

36 Robert O. Keohane, ed., *Neorealism and Its Critics* (New York: Columbia University Press, 1986), 8. "There is an optimistic assumption lurking in liberal internationalism that states can overcome constraints and cooperate to solve security dilemmas, pursue collective action, and create an open, stable system." G. John Ikenberry, "Liberal Internationalism 3.0: America and Dilemmas of Liberal World Order," in *Liberal World Orders,* ed. Tim Dunne et al. (New York: Oxford University Press, 2013), 25.

37 Charles W. Kegley, Jr., ed., *Controversies in International Relations Theory: Realism and the Neoliberal Challenge* (New York: St. Martin's Press, 1995), 4. "[T]here is no single canonical liberalism, but merely a liberal tradition, which has always derived its temporal manifestations from how it is practiced and how it is imagined." Trine Flockhart, "Liberal Imaginations: Transformative Logics of Liberal Order," in *Liberal World Orders*, ed. Tim Dunne et al. (New York: Oxford University Press, 2013), 70.

38 Mark W. Zacher and Richard A. Matthew, "Liberal International Theory: Common Threads, Divergent Strands," in *Controversies in International Relations Theory: Realism and the Neoliberal Challenge*, ed. Charles W. Kegley, Jr. (New York: St. Martin's Press, 1995), 118. These groups may include labor unions, political parties, trade associations, multinational corporations, influential nongovernmental organizations, and multilateral agencies such as the World Trade Organization or the International Monetary Fund. They can even encompass transnational criminal cartels.

39 Mark W. Zacher and Richard A. Matthew, "Liberal International Theory: Common Threads, Divergent Strands," in *Controversies in International Relations Theory: Realism and the Neoliberal Challenge*, ed. Charles W. Kegley, Jr. (New York: St. Martin's Press, 1995), 118. Human and state interests are determined by bargaining power among interest groups, but the definition of those interests are affected by a variety of characteristics. "At the domestic level they include the nature of the economic and political systems, economic interactions, and personal values; at the international level there are technological capabilities that allow states to affect each other in different ways, patterns of interactions and interdependencies, transnational sociological patterns, knowledge, and international institutions." Ibid at 119.

40 G. John Ikenberry, "Liberal Internationalism 3.0: America and Dilemmas of Liberal World Order," in *Liberal World Orders*, ed. Tim Dunne et al. (New York: Oxford University Press, 2013), 25.

41 Robert O. Keohane, *International Institutions and State Power* (Boulder, CO: Westview Press, 1989), 11.

42 Christopher Hobson and Milja Kurki, "Democracy Promotion as a Practice of Liberal World Order," in *Liberal World Orders*, ed. Tim Dunne et al. (New York: Oxford University Press, 2013), 196.

43 Robert Jervis, "Unipolarity: A Structural Perspective," in *International Relations Theory and the Consequences of Unipolarity*, ed. G. John Ikenberry et al. (New York: Cambridge University Press, 2011), 269.

44 John M. Hobson and Martin Hall, "Imperialism and Anti-Imperialism in Eurocentric Liberal International Theory," in *Liberal World Orders*, ed. Tim Dunne et al. (New York: Oxford University Press, 2013), 139.

45 For adherents of the so-called English school of international relations, for example, hegemony by a single great power is antithetical to the order of sovereign states rather than being a source of survival. Tim Dunne and Trine Flockhart, eds, *Liberal World Orders* (New York: Oxford University Press, 2013), 12.

46 G. John Ikenberry, "Liberal Internationalism 3.0: America and Dilemmas of Liberal World Order," in *Liberal World Orders*, ed. Tim Dunne et al. (New York: Oxford University Press, 2013), 25.

47 Paul W. Schroeder, "From Hegemony to Empire: The Fatal Leap," in *Imbalance of Power: U.S. Hegemony and International Power*, ed. William I. Zartman (Boulder, CO: Lynne Rienner Publishers, 2009), 64.

48 Paul W. Schroeder, "From Hegemony to Empire: The Fatal Leap," in *Imbalance of Power: U.S. Hegemony and International Power*, ed. William I. Zartman (Boulder, CO: Lynne Rienner Publishers, 2009), 64–5.

49 Robert Gilpin, *Global Political Economy: Understanding the International Economic Order* (Princeton, NJ: Princeton University Press, 2001), 85. Keohane argued that international regimes and cooperation among the major economic powers would replace declining American leadership as the basis of the liberal international economic order. Ibid at 84–5.

50 Robert Gilpin, *Global Political Economy: Understanding the International Economic Order* (Princeton, NJ: Princeton University Press, 2001), 84. "Among the tasks performed by regimes are reduction of uncertainty, minimization of transaction costs, and prevention of market failures." Ibid.

51 Robert O. Keohane, *International Institutions and State Power* (Boulder, CO: Westview Press, 1989, 75. A more expansive definition of regimes would include "those arrangements for issue areas that embody implicit rules and norms insofar as they actually guide behavior of important actors in a particular issue area." Ibid at 76.

52 Robert O. Keohane, *International Institutions and State Power* (Boulder, CO: Westview Press, 1989), 78.

53 Robert Gilpin, *Global Political Economy: Understanding the International Economic Order* (Princeton, NJ: Princeton University Press, 2001), 84. "[E]ven if U.S. hegemonic leadership may have been a crucial factor in the creation of some contemporary international economic regimes, the continuation of hegemony is not necessarily essential for their continued viability." Robert O. Keohane, *After Hegemony* (Princeton, NJ: Princeton University Press, 1984), 85.

54 Howard H. Lentner, "Hegemony and Power in International Politics," in *Hegemony and Power*, ed. Mark Haugaard et al. (Lanham, MD: Lexington Books, 2006), 98. "The military conditions for economic hegemony are met if the economically preponderant country has sufficient military capabilities to prevent incursions by others that would deny it access to major areas of its economic activity." Robert O. Keohane, *After Hegemony* (Princeton, NJ: Princeton University Press, 1984), 40.

55 Howard H. Lentner, "Hegemony and Power in International Politics," in *Hegemony and Power*, ed. Mark Haugaard et al. (Lanham, MD: Lexington Books, 2006), 91.

56 Ian Clark, *Hegemony in International Society* (Oxford: Oxford University Press, 2011), 19. "[A] class is dominant in two ways, namely it is 'leading' and 'dominant'." Antonio Gramsci, "First Prison Notebook, Section 44," in *Prison Notebooks Vol. I*, ed. and trans. Joseph A. Buttigieg (New York: Columbia University

Press, 1992), 136. "[I]n order to exercise political leadership or hegemony one must count not solely on the power and material force that is given by the government." Ibid at 137.

57 Henri Goverde, "Mars and Venus in the Atlantic Community: Power Dynamics Under Hegemony," in *Hegemony and Power*, ed. Mark Haugaard et al. (Lanham, MD: Lexington Books, 2006), 110. In Gramsci's writings, hegemony is used as a master concept to explain the ability of the bourgeoisie to dominate modern capitalist society. "Gramsci argued that the bourgeoisie occupied the position of a hegemon because they managed to present their particular interests as universal for society as a whole. Through the language of universality they gained support from other classes and, in this manner, effectively organizationally outflanked potential proletariat opposition." Mark Haugaard, "Power and Hegemony in Social Theory," in *Hegemony and Power*, ed. Mark Haugaard et al. (Lanham, MD: Lexington Books, 2006), 45.

58 Robert W. Cox, "Social Forces, States and World Orders: Beyond International Relations Theory," in *Neorealism and Its Critics*, ed. Robert O. Keohane (New York: Columbia University Press, 1986), 246. "[T]he fact of hegemony presupposes that the interests and tendencies of those groups over whom hegemony is exercised have been taken into account and that a certain equilibrium is established. It presupposes, in other words, that the hegemonic group should make sacrifices of an economic-corporate kind." Antonio Gramsci, "Fourth Prison Notebook, Section 38," in *Prison Notebooks Vol. II*, ed. and trans. Joseph A. Buttigieg (New York: Columbia University Press, 1996), 183.

59 Robert W. Cox, "Gramsci, Hegemony and International Relations: An Essay in Method," *Millennium: Journal of International Studies,* Vol. 12, No. 2 (1983): 165.

60 Robert O. Keohane, *International Institutions and State Power* (Boulder, CO: Westview Press, 1989), 52. "Marxists have often used the concept of hegemony, implicitly defined simply as dominance, as a way of analyzing the surface manifestations of world politics under capitalism." Robert O. Keohane, *After Hegemony* (Princeton, NJ: Princeton University Press, 1984), 42.

61 Robert O. Keohane, *After Hegemony* (Princeton, NJ: Princeton University Press, 1984), 45. "We should not assume that leaders of secondary states are necessarily the victims of 'false consciousness' when they accept the hegemonic ideology, or that they constitute a small, parasitical elite that betrays the interests of the nation to its own selfish ends" but, in some cases, "it may be not only in the self-interest of peripheral elites, but conducive to the economic growth of their countries, for them to defer to the hegemon." Ibid.

62 Mark Haugaard, "Power and Hegemony in Social Theory," in *Hegemony and Power*, ed. Mark Haugaard et al. (Lanham, MD: Lexington Books, 2006), 47.

63 Philip G. Cerny, "Dilemmas of Operationalizing Hegemony," in *Hegemony and Power*, ed. Mark Haugaard et al. (Lanham, MD: Lexington Books, 2006), 70. "The historical unity of the ruling classes is found in the state, and their history is essentially the history of states and groups of states." Antonio Gramsci, "Third Prison Notebook, Section 90," in *Prison Notebooks Vol. II*, ed. and trans. Joseph A. Buttigieg (New York: Columbia University Press, 1996), 91.

64 Robert W. Cox, "Gramsci, Hegemony and International Relations: An Essay in Method," *Millennium: Journal of International Studies,* Vol. 12, No. 2 (1983): 172. Cox also argues that international organizations also serve to co-opt elites from subaltern countries and absorb counter-hegemonic ideas.

65 Marcel Nelson, *A History of the FTAA: From Hegemony to Fragmentation* (New York: Palgrave Macmillan, 2015), 30. "[H]egemonic world orders are founded by powerful states that portray their interests as being universally compatible with the interests of other states" and "this universality is premised on the emergence of a global civil society founded on an expanding global mode of production." Ibid.

66 Dominant states must credibly commit to limit their authority and power through multilateralism and other mechanisms in order to entice subordinates to enter and remain in such a relationship, which "[i]n a wholly anarchic world . . . is an oxymoron." David A. Lake, *Hierarchy in International Relations* (Ithaca, NY: Cornell University Press, 2009), 14. "To earn and sustain their authority, dominant states must (1) produce political orders that benefit subordinates, even when they have no immediate interests in doing so; (2) discipline subordinates who violate rules and, especially, threaten or reject their authority; and (3) commit credibly not to abuse the authority they have been granted." Ibid at 93.

67 David A. Lake, *Hierarchy in International Relations* (Ithaca, NY: Cornell University Press, 2009), 34. "[A]uthority relationships are not devoid of coercion but are defined by the status or legitimacy of force when it is used." Ibid at 8. "Authority differs from simple coercion in the bundle of accepted rights and duties—the legitimacy—of the particular relationship within which coercion is used." Ibid. "Legitimacy is, by its nature, a social and relational phenomenon" and "only has meaning in a particular social context" and "can only be given by others." Martha Finnemore, "Legitimacy, Hypocrisy, and the Social Structure of Unipolarity: Why Being a Unipole Isn't All It's Cracked Up to Be," in *International Relations Theory and the Consequences of Unipolarity*, ed. G. John Ikenberry et al. (New York: Cambridge University Press, 2011), 71.

68 David A. Lake, *Hierarchy in International Relations* (Ithaca, NY: Cornell University Press, 2009), 34. Subordinate states may benefit from lower levels of defense spending, or enhanced economic opportunities because of the dominant state enforcing a liberal economic policy of free trade.

69 David A. Lake, *Hierarchy in International Relations* (Ithaca, NY: Cornell University Press, 2009), 15. Lake further notes that hierarchy, as is true of anything that is political, is always contested terrain. "[R]uler and ruled will continuously struggle over the nature, meaning, and limits of the authority possessed by the former and conferred by the latter." Ibid at 34. Hierarchy is always "a shifting and dynamic relationship." Ibid at 92.

70 Gordon Connell-Smith, *The United States and Latin America: An Historical Analysis of Inter-America Relations* (London: Heinemann Educational Books, 1974), 268. One of those expansionists was Senator Henry Cabot Lodge of Massachusetts, who insisted that in the Western Hemisphere the United Sates had to be "supreme" and intervene in order to prevent South America from sharing the fate of Africa, where the European powers were engaged in a race to acquire colonies and resources. William C. Widenor, *Henry Cabot Lodge and the Search for an American Foreign Policy* (Berkeley: University of California Press, 1980), 106–7.

71 John J. Mearsheimer, *The Tragedy of Great Power Politics* (New York: W.W. Norton & Co., 2001), 41. Underscoring that point, Daniel Deudney notes: "the widespread characterization of the contemporary international system as unipolar is significantly unfounded. The paramount military capability of nuclear weapons is not distributed in a unipolar pattern. The system is at least bipolar and perhaps multipolar." Daniel Deudney, "Unipolarity and Nuclear Weapons," in *International Relations Theory and the Consequences of Unipolarity*, ed. G. John Ikenberry et al. (New York: Cambridge University Press, 2011), 314.

72 Ian Clark, *Hegemony in International Society* (Oxford: Oxford University Press, 2011), 23.

73 Ian Clark, *Hegemony in International Society* (Oxford: Oxford University Press, 2011), 3.

74 Stephen M. Walt, "Alliances in a Unipolar World," in *International Relations Theory and the Consequences of Unipolarity*, ed. G. John Ikenberry et al. (New York: Cambridge University Press, 2011), 100.

75 See, e.g., Ian Clark, *Hegemony in International Society* (Oxford: Oxford University Press, 2011), 123. The "majority opinion is staunchly that the United States did indeed emerge as a hegemon at the end of the Second World War. The only major issue that has troubled this consensus is how to comprehend an American hegemony from which the socialist world was evidently excluded." See also Robert Gilpin, "The Rise of American Hegemony," in *Two Hegemonies: Britain 1846–1914 and the United States 1941–2001*, ed. Patrick Karl O'Brien et al. (Aldershot, UK: Ashgate Publishing, 2002), 166–7. The U.S., as a leader or hegemonic power, "led the world economy following WW II." Ibid at 167.

76 David P. Calleo, "Reflections on American Hegemony in the Postwar Era," in *Two Hegemonies: Britain 1846–1914 and the United States 1941–2001*, ed. Patrick Karl O'Brien et al. (Aldershot, UK: Ashgate Publishing, 2002), 253. "At the same time, the process was not without real costs, and it is those costs which keep alive the issue of decline. The constant monetary instability that has accompanied the use of these formulas [i.e., loose fiscal and/or loose monetary policy] has not been good for the American economy's long-term health. It is very difficult for capital markets to work properly under conditions of perennial monetary instability. Such conditions encourage the tendency to focus on speculation and quick profit, rather than on national long-term investment." Ibid.

77 John M. Hobson, "Two Hegemonies or One?" in *Two Hegemonies: Britain 1846–1914 and the United States 1941–2001*, ed. Patrick Karl O'Brien et al. (Aldershot, UK: Ashgate Publishing, 2002), 318. In particular, the United States supported the establishment of a European Payments Union that avoided use of hard currency for intra-European trade as well as the European Economic Community, even though both were discriminatory against U.S. exports. It also promoted the Marshall Plan (without demanding reciprocity), and undertook the role of "lender of last resort," by providing badly needed investment capital to Europe and Japan in the aftermath of WW II. Ibid at 318–19.

78 G. John Ikenberry, "The Liberal Sources of American Unipolarity," in *International Relations Theory and the Consequences of Unipolarity*, ed. G. John Ikenberry et al. (New York: Cambridge University Press, 2011), 228–9. The liberal character of this hegemonic order provided access points and opportunities for political communication and reciprocal influence. Ibid at 231.

79 The expectation of hegemonic theorists is that hegemonic states will tend to take on more responsibilities and roles than their power capabilities and resources can ultimately support. Daniel Deudney, "Unipolarity and Nuclear Weapons," in *International Relations Theory and the Consequences of Unipolarity*, ed. G. John Ikenberry et al. (New York: Cambridge University Press, 2011), 300. In addition, over time, it becomes increasingly difficult for a strong power to live by the rules of the institutions it created when it becomes inconvenient, thus undermining the entire system and ultimately delegitimizing the unipole's hegemony. Barry K. Posen, "From Unipolarity to Multipolarity: Transition in Sight?" in *International Relations Theory and the Consequences of Unipolarity*, ed. G. John Ikenberry et al. (New York: Cambridge University Press, 2011), 337.

80 There is a contrarian view that the end of the Bretton Woods regime actually denoted a reaffirmation of U.S. hegemony rather than its demise. See, e.g., Ian Clark, *Hegemony in International Society* (Oxford: Oxford University Press, 2011), 128, quoting Nye: "[I]f hegemonic economic behavior is the ability to change the rules of the international game, then 1971 did not mark the end of U.S. economic hegemony." On the other hand, the United States was powerless to prevent the 1973–4 Arab oil embargo. Threats of "military intervention were countered by Arab threats of preemptive sabotage" and a larger Soviet naval presence in the eastern Mediterranean than that enjoyed by the United States. See, James Macdonald, *When Globalization Fails* (New York: Farrar, Straus and

Giroux, 2015), 208. "As the embargo took its toll, a number of countries shifted their foreign policies in a direction more congenial to the Arab point of view." Ibid at 209.

81 Paul Schroeder, for example, argues that the U.S. invasion of Iraq in 2003 undermined the possibility of a useful U.S. hegemony and contributed "to a growth of Hobbesian disorder in the Middle East and the world that the pursuit of a sane hegemony could have avoided." Paul W. Schroeder, "From Hegemony to Empire: The Fatal Leap," in *Imbalance of Power: U.S. Hegemony and International Power*, ed. I. William Zartman (Boulder, CO: Lynne Rienner Publishers, 2009), 61.

82 Philip G. Cerny, "Dilemmas of Operationalizing Hegemony," in *Hegemony and Power*, ed. Mark Haugaard et al. (Lanham, MD: Lexington Books, 2006), 81.

83 See, e.g., Philip G. Cerny, "Dilemmas of Operationalizing Hegemony," in *Hegemony and Power*, ed. Mark Haugaard et al. (Lanham, MD: Lexington Books, 2006), 73.

84 Tom Long, *Latin America Confronts the United States: Asymmetry and Influence* (New York: Cambridge University Press, 2015), 3. Long cites Brazilian President Juscelino Kubitschek's Operation Pan America which connected his development goals with the Cold War, as an example of how a Latin American leader influenced U.S. policy. "By drawing a line between underdevelopment, instability, and communism, Kubitschek hoped to raise the profile of underdevelopment in Latin America and define it in a way that made it a U.S. national security interest." Ibid at 70. Although Kubitschek's original proposal fell on the deaf ears of the Eisenhower administration, it bore fruit under the subsequent Kennedy White House, and is widely credited as serving as the inspiration for the Alliance for Progress.

85 John J. Mearsheimer, *The Tragedy of Great Power Politics* (New York: W.W. Norton & Co., 2001), 239. For Henry Cabot Lodge, "[t]he *sine qua non* of an assertive foreign policy was a rigid enforcement of the Monroe Doctrine." William C. Widenor, *Henry Cabot Lodge and the Search for an American Foreign Policy* (Berkeley: University of California Press, 1980), 105.

86 Mark Eric Williams, *Understanding U.S.–Latin American Relations* (New York: Routledge, 2012), 49. "Manifest Destiny was a close cousin of *social Darwinism*" which "argued that civilized societies had a moral obligation to help the less evolved reach a higher state of being." Ibid at 86.

87 The provisions of the Platt amendment are found in the Treaty between the United States and the Republic of Cuba Embodying the Provisions Defining Their Future Relations as Contained in the Act of Congress Approved March 2, 1901, signed 05/22/1903: General Records of the United States Government, 1778–2006, RG 11. Washington, DC: National Archives. Available at: www.ourdocuments.gov

88 Theodore Roosevelt's Annual Message to Congress for 1904, House Records HR 58A-K2; Records of the U.S. House of Representatives; Record Group 233. Washington, DC: Center for Legislative Archives (National Archives). Available at: www.ourdocuments.gov

89 Theodore Roosevelt, *An Autobiography* (New York: The Macmillan Company, 1913), 547. "The great and prosperous civilized commonwealths such as the Argentine, Brazil, and Chile, in the Southern half of South America, have advanced so far that they no longer stand in any position of tutelage toward the United States. They occupy toward us precisely the position that Canada occupies. Their friendship is the friendship of equals for equals. My view was that as regards these nations there was no more necessity for asserting the Monroe Doctrine then there was to assert it for Canada. They were competent to assert it for themselves."

90 Carlos Gustavo Poggio Teixeira, *Brazil, the United States, and the South American Subsystem* (Lanham, MD: Lexington Books, 2012), 59.

91 John Edwin Fagg, *Pan Americanism* (Malabar, FL: Robert E. Krieger Publishing Company, 1982), 48. Interestingly, FDR had previously been associated with the

1914 U.S. occupation of Veracruz as well as the interventions in Haiti and the Dominican Republic while he served as U.S. Secretary of the Navy.

92 The full text of FDR's Inaugural Address of March 4, 1933 is available at the website of the American Presidency Project at: www.presidency.ucsb.edu/ws/index.php?pid=14473. The term "Good Neighbor" had actually been coined by FDR's predecessor, Herbert Hoover, as an antidote to dollar diplomacy. Herbert Hoover took advantage of the long period between his election in November 1928 and his inauguration the following March to embark on a trip to Central and South America. While there, he experienced in the flesh the hostility U.S. interventionist policies had engendered throughout the region, and saw how this was harming U.S. business. Other than withdrawing the U.S. Marines from Nicaragua and beginning the process in Haiti, however, the Great Depression distracted him from implementing any bold new foreign policy for the Americas.

93 This is not to imply that the Roosevelt administration ignored both nationalizations, but it used diplomatic as well as subtle and low-key economic pressure to get both governments to offer, after a number of years, a respectable level of monetary compensation for the detrimentally impacted U.S. oil companies. It also helped that American oil prospectors discovered petroleum in Saudi Arabia in 1938.

94 "Between early 1982 and the end of 1983, the Guatemalan army destroyed some 400 towns and villages, drove 20,000 rural people out of their homes and into camps, killed between 50,000 and 75,000 mostly unarmed indigenous farmers and their families, and violently displaced over a million people." Stephen Schlesinger and Stephen Kinzer, *Bitter Fruit* (Cambridge, MA: Harvard University Press, 2005), x. "As the atrocities escalated, the U.S. government gave repeated and dramatic evidence of its support for the Ríos Montt government" by resuming economic aid to Guatemala in October 1982 terminated by the Carter administration, and "[i]n January 1983, the U.S. government lifted its embargo on the sale of arms to Guatemala and sent US\$ 6.3 million in spare parts for helicopters, the same helicopters that had already begun to appear in accounts of army massacres of entire villages." Ibid.

95 Mark Eric Williams, *Understanding U.S.–Latin American Relations* (New York: Routledge, 2012), 180.

96 "The CIA contributed \$1.20 per Chilean voter to the anti-left propaganda effort, over twice as much as the \$0.54 per U.S. voter that Lyndon Johnson and Barry Goldwater jointly spent in their own presidential campaigns that year." J. Samuel Valenzuela and Arturo Valenzuela, "Chile: The Development, Breakdown, and Recovery of Democracy," in *Latin America: Its Problems and Its Promise: A Multidisciplinary Introduction*, ed. Jan Knippers Black (Boulder, CO: Westview Press, 2011), 498. In addition to funding more than half of Frei's 1964 campaign budget, the CIA conducted 15 other operations in Chile, including covert creation of and support for numerous civic organizations to influence and mobilize key voting sectors, and a massive US\$3 million anti-Allende propaganda campaign that included political posters, pamphlets, and radio advertising spots. Peter Kornbluh, *The Pinochet File* (New York: The New Press, 2004), 4.

97 David W. Dent, *The Legacy of the Monroe Doctrine: A Reference Guide to U.S. Involvement in Latin America and the Caribbean* (Westport, CT: Greenwood Press, 1999), 294. By the mid-1980s, economic production in Nicaragua had declined to 1960 levels; by 1987 defense spending swallowed up 62 percent of Nicaragua's state budget; and by 1988 inflation had reached 33,000 percent. Mark Eric Williams, *Understanding U.S.–Latin American Relations* (New York: Routledge, 2012), 256.

98 David W. Dent, *The Legacy of the Monroe Doctrine: A Reference Guide to U.S. Involvement in Latin America and the Caribbean* (Westport, CT: Greenwood Press, 1999), 166.

99 David W. Dent, *The Legacy of the Monroe Doctrine: A Reference Guide to U.S. Involvement in Latin America and the Caribbean* (Westport, CT: Greenwood Press, 1999), 307. Noriega had also ignored Panamanian banks laundering money for the Colombian cocaine cartels and their Peruvian suppliers.
100 David W. Dent and Larman C. Wilson, *Historical Dictionary of Inter-American Organizations, Second Edition* (Plymouth, UK: Scarecrow Press, 2014), 257. After serving half of his 30-year sentence in a U.S. federal prison in Florida, Noriega was extradited by the U.S. to France, where he was convicted of money laundering in 2010. Extradited to Panama at the end of 2011, he stood trial again and was convicted of many misdeeds during his time in power. He died on May 29, 2017 in a Panamanian prison.

Bibliography

Clark, Ian. *Hegemony in International Society*. Oxford: Oxford University Press, 2011.

Connell-Smith, Gordon. *The United States and Latin America: An Historical Analysis of Inter-America Relations*. London: Heinemann Educational Books, 1974.

Cox, Robert W. "Gramsci, Hegemony and International Relations; An Essay in Method." *Millennium: Journal of International Studies* Vol. 12, No. 2 (1983): 162–175.

Dent, David W. *The Legacy of the Monroe Doctrine: A Reference Guide to U.S. Involvement in Latin America and the Caribbean*. Westport, CT: Greenwood Press, 1999.

Dent, David W. and Larman C. Wilson. *Historical Dictionary of Inter-American Organizations, Second Edition*. Plymouth, UK: Scarecrow Press, 2014.

Dunne, Tim and Trine Flockhart, eds. *Liberal World Orders*. New York: Oxford University Press, 2013.

Fagg, John Edwin. *Pan Americanism*. Malabar, FL: Robert E. Krieger Publishing Company, 1982.

Gilpin, Robert. *Global Political Economy: Understanding the International Economic Order*. Princeton, NJ: Princeton University Press, 2001.

Gramsci, Antonio. *Prison Notebooks Vol. I*. Joseph A. Buttigieg, ed. and trans. New York: Columbia University Press, 1992.

Gramsci, Antonio. *Prison Notebooks Vol. II*. Joseph A. Buttigieg, ed. and trans. New York: Columbia University Press, 1996.

Guzzini, Stefano. *Power, Realism and Constructivism*. New York: Routledge, 2013.

Hansen, Birthe and Bertel Heurlin, eds. *The New World Order: Contrasting Theories*. New York: St. Martin's Press, 2000.

Haugaard, Mark and Howard H. Lentner, eds. *Hegemony and Power*. Lanham, MD: Lexington Books, 2006.

Ikenberry, G. John, Michael Mastanduno, and William C. Wohlforth, eds. *International Relations Theory and the Consequences of Unipolarity*. New York: Cambridge University Press, 2011.

Kegley Jr., Charles W., ed. *Controversies in International Relations Theory: Realism and the Neoliberal Challenge*. New York: St. Martin's Press, 1995.

Keohane, Robert O. *After Hegemony*. Princeton, NJ: Princeton University Press, 1984.

Keohane, Robert O., ed. *Neorealism and Its Critics*. New York: Columbia University Press, 1986.

Keohane, Robert O. *International Institutions and State Power*. Boulder, CO: Westview Press, 1989.

Knippers Black, Jan, ed. *Latin America: Its Problems and Its Promise: A Multidisciplinary Introduction*. Boulder, CO: Westview Press, 2011.

Kornbluh, Peter. *The Pinochet File*. New York: The New Press, 2004.

Lake, David A. *Hierarchy in International Relations*. Ithaca, NY: Cornell University Press, 2009.

Long, Tom. *Latin America Confronts the United States: Asymmetry and Influence*. New York: Cambridge University Press, 2015.

Macdonald, James. *When Globalization Fails*. New York: Farrar, Straus and Giroux, 2015.

Mearsheimer, John J. *The Tragedy of Great Power Politics*. New York: W.W. Norton & Co., 2001.

Nelson, Marcel. *A History of the FTAA: From Hegemony to Fragmentation*. New York: Palgrave Macmillan, 2015.

O'Brien, Patrick Karl and Armand Cleese, eds. *Two Hegemonies: Britain 1846–1914 and The United States 1941–2001*. Aldershot, UK: Ashgate Publishing, 2002.

Poggio Teixeira, Carlos Gustavo. *Brazil, the United States, and the South American Subsystem*. Lanham, MD: Lexington Books, 2012.

Roosevelt, Franklin Delano. "Inaugural Address of Franklin D. Roosevelt." Delivered in Washington, DC on March 4, 1933. Accessed July 27, 2017: www.presidency.ucsb.edu/ws/index.php?pid=14473.

Roosevelt, Theodore. *An Autobiography*. New York: The Macmillan Company, 1913.

Schlesinger, Stephen and Stephen Kinzer. *Bitter Fruit*. Cambridge, MA: Harvard University Press, 2005.

Theodore Roosevelt's Annual Message to Congress for 1904, House Records HR 58A-K2; Records of the U.S. House of Representatives; Record Group 233. Washington, DC: Center for Legislative Archives (National Archives).

Treaty between the United States and the Republic of Cuba Embodying the Provisions Defining Their Future Relations as Contained in the Act of Congress Approved March 2, 1901, signed 05/22/1903: General Records of the United States Government, 1778–2006, RG 11. Washington, DC: National Archives.

Waltz, Kenneth N. *Theory of International Politics*. New York: Random House, 1979.

Waltz, Kenneth N. *Realism and International Politics*. New York: Routledge, 2008.

Widenor, William C. *Henry Cabot Lodge and the Search for an American Foreign Policy*. Berkeley: University of California Press, 1980.

Williams, Mark Eric. *Understanding U.S.–Latin American Relations*. New York: Routledge, 2012.

Zartman, I. William, ed. *Imbalance of Power: U.S. Hegemony and International Power*. Boulder, CO: Lynne Rienner Publishers, 2009.

2 The Inter-American System under the Aegis of United States Hegemony

Introduction

An examination of the inter-American system—the umbrella term for a network of institutions, legal principles, and procedures, which began in the late nineteenth century and evolved throughout the twentieth century—provides the perfect bellwether for charting the rise and exercise of American hegemony in the Western Hemisphere, as well as any decline. This particular chapter examines the inter-American system during the heyday of U.S. hegemony in the Americas. The system traces its origins to the invitation issued by then U.S. Secretary of State James G. Blaine in 1889 to the governments of all the sovereign republics of the Western Hemisphere to send representatives to the first International Conference of American States. That conference took place in Washington, DC between January and April 1890.

An underlying premise for the 1890 conference was a desire by Washington, DC to establish a hemispheric venue to prevent the eruption of wars over boundary disputes in the Americas that might provoke European intervention. This objective was very much in keeping with the spirit of the Monroe Doctrine that proclaimed the independent states of the Americas off-limits for European colonization.[1] Holding the conference in the United States also provided an opportunity for the host country to impress upon visiting delegates its growing industrial and military prowess, as side excursions to visit other cities and factories were part of the conference agenda. In addition to geopolitical considerations, the United States was interested in increasing its exports to Latin America and securing access to important commodities produced in the region. One of the specific proposals tabled by the United States was the establishment of a Western Hemisphere customs union similar to the one that existed at the time among the German states in Europe. The United States also proposed that any disputes that might arise among the nations of the Americas be submitted to binding arbitration.

Despite footing the bill for the first inter-American conference, the United States was only entitled to one vote. Hence, the proposals for a hemispheric customs union and for submitting boundary disputes to binding arbitration did not pass, as a majority of the Latin American delegates rejected them. One reason for the failure of the proposed customs union was a concern that it was an effort to tie Latin American raw materials to U.S. markets at the expense of more lucrative European ones.[2] Echoing some of the same concerns that would be raised to oppose the Free Trade Area of the Americas initiative a century later, there was also unease that Blaine's proposal for a customs union would solidify U.S. manufacturing prowess, to the detriment of Latin American industrialization.[3] Suspicions regarding U.S. intentions were exacerbated by the fact the U.S. Congress, demonstrating a complete disregard for the upcoming conference, approved a rise in import tariffs in December 1889 that negatively affected Latin American exports to the United States.[4] Binding arbitration was rejected because of apprehension that it might lead to a reversal of some countries' recent territorial gains through wars. This was a particular worry for Chile following its acquisition of the highly lucrative nitrate-rich provinces of Peru and Bolivia in the War of the Pacific (1879–1884).

Although the Washington, DC conference of 1890 ended without any plans for a future inter-American meeting, U.S. President McKinley prodded Mexico (then under Porfirio Díaz's authoritarian rule) to hold another in Mexico City in 1901–1902. At that second conference, the conferees (as was the case with the delegates in 1890) called for the creation of an inter-American bank—something that would not happen until the establishment of the Inter-American Development Bank at the end of the 1950s. They also endorsed a U.S. proposal to build a canal across the Panamanian isthmus, and passed resolutions concerning patents and copyrights protection and the mutual recognition of professional titles.[5] Furthermore, the delegates were updated on the progress of a Pan-American Railway that would run from North to South America. Although that railway was never completed, it did serve as the precursor for the Pan-American Highway originating in Alaska and ending in Argentina, which (but for the Darian Gap in Panama) was finally finished in 1963. The most significant outcome of the Mexico City conference, however, was the authorization to create the precursor to what eventually became the Pan American Health Organization (PAHO).

Little of substance came out of the Third International Conference of American States in Rio de Janeiro in 1906, and there was no discussion of U.S. involvement in the independence movement that led to Colombia's loss of Panama in 1903. In fact, what is most remarkable is that the discussions at the initial three inter-American conferences never broached the issue that was of most concern to the Latin American countries, namely the growing economic and military power of the United States and its ability to do what it pleased in the Caribbean Basin. This underscores the fact that, regardless of the country hosting an inter-American conference, it was always the U.S. delegation that maintained a firm grip on the agenda. In addition, the inter-American conferences were viewed as an opportunity for the host country to show off its material progress more than for addressing issues that might bring discomfort and embarrassment to some of the guests. Brazil's decision to host the third conference in 1906 was itself part of a strategy to pose as a willing ally of the United States, sharing its goals in the hemisphere, in order to gain an advantage over

Argentina in its quest for diplomatic leadership in South America.[6] Carlos Gustavo Poggio Teixeira argues that Brazil wanted to be viewed by Washington, DC as a co-guarantor of the Monroe Doctrine in South America and thus it pursued an unwritten alliance with the United States, meaning that each country would take care of its respective regional subsystem.[7]

The Pan-American Union

At the Fourth International Conference of Inter-American States, held in Buenos Aires in 1910, the decision was made to establish a new organization called the Pan-American Union, headquartered in Washington, DC. The U.S. Secretary of State of the time would automatically become chair of the new organization. Construction of the building in Washington, DC that would serve as the headquarters of the Pan-American Union and later house the Organization of American States (OAS) began that same year.[8] Buenos Aires was an interesting choice of venue for the conference, given that Argentina could always be counted on to provide a contrarian position to most of the United States' proposals at these early inter-American conferences. The explanation for Argentina's testy relationship with the United States was based on the former country's fabulous wealth and well-educated population at the start of the twentieth century. Given this, Argentina viewed itself as the natural leader of Latin America, with just as much right as the United States to be the hegemon of the Western Hemisphere. In addition, Argentina had much closer economic and cultural ties to Europe than it did to the United States, a country that directly competed with Argentina in terms of commodities in the global market.

World War I meant the Fifth International Conference of American States was postponed until 1923. It took place in Santiago, in a climate of strained relations between the United States and its neighbors to the south as a result of repeated invasions of countries in the Caribbean Basin and occupations of the Dominican Republic, Haiti, and Nicaragua. "[D]elegates from Haiti and the Dominican Republic joined forces to protest, distributed pamphlets to all the delegates, and aired their grievances in the Latin American press."[9] The Latin American states, led by the Uruguayan president, presented a plan to make the Monroe Doctrine a multilateral instrument so that each republic would commit itself to intervene to aid a fellow American state in the event of an extrahemispheric attack.[10] The United States, however, refused to accept any proposal that would limit its hegemony through a non-exclusive interpretation of the very doctrine that underpinned it. The U.S. delegation also rejected draft legal instruments to prevent interventions in other sovereign states' internal affairs which had been submitted by a committee of jurists from throughout the Americas that was formed after the 1906 inter-American conference in Rio de Janeiro. The delegates in Santiago did agree, however, to sign a Treaty to Avoid and Prevent Conflicts between the American States.[11]

The Sixth International Conference of American States, in Havana in 1928, was dominated by denunciations—although, conspicuously, not from Brazil—of the U.S. re-occupation of Nicaragua, and a Mexican proposal that the head of the Pan-American Union be replaced annually on a rotating basis and not be limited to the U.S. Secretary of State. In deference to U.S. President Calvin Coolidge, who spoke at the conference, however, neither the Mexican proposal nor another put forward by El Salvador prohibiting interference in the internal affairs of another country garnered sufficient votes for approval. The U.S. chief delegate, former U.S. Secretary of State Charles Evans Hughes, managed to postpone a final vote on the non-intervention resolution until the next inter-American conference, scheduled to be held in the Uruguayan capital.[12] Interestingly, Coolidge's visit to Havana would be the last by a sitting American president until the historic March 2016 visit by President Obama, seeking to re-establish diplomatic relations with Cuba after they were broken off following Castro's 1959 revolution.

Despite Latin American frustration regarding the United States' lack of commitment to a set of legal principles that would respect national sovereignty and prohibit unilateral interventions, support for the Pan-American Union held. That was primarily because of so-called second-dimension initiatives of mutual hemispheric interest, including scientific cooperation, as well as efforts to improve sanitary conditions, expand trade, enhance the rights of women and children, and protect intellectual property rights.[13]

The Seventh International Conference of American States, held in Montevideo in 1933, coincided with Franklin Delano Roosevelt's first year in office. In keeping with the new U.S. Good Neighbor policy, U.S. Secretary of State Cordell Hull accepted a proposal long resisted by the United States that forbade intervention in the internal and external affairs of the American republics. The U.S. delegation, however, did enter a reservation that its rights under generally accepted principles of international law were not abrogated, these being to protect the lives and property of U.S. citizens and for reasons of self-defense.[14] The Americans also subscribed to the Convention on the Rights and Duties of States, which gave the Latin Americans all they had clamored for in the past, including recognition of the Calvo Doctrine, the legal equality of the republics, the inviolability of territory, and the non-recognition of territorial claims acquired by force.[15] The Convention on the Rights and Duties of States further mandated that any disputes that might arise among any countries in the Americas had to be resolved by peaceful means. Despite the latter obligation, the Pan-American Union proved itself incapable of resolving three major conflicts that engulfed the South American nations in the 1930s and early 1940s. These included the Chaco War (1932–1935) between Bolivia and Paraguay, the border dispute over the town of Leticia between Colombia and Peru (1932–1933), and a second border dispute in 1941 near the same remote Amazonian region, but this time involving Ecuador and Peru. For some commentators, the lack of an effective hemispheric mechanism to resolve these border disputes underscored that the Pan-American Union remained a creature of the United States, designed to serve its own national interests.[16]

At a special Inter-American Conference for the Maintenance of Peace in Buenos Aires in 1936 attended by U.S. President Franklin Delano Roosevelt, the delegates signed the Convention for the Maintenance, Preservation, and Re-establishment of Peace, which provided for consultations if any one of them felt threatened by an outside aggressor. The delegates also adopted a protocol that declared inadmissible the intervention of any one state, directly or indirectly, in the internal affairs of another for whatever reason, thereby abrogating the reservation the United States had made in Montevideo in 1933 when it finally accepted that intervention in the sovereign affairs of another country was impermissible.[17] In order to oversee compliance with this new treaty, the Meeting of Consultation of Ministers of Foreign Affairs was created to deal with any urgent matters affecting peace and security.[18]

The Eighth International Conference of American States convened in Lima in 1938, under gathering war clouds in both Asia and Europe. Japan had already invaded and established a puppet regime in Manchuria, and both Austria and the Sudetenland were now part of the Third Reich. The major achievement of the Lima conference was a commitment that the member states of the Pan-American Union would consult among themselves if any one of them charged that a danger to the peace had arisen, with remedial measures including the use of military force.[19] The United States invoked this provision after war broke out in Europe in 1939, at the first Meeting of Consultation of the Ministers of Foreign Affairs in Panama. That meeting proclaimed the neutrality of the American republics and established a zone of neutral seas that extended from Canada to Antarctica and up to 300 miles offshore on either the Atlantic or the Pacific Oceans. While each country was obligated to patrol its own coasts to enforce this neutrality pledge, only the United States had the resources to patrol all of it, implying the need for bases in Latin America.[20] In a first, the United States also pledged at the Panama meeting to provide economic assistance to Latin American governments facing hardships that might arise from the war. Until then, the U.S. government had always managed to avoid making any type of financial commitment to assist other republics in the Americas.

Following the U.S. declaration of war on the Axis powers on December 7, 1941, the Roosevelt administration worked through the Pan-American Union to get member states to move beyond declarations of neutrality. Instead, the U.S. wanted member states to apply pressure on domestic Axis interests and break diplomatic relations with the Axis powers. Although the United States succeeded early on in getting most countries in the hemisphere to recall their ambassadors from the Axis countries (Argentina and Chile being notable exceptions), in the end only Brazil joined the war effort, sending troops who participated in the Italian campaign. Chile and Argentina were among the last countries in the Americas to declare war on the Axis countries, doing so in the last months of the war in order to ensure invitations to the planned post-war conference in San Francisco that resulted in the creation of the United Nations.

The Organization of American States (OAS)

The end of World War II sparked a debate among Western Hemisphere governments as to whether the inter-American system should be abolished in favor of a new multilateral arrangement that eventually became the United Nations (UN). At the insistence of the Latin American countries, the inter-American system was retained, thereby providing the impetus for creation of the Organization of American States (OAS) in 1948. One reason the Latin Americans were so interested in preserving the inter-American system and institutionalizing it further was that they viewed it as a more effective way of inhibiting U.S. power in their region than a multilateral organization would be. This, in turn, is widely attributed to Latin America's bitter experience with the League of Nations and its inability to prevent encroachments on national sovereignty or stop the region's border disputes from degenerating into wars.

In 1947, even before the establishment of the OAS, the nations of the Western Hemisphere signed the Inter-American Treaty of Reciprocal Assistance (aka the Rio Treaty), by which an attack on any signatory country in the Americas was deemed an attack on the others.[22] Such an incident would trigger a collective response to assist the victim, although the use of military force against the aggressor was not required: retaliatory actions could also include diplomatic or economic measures. The impetus behind the Rio Treaty was the new state of tension that had arisen between former World War II allies the United States and the Soviet Union. One commentator has called the Rio Treaty "a fig leaf for the Monroe Doctrine," although recognizing that it imposed restraints on the United States as well.[23] Early misgivings that the Rio Treaty would subordinate the foreign and military policies of the Latin American states to U.S. priorities were borne out by subsequent events.

In addition to military-related obligations that might arise under the Rio Treaty, the United States continued to have hemispheric or strictly bilateral military arrangements with countries throughout the Americas that had originated during World War II. In particular, the Inter-American Defense Board, created during the war, became the principal body of the inter-American military system.[24] In 1951, the U.S. Congress passed the Military Defense Assistance Act so that Latin American military establishments would be equipped mainly with U.S. arms and encouraged to accept U.S. training, organization, and doctrine as a useful mechanism for denying European arms sellers entry into Latin American markets.[25] The focus of this military assistance was primarily bilateral in nature. An Inter-American Defense College established in 1962 offered training in internal defense and development, counter-insurgency, and civil actions such as building schools, health clinics, and roads in an attempt to prevent the outbreak or contain the spread of Castro-inspired guerilla movements.[26] The National Security Doctrine's widespread dissemination in the 1960s through training provided to Latin American military personnel at the School of the Americas in the Panama Canal Zone (before it was transferred to Fort Benning, Georgia in 1984) emphasized internal security threats viewed through a Cold War lens. These viewpoints helped contribute to the massive human rights violations suffered in the region when numerous Latin American countries came under military rule, with any type of dissent viewed as a potential national security threat.

The Ninth International Conference of American States convened in Bogotá in early 1948. While the conference was going on, the Colombian presidential candidate for the Liberal Party, Jorge Eliécer Gaitán, was gunned down on a Bogotá street. His assassination set off riots in the major Colombian cities and initiated the long period of political violence that engulfed Colombia for the rest of the twentieth century and into the new millennium. The delegates attending the conference were forced to conclude their meeting in a schoolhouse in the suburbs of the Colombian capital. Before dispersing, they signed the OAS Charter, thereby replacing the old Pan-American Union. Unsurprisingly, given past U.S. behavior in the hemisphere, the OAS Charter contains numerous references and provisions prohibiting direct or indirect intervention in the internal and external affairs of the member states in whatever form. Unlike the founding documents of other regional organizations, the OAS Charter also includes clear references to the endorsement of representative democracy, although it would be decades before this would be honored in actual practice.[27] The original OAS Charter has been amended four times since the first version came into force in 1951 (with the last amendments made in 1993). "The impetus for the amendments was the Latin American states' desire to strengthen the economic and social provisions, their priority, and weaken the political and security provisions, the U.S. priority."[28]

The governing body of the OAS is the General Assembly, which convenes each country's representatives on an annual basis to make decisions related to the structure, funding, and guiding priorities of the OAS. It may also meet in special sessions during the course of the year. The General Assembly eventually replaced the former International Conferences of American States after the tenth, and last, such conference took place in Caracas in 1954. Although most decisions of the General Assembly require the affirmative vote of a majority to pass, approval of measures related to institutional structure, budgetary matters, and fundamental goals of the organization (such as the preservation of representative democracy in a particular member state) require a two-thirds affirmative vote. A Permanent Council made up of ambassadors from each of the member states oversees the routine business of the OAS. As is also true of the General Assembly, every country's vote is equal and no nation exercises veto power. The Permanent Council, which usually meets twice a month in Washington, DC, is chaired for a six-month term by an ambassador of a member state on a rotating basis according to the country's alphabetical order (in Spanish). The Permanent Council's decisions—such as the imposition of collective security measures—require a two-thirds affirmative vote, a not-so-subtle attempt to control the disproportionate influence of the United States and its capacity to use economic or political pressure to try to put together a simple majority.[29] Among the Permanent Council's specific duties is the election of the Secretary

General and the Assistant Secretary General, who in turn oversee the work of the various OAS technical bodies and agencies as well as ensure implementation of OAS initiatives. In a reflection of the OAS's long tradition of heightened concerns over national sovereignty, the Secretary General and the Assistant Secretary General cannot undertake independent initiatives unless explicitly authorized by the Permanent Council and/or General Assembly or upon the consent of the member state, which is the target of such an initiative.[30] Other OAS bodies include the Inter-American Council for Integral Development and a host of specialized agencies and entities immersed in various topics of hemispheric interest (e.g., defense, drugs, human rights, legal reform, telecommunications, etc.) as well as affiliated organizations such as PAHO. The organizational culture of the OAS emphasizes consensual decision making, which reinforces the notion of equality between states and serves as a constraint on intervention in domestic affairs.[31]

The Tenth (and last) International Conference of American States was held in Caracas in March 1954. Efforts by the United States to contain the spread of Communism in the Western Hemisphere dominated the agenda. The United States was particularly concerned that the reformist government of Jacobo Árbenz of Guatemala was a tool of Moscow-inspired intrigue meriting a decisive response. The Eisenhower administration therefore sought approval of a declaration authorizing appropriate action against any government in the Americas that fell under the domination or control of the international Communist movement, which was thereby considered to constitute a threat to the sovereignty and political independence of the American states and endanger peace in the hemisphere.[32] The embattled Guatemalan government made an impassioned plea for support and received a standing ovation. In the end, though, it was unable to prevent the passage of the declaration, thereby sealing Guatemala's fate. The fact that the Guatemala matter had ended up in the OAS was itself the result of maneuvering by the U.S. to move the issue away from the UN Security Council (to whom the Guatemalans had initially appealed), where the Americans had less ability to influence things. At the OAS, only Guatemala voted against the U.S.-sponsored declaration (Argentina and Mexico abstained). The other governments acquiesced to U.S. pressure in the hopes of currying favor and securing possible U.S. economic assistance—something that did not happen.[33] Massive aid for economic development in Latin America would have to wait until Fidel Castro took power in Cuba and President John F. Kennedy proposed an Alliance for Progress in 1961.

Having quashed Guatemala's incipient experiment with representative democracy through a CIA-directed military coup in 1954, U.S. President Dwight Eisenhower convened a meeting with 18 other heads of state from Latin America, under the auspices of the OAS, in Panama in 1956. The main purpose of the event was to solidify support for the U.S. Cold War effort against global Communism. Many of the Latin American presidents who attended did so in the hope of securing U.S. funding for the economic and social development of their nations. Once again, the U.S. delegation skillfully sidestepped the aid issue and avoided making any financial commitments regarding funding economic development projects. The U.S. position was that the best way to ensure economic development in Latin America was for governments to adopt policies that encouraged private-sector initiative. By mid-January 1959, however, Eisenhower had finally acquiesced to Latin American demands for the establishment of the Inter-American Development Bank.[34]

On the heels of Fidel Castro's blossoming alliance with the Soviet Union, the Kennedy administration proposed an Alliance for Progress in 1961 to encourage political stability and economic development in other Latin American countries as a way to make them less susceptible to a Communist takeover. The intellectual author of the Alliance for Progress was actually Brazilian President Juscelino Kubitschek, who had proposed something similar as far back as 1956. Kubitschek had argued that substantial U.S. economic aid was required to address widespread poverty in Latin America and prevent desperate masses from turning to Communism as a solution.[35] Under the Alliance for Progress, the expectation was that Latin American countries would implement a whole series of important reforms, including overhauling tax systems, land redistribution, improving health and education systems, and strengthening democratic institutions, in exchange for funding from the United States.[36] Despite U.S. pledges to provide the bulk of US$20 billion in assistance over a ten-year period, the Alliance for Progress soon foundered—the victim of bureaucratic infighting in Washington, DC, poor planning, and resistance to serious reforms by local elites. In addition, between 1961 and 1965, military governments replaced elected civilians in at least nine countries in the Western Hemisphere. As one critic noted, the Alliance contemplated a partnership where there existed only a hegemonic relationship and it soon degenerated into a crony capitalist scheme where loans extended to Latin American governments were tied to purchases of U.S. goods and equipment.[37]

At the January 1962 OAS Meeting of Consultation of Foreign Ministers in the Uruguayan resort city of Punta del Este, Venezuelan President Rómulo Betancourt claimed that Cuba was supporting an armed movement attempting to destabilize his country's government.[38] The Kennedy administration hoped to use the meeting to expel Cuba from the OAS, but it had to settle for a suspension of Cuba's participation on the basis that a Communist form of government was incompatible with the inter-American system. The three largest countries in Latin America (Argentina, Brazil, and Mexico) voted against the motion, along with Bolivia, Chile, and Ecuador. Fidel Castro responded by belittling the OAS as the U.S. Secretariat for the Colonies and a house of prostitution.[39] The United States received more support later that year when it asked the OAS Permanent Council to approve a declaration demanding that Russian missiles installed in Cuba be deemed as "offensive" in nature and removed immediately. The vote was unanimous in favor of the U.S.-sponsored declaration. The document also authorized the use of force under the Rio Treaty (although Brazil, Mexico, and Bolivia abstained on this part of the declaration). In response to Venezuelan allegations of renewed Cuban involvement in efforts to overthrow the government in Caracas, the OAS Meeting of Consultation of Foreign Ministers approved a U.S.-supported initiative in 1964 to have all member states break diplomatic relations with Havana and suspend most of their trade with Cuba. All the OAS member states but Mexico eventually complied (although four countries—Bolivia, Chile, Mexico, and Uruguay—voted against the original motion).

In January 1964, violence erupted in Panama after a group of Panamanian students marched into the U.S. Canal Zone to hoist their country's flag alongside a U.S. flag that a group of American students had illegally hoisted hours before. In the scuffle that ensued, the American students ripped the Panamanian flag to shreds. This infuriated Panamanians, already resentful that the Canal Zone had split their country in two and that the Zone's residents enjoyed a much higher standard of living than that of the average Panamanian. In response to the destruction of their country's flag, a group of Panamanians led by university students attempted to march into the Canal Zone, but were repelled by U.S. troops. At least 24 Panamanian civilians lost their lives in the subsequent rioting. The Panamanian government responded by breaking diplomatic relations with Washington, DC and referring the matter of establishing Panamanian sovereignty over the Canal Zone to the OAS. Although President Lyndon Johnson quickly negotiated a new treaty that recognized Panama's eventual sovereignty over the Canal Zone, the U.S. Senate refused to ratify it. The Nixon administration attempted to revive efforts to negotiate a new canal treaty but only achieved agreement on a set of negotiating principles. His successor Jimmy Carter had better luck, undoubtedly influenced by the fact that the Panama Canal was by then viewed as strategically obsolete by many in the defense establishment. The United States and Panama finally signed two treaties in September 1977, at an elaborate ceremony at OAS headquarters attended by most of the Hemisphere's heads of state. The first treaty was about the operation and defense of the canal, which would remain in effect until Panama assumed full control of the Panama Canal Zone on January 1, 2000. The second required the permanent neutrality and international status of the canal following its handover to full Panamanian control. The treaties were approved by a large majority of Panamanians in an October 1977 referendum, and narrowly achieved the two-thirds majority (68–32) required for ratification by the U.S. Senate. Many U.S. senators who had voted to ratify the treaties found themselves out of a job following the November 1978 elections. "Although highly unpopular in conservative, U.S. political circles, Washington's appeasement of Panama kept the canal issue from blossoming into a unifying cause that might solidify regional anti-U.S. sentiments even more."[40]

In 1965, the Johnson administration sought a resolution that would authorize stationing an inter-American peace force in the Dominican Republic. In making such a request, the U.S. was asking the OAS to approve its earlier invasion of the Dominican Republic in response to the violence that engulfed the country following an attempt by supporters of Juan Bosch to restore him to power. Bosch had been elected president in an OAS-monitored election in 1962, but was overthrown several months later in a military coup supported by the country's economic elites. The U.S. claimed Bosch was supported by Communists, who would come to dominate his government once restored to power. The resolution proposed by the United States at the OAS barely achieved the two-thirds majority required to pass and was opposed by Chile, Mexico, Uruguay, and Venezuela. With the exception of some 3,000 Brazilian soldiers, the remaining 20,000 or so members of the inter-American peace force that was eventually posted to the Dominican Republic consisted almost exclusively of U.S. military personnel. The foreign soldiers remained in the country until the 1966 inauguration of Joaquín Balaguer, a Trujillo loyalist, and the interim president following the dictator's assassination in 1961. The U.S. intervention in the Dominican Republic dealt "a severe blow to the inter-American system, which was treated in the crisis as a mere rubber stamp of [U.S.] policies which its critics have long held it to be."[41]

One of the few success stories of the OAS during the 1960s was its speedy resolution of the so-called Soccer War between Honduras and El Salvador in 1969. The catalyst for the conflict was riots that broke out between Honduran and Salvadoran fans following a soccer match, after months of rising tension due to the large numbers of Salvadoran peasants crossing the border to settle in less densely populated Honduras. In response to the violence, Salvadoran troops invaded Honduras, ostensibly to protect their co-nationals against escalating attacks from Hondurans. Utilizing provisions in the Rio Treaty on mutual defense, the OAS sent an observer mission to Honduras, got both countries to agree to a ceasefire, and quickly convinced El Salvador to withdraw its soldiers from Honduras after the OAS threatened to impose sanctions. The United States also imposed an arms embargo on both countries as they had violated their bilateral military assistance programs with Washington, DC by utilizing weapons obtained from the Americans against each other, instead of against an extra-regional foe.

Another OAS success story—although it took decades to manifest itself as such—was the signing of the 1967 Treaty of Tlatelolco, which declared Latin America and the Caribbean to be a nuclear weapons-free zone. Many governments saw the treaty as a U.S.-inspired initiative to monopolize its nuclear arms capabilities and assert its hemispheric hegemony, even though it had been tabled by Mexico (which subsequently garnered the Mexican diplomat, Alfonso Garcia Robles, who came up with the idea of the Nobel Peace Prize in 1982). Argentina, Brazil, and Chile—all of which were at the time under military governments that sought to acquire nuclear weapons—were among the last countries to ratify the treaty, in 1994.

All the leaders of all the sovereign states in the Americas gathered for a summit in the Uruguayan resort city of Punta del Este in 1967. Argentine President Arturo Illia had originally proposed the meeting (before his overthrow in a military coup in 1966), and it was seconded by his Chilean counterpart Eduardo Frei Montalva. Lyndon Johnson, the U.S. president of the period, enthusiastically pushed his diplomats to hammer out a substantive agenda and there were expectations that it could resuscitate the by then moribund Alliance for Progress.[42] Although the United States showed itself to be accommodating to Latin American demands, even accepting a proposal to create a strictly Latin American common market similar to the one that existed in Western Europe, the summit produced little of substantive and long-lasting value. One important reason for this was that many of the ambitious goals and action items that came out of the Punta del Este meeting were often left unattached to procedures or institutions capable of transforming them into deeds.[43]

Trinidad and Tobago became the first English-speaking Caribbean nation to join the OAS in 1967, followed by Jamaica and Barbados. Thereafter the OAS experienced a dramatic increase in membership throughout the 1970s and 1980s as more British colonies in the Caribbean gained their independence.[44] Dutch-speaking Suriname became an OAS member state in 1977. Canada joined in 1990, finally overcoming its fear that by joining the U.S.-dominated OAS its foreign policy independence in the Americas would be subsumed by its bigger neighbor.[45] The increase in membership from the Caribbean resulted in revisions to the OAS Charter, including rules on eligibility for admission, a greater emphasis on economic and social development issues, and a reduction of the OAS Secretary General's tenure from one ten-year term to a five-year term (subject to re-election).

During the 1970s, some U.S. government officials began to question the value of continued United States membership in the OAS. One reason for this was that the meetings of the General Assembly and Permanent Council had become fora for criticizing U.S. foreign policy, including Washington, DC's unwillingness to funnel significant aid to the region for economic development. In addition, the OAS no longer compliantly rubber-stamped U.S.-sponsored resolutions. Instead, the Latin American governments were now tabling their own resolutions, which frequently went against U.S. policy objectives. For example, in 1975 the OAS General Assembly authorized those member states wanting to re-establish trade and diplomatic relations with Havana to do so. That same year, the United States found itself alone in opposing an effort to amend the Rio Treaty on mutual defense to include a provision that "for the maintenance of peace and security in the Hemisphere, it is also necessary to guarantee collective economic security for the development of the American states."[46] In 1979, as the demise of the Somoza dictatorship appeared imminent, a U.S.-sponsored resolution at the OAS to establish a government of national reconciliation in Nicaragua and an inter-American peacekeeping force was resoundingly defeated.[47] Latin American nations also made various attempts in the 1970s to curtail U.S. influence by establishing alternative entities that excluded the United States, such as the *Sistema Económico Latinoamericano* or SELA, based in Caracas. For Mark Eric Williams, enhanced Latin American assertiveness in the 1970s could be explained by a widespread perception of hegemonic disequilibrium following the collapse of the Bretton Woods monetary exchange system, U.S. military setbacks in Southeast Asia, and the newfound wealth of Latin American oil producers as a result of OPEC's price hikes.[48]

Whatever doubts some Nixon and Ford administration officials may have harbored about the effectiveness of working through the OAS in order to achieve U.S. policy objectives, Jimmy Carter's election in 1976 led to a reappraisal, given the administration's strong support for the promotion of human rights in the Western Hemisphere. Even before Carter's arrival in the White House, the U.S. Congress had already made it the policy of the United States to promote and encourage increased respect for human rights and fundamental freedoms for all persons.[49] The International Security Assistance and Arms Export Control Act of 1976, for example, required that the executive branch ensure that U.S. military assistance not be provided to governments that systemically violated human rights. Congress also required the U.S. State Department to submit annual human rights reports for each country that received any type of U.S. military and financial assistance. In 1974, the Committee on Foreign Affairs of the U.S. House of Representatives formally recommended that the U.S. State Department propose that the OAS strengthen the powers of the Inter-American Commission on Human Rights.[50]

Human Rights in the Inter-American System

In addition to approving the Charter that brought the OAS into existence, the delegates in Bogotá in 1948 had approved an American Declaration of the Rights and Duties of Man. An Inter-American Commission on Human Rights—made up of seven experts chosen by the OAS General Assembly—was established in 1959 to oversee compliance with the provisions of the American Declaration as well as human rights obligations found in the OAS Charter. Since 1966, individuals and, subsequently, any non-governmental organization (NGO) legally recognized in one or more OAS member state have the right to present petitions to the Commission alleging human rights abuses. An American Convention on Human Rights was adopted in 1969 (although it did not come into force until almost a decade later), while an American Court of Human Rights, headquartered in San José, Costa Rica, was set up to enforce provisions of the Convention and additional human rights obligations found in other OAS documents. The Court has seven judges, selected in their individual capacities by the General Assembly for a six-year term. Unlike the Inter-American Commission on Human Rights, the Court only has jurisdiction over those OAS member states that have ratified the Convention as well as explicitly accepted the compulsory jurisdiction of the Inter-American Court of Human Rights.

Over the decades, from its beginnings as a government-run diplomatic entity with an ill-defined mandate to promote human rights in the region, the inter-American human rights system emerged as a legal regime formally empowering citizens to bring suit challenging the domestic activities of their own governments.[51] Despite perennial financial constraints, the inter-American human rights system has proven to be remarkably effective. One reason for this is that the Inter-American Commission on Human Rights and the Court in San José, Costa Rica do not need to establish consensus among member states before they take action, whether in the pivotal role of condemnation or in providing an early warning on situations that threaten to undermine the consolidation of democracy and the rule of law.[52] By championing the inter-American human rights system, the U.S. government was able to push an important foreign policy agenda that was not viewed as imposing its standards or values on other societies but rather was universal and guaranteed under international law. However, "[f]rom their insistence on a full range of rights, including socio-economic rights, to their lobbying for intrusive mandates for human rights institutions to intervene in the domestic affairs of states, the positions of Latin American government representatives have not necessarily reflected US policy preferences."[53] For example, in 1988 the General Assembly approved the Additional Protocol to the American Convention on Human Rights in the Area of Economic, Social, and Cultural Rights, to the great consternation of the Reagan administration.

By the early 1980s, the economic dynamics that had encouraged a diplomatic challenge to U.S. hegemony in the inter-American system a decade earlier began to unravel. Contributing to this shift was the hike in international oil prices that detrimentally affected the majority of Latin American countries who were not petroleum producers. Soon thereafter, the Reagan administration sought to tame domestic U.S. inflation by restricting the country's money supply through a sharp rise in interest rates. This sparked a global recession and a collapse in commodity prices. For most Latin American governments, which had heavily borrowed money during the 1970s at variable interest rates that were then low, the sharp rise in interest rates became unsustainable, as revenue obtained from traditional commodity exports also collapsed. As a result, most Latin American countries found themselves forced to reschedule interest payments and obtain new credit lines from the International Monetary Fund in order to make interest payments on existing loan obligations. This new credit often came with conditions, such as adopting austerity measures, privatizing state-owned enterprises, lowering tariff barriers on imports, and eliminating restrictions on foreign investment. Throughout much of the 1980s, Latin American states became so absorbed with domestic problems that, rather than challenging U.S. influence, debt negotiations comprised the bulk of their policy agendas.[54]

In April 1982, Argentina's military rulers invaded the Malvinas, or Falkland Islands, and South Georgia in the South Atlantic, as part of a desperate move to whip up nationalist fervor and distract attention from a collapsing economy. From elementary school onwards, Argentines are taught that the Malvinas belong to Argentina and were illegally appropriated by Great Britain in 1833. In fact, even today, maps in Argentina do not acknowledge British control over the islands. As British war ships streamed to confront the Argentine military in the South Atlantic, Buenos Aires frequently invoked the Monroe Doctrine as requiring the United States to come to Argentina's defense. The United States first tried to have the matter resolved at the OAS, but soon gave up when the United Kingdom preferred referral of the matter to the UN. Although initially espousing neutrality, the Reagan administration soon commenced covert support for Margaret Thatcher's efforts to recapture the lost territory by, among other things, providing the British with intelligence assistance. By the time British military forces arrived in the South Atlantic several weeks later, the United States was now openly siding with its NATO ally and providing London with military aid. An OAS resolution, *inter alia*, criticized the United States for abandoning and betraying the inter-American system, including the mutual defense obligations of the Rio Treaty.[55] Although it would take another few decades for U.S. politicians, particularly conservatives, to acknowledge it, the U.S. failure to come to Argentina's defense in 1982 effectively abrogated the Monroe Doctrine. John Kerry, U.S. Secretary of State, finally made this official in November 2013 when, during a speech at the OAS, he acknowledged that the era of the Monroe Doctrine was over.[56] The entire Malvinas incident also highlighted, once again, that the inter-American system, including the Rio Treaty, was designed to primarily further U.S. interests and objectives in the Western Hemisphere.

When President Reagan ordered the invasion of Grenada in October 1983, it had the blessing of the tiny island nations that made up the newly minted Organization of Eastern Caribbean States, or OECS (Antigua and Barbuda, Dominica, Grenada, Saint Kitts and Nevis, Saint Lucia, and Saint Vincent and the Grenadines). The OECS countries also contributed a few hundred personnel to what was a predominantly U.S. force. The OAS, on the other hand, was completely sidelined—much to the consternation of the Latin American member states, who argued that the OAS, not the OECS, was the appropriate body to seek authorization for the invasion (particularly given that the United States was not even a member of the OECS).

As civil wars engulfed El Salvador, Guatemala, and Nicaragua throughout the 1980s, the OAS initially played a role in trying to restore peace in Central America through its institutional support of the Contadora Group of countries (Colombia, Mexico, Panama, and Venezuela) and their support group of nations (Argentina, Brazil, Peru, and Uruguay). Costa Rican President Oscar Arias eventually used the Contadora framework to facilitate a peace agreement that won the backing of the five Central American governments in 1987, and garnered Arias the Nobel Peace Prize that same year.[57] In 1989, the Central

American presidents asked the Peruvian UN Secretary General, Javier Pérez de Cuellar, to establish a UN Observer Group in Central America (ONUCA) to disarm and facilitate the repatriation of the Contras based in Honduras. The UN provided an election observer mission for the 1990 presidential election in Nicaragua as well. The UN was also responsible for ending El Salvador's civil war and brokering the peace initiative in neighboring Guatemala. In addition, it was the UN that assumed major responsibility for peacekeeping operations in Haiti following President Jean-Bertrand Aristide's restoration to office in 1994, although the OAS had played an initial role in Haiti when member states imposed a trade embargo on the country after Aristide was overthrown in a military coup in September 1991.[58]

In February 1988, General Manuel Noriega removed the civilian president of Panama and assumed full control of the country (although he had been the country's *de facto* ruler since at least 1983). The Reagan administration responded by imposing economic sanctions on Panama and suspending military aid. Weeks later, a federal court in Florida indicted Noriega on drug-trafficking charges. Following George H.W. Bush's inauguration in January 1989, the new administration decided to work through the OAS in response to Noriega's decision to annul the results of the May 1989 Panamanian presidential election. An OAS mediation team made a number of visits to Panama to negotiate with Noriega regarding the establishment of a transitional government to be put in place until new elections could be held, but Noriega refused to make any concessions until Washington, DC first lifted the economic sanctions it had imposed under Reagan. When the United States refused to do this, the OAS found itself without any carrots to entice Noriega to give up power, and soon abandoned its mediation efforts. Following the shooting death of a U.S. Marine officer at the hands of the Panamanian Defense Forces and the subsequent escalation in tensions between U.S. and Panamanian military personnel near the Canal Zone in December 1989, President Bush ordered the invasion of Panama by a force made up of 20,000 U.S. troops. Their main objective was to arrest Noriega and bring him back to the United States to be tried for drug trafficking and corruption charges. "Because the United States had not consulted any Latin American government about its invasion plans, regional opposition—quick, sharp, and uniform—cut through ideological divisions, and united governments that were friendly and less friendly toward Washington."[59] A subsequent OAS resolution approved by 20 countries, with seven abstentions, condemned the U.S. invasion of Panama and demanded the immediate withdrawal of U.S. troops. The United States provided the lone dissenting vote.

Despite the condemnation of the U.S. invasion of Panama, 1989 was also the year that the General Assembly meeting in Washington, DC approved Resolution 991 permitting the OAS—at the request of a host country—to send missions to observe all stages of a domestic electoral process, and for the Secretary General to report on the results of this on-site monitoring.[60] Although the OAS had been providing election observer missions for member states that requested them since 1962, these had been done on an *ad hoc* basis and under limited circumstances. In 1990, a Unit for the Promotion of Democracy was established at the OAS to oversee the planning and preparation of election observer missions that would henceforth focus on the quality of the entire electoral process. The 1990s began with an unprecedented situation in the Western Hemisphere. A long period of economic stagnation sparked by the debt crisis of the 1980s, followed by the collapse of the Soviet Union, convinced governments throughout the Americas of the merits of market-oriented policies long advocated by the United States as remedies for Latin America's chronic underdevelopment. Furthermore, the leaders of all the hemisphere's nations (with the exceptions of Fidel Castro's Cuba, and Haiti between September 1991 and October 1994) were democratically elected civilians. The latter fact helps to explain why, on June 5, 1991, the OAS General Assembly, meeting in Santiago, Chile, was able to approve Resolution 1080 on Representative Democracy. In particular, the resolution called for OAS members to respond collectively to the sudden or irregular interruption of the democratic political institutional process or of the legitimate exercise of power by a democratically elected government in any of the Organization's member states.[61] One year after Resolution 1080's approval, the OAS General Assembly adopted the Protocol of Washington, which entered into force in 1997 and authorized the OAS to suspend a member state whose democratically constituted government had been overthrown by force.[62]

Resolution 1080 and the Protocol of Washington marked an important shift from the almost fanatical—albeit understandable—adherence among the Latin American member governments of the OAS to the principle of non-interference in the internal affairs of another sovereign state. Resolution 1080 was first invoked in response to Haitian President Aristide's overthrow by the military in September 1991, although it was the U.S. military, acting through the UN, that was primarily responsible for Aristide's return to the presidency in September 1994. Resolution 1080 was also invoked in response to efforts by Peruvian President Alberto Fujimori in 1992, and Guatemalan President Jorge Serrano in 1993, to impose authoritarian rule. The power grab was resolved in Peru by elections for a constituent assembly at the end of 1992 to draft a new constitution (which resulted in new presidential elections that Fujimori won). In the Guatemalan case, Serrano was replaced by the country's human rights ombudsman as president after the Guatemalan Congress determined the vice-president was ineligible to succeed Serrano due to his involvement in the president's attempt to assume dictatorial powers. Resolution 1080 was also invoked in 1996 when the head of the Paraguayan armed forces, General Lino Oviedo, refused to obey an order from President Juan Carlos Wasmosy to step down, thereby signaling his intent to take power through a military coup. The political crisis in Paraguay was resolved when the presidents of the other MERCOSUR countries (Argentina, Brazil, and Uruguay) made clear they would suspend Paraguay's membership in the regional economic integration scheme unless the democratic order in the country was preserved. Paraguay's heavy dependence on trade with its larger neighbors soon dissipated any support for Oviedo's threat to take power, and he was eventually imprisoned.

When the Clinton administration decided, at the end of 1993, to revive the concept of the old inter-American conferences with a Summit of the Americas in Miami in 1994, all the elected leaders in the hemisphere accepted the U.S. invitation. Accompanied by his democratically elected counterparts from 33 other countries (Cuba being the only notable exclusion), U.S. President Clinton pledged with them to implement 23 initiatives and some 150 action items ranging from the promotion of representative democracy and sustainable development to the eradication of poverty and discrimination. The summit also elevated new issues, such as anticorruption, money laundering, civil society, and women's rights, onto the hemispheric agenda and dramatically expanded the scope for collective action in the region.[63] To the chagrin of the Clinton administration, which had just emerged from a bruising battle with fellow Democrats in the U.S. Congress to get the North American Free Trade Agreement (NAFTA) ratified, the Latin American and Caribbean leaders insisted that trade be at the top of the agenda. As a result, the Miami summit ended with a commitment to prepare the groundwork for negotiating a Free Trade Area of the Americas. In order to ensure oversight of implementation of the mandates coming out of the Summit of the Americas process, a Summit Implementation Review Group was formed, with national representation at the vice-ministerial level as well as with officials from the OAS, the Inter-American Development Bank, the UN's Economic Commission on Latin America and the Caribbean, and PAHO. As a direct outgrowth of one of the initiatives raised at the First Summit of the Americas in Miami, a special OAS group issued the text for an Inter-American Convention against Corruption in March of 1996, which 21 countries immediately signed.[64]

Conclusion

The establishment of the Pan-American Union and the subsequent OAS would appear to be the embodiment of international liberalism. The Pan-American Union sought, as the OAS still does today, to foster dialogue among the American republics in an effort to promote peace and understanding and avoid outbreaks of war. The OAS Charter, in particular, emphasizes core liberal values such as respect for sovereignty and non-interference in the internal and external affairs of member states. It even endorses representative democracy as the ideal form of governance in the Americas.

Despite its liberal façade, for much of its existence the inter-American system has better reflected a realist perception of the world. It was born as a mechanism for the United States to keep other powers out of the Western Hemisphere in order to ensure its own national security and promote its economic predominance over the region. This is most apparent in the Inter-American Treaty of Reciprocal Assistance or Rio Treaty. Only actual or perceived threats to the United States have merited the invocation of its collective security obligations. When Argentina tried to invoke the Rio Treaty after Margaret Thatcher sent a British fleet to retake the disputed Malvinas, which Argentina had always claimed as its territory, the United States rebuffed the request. The type of government or the economic system that a member state could pursue in order to be considered a member of the inter-American system in good standing were also defined by the hegemon. In addition, for decades the United States resisted any attempt to include economic development as key to securing the peace and security of the Western Hemisphere.

Realist theory also helps to explain the Cold War paradox of a U.S. government that claimed to support the spread of democracy, but frequently found itself allied with brutal and repressive dictatorships throughout Latin America and the Caribbean:

> Although the United States may have preferred to see democratic regimes develop in the region, if faced with the trade-off between embracing a right-wing, anti-communist dictatorship or enduring a (sometimes perceived) communist state—even one whose government was democratically elected—security dictated the former.[65]

Realist theory is, however, unable to explain cases in which the United States was unable to get the OAS to go along with positions it favored but, for whatever reason, chose not to act unilaterally.

The inter-American system does fit comfortably within the parameters of the neo-realist quest for balance of power. The primary objective of Latin American participation in the Pan-American Union and the OAS was to enhance national sovereignty by acting as a collective counterweight to unbridled United States hegemony. At the same time, the inter-American system is in keeping with neo-realist theory that states will enter into alliances or mutual defense pacts directed against a serious and imminent threat to their security, as happened when the American republics lined up with the United States during World War II and in the first decades of the Cold War.

The inter-American system, particularly after the creation of the OAS, provides support for hegemonic stability theory, or HST, as well. As the undisputed hegemon of the Western Hemisphere after World War II, the United States did not have to accept the restrictions the OAS Charter imposed on its ability to intervene unilaterally in other countries. In doing so, the United States was providing a public good, namely a rules-based system to govern inter-American relations that would better support its ultimate goals of enhanced commerce, political stability, and regional peace and security. Discussion of whether the inter-American system can survive the decline of U.S. hegemony in the Western Hemisphere, and therefore fulfill predictions that flow out of international regime theory, will have to wait until the next chapter.

The heyday of the inter-American system as a prototype of international liberalism is best associated with FDR's Good Neighbor policy, as well as the presidencies of Jimmy Carter and Bill Clinton. Although the United States remained a regional hegemon, these administrations saw themselves as fulfilling the crucial "first among equals" role required to manage and maintain some degree of order and decision-making capacity within the inter-American system. The Good Neighbor policy, in particular, reflected a genuine effort on the part of the FDR administration to avoid engaging in many of the practices that had caused so much anti-American sentiment throughout Latin America and the Caribbean in previous decades and had ultimately had a negative impact on U.S. business interests in the region. By the late 1930s, gathering war clouds in Europe and Asia arising from the bellicose actions of Germany, Italy, and Japan had made it imperative for the United States to maintain good relations with its Latin American neighbors. The region was a source of key mineral and agricultural products that would be in great demand in any successful engagement in sustained armed conflict. South America's Southern Cone was also home to large populations of persons of German, Italian, and (in the case of Brazil) Japanese nationality or ancestry. The United States therefore could not risk alienating major countries such as Argentina, Brazil, Chile, or Mexico and having them side or trade with nations from outside the Americas that it might soon find itself confronting militarily. That concern also provides an important explanation of why the FDR administration preferred to downplay the Mexican nationalization of American oil interests in 1938.

Carter's emphasis on making human rights a centerpiece of U.S. foreign policy *vis-à-vis* Latin America reflected the priorities of his political party, which controlled both chambers of the Federal Congress at the time and had already made clear the importance it attached to the promotion of international human rights. It also marked a way for Carter to distinguish his presidency from that of his disgraced predecessor, which was associated with, among other things, the military dictatorship that came to power in Chile in 1973. For its part, the Clinton presidency coincided with the end of the Cold War and the triumph of the international liberal order of free markets and representative democracy. For a brief period, at least, there seemed to be no alternative to the liberal order long promoted by successive administrations in Washington, DC, leading Francis Fukuyama to provide the iconic label that characterized this phenomenon as "The End of History."

The glue that held the inter-American system together for as long as it did, even when the United States was blatantly violating its obligations under the OAS not to engage in unilateral interventions such as the overthrow of Jacobo Árbenz in Guatemala in 1954, is supplied by Antonio Gramsci's notions of hegemony. During the first two decades of the Cold War, at least, the national interests of United States and Latin American political elites were not fundamentally antagonistic.[66] Whatever restraints the Rio Treaty and the OAS Charter may have theoretically imposed on U.S. unilateralism within the Western Hemisphere, the fact is that, during the 1950s and 1960s, the OAS anathematized Marxists and implicitly authorized the relaxation of non-intervention norms as a means of cauterizing the revolutionary threat.[67] Accordingly, the inter-American system was serving the fundamental interests of a transnational capitalist class to confront a common mortal danger, overriding parochial concerns related to national sovereignty and non-intervention.

Notes

1 The territory in the Americas of the newly independent nations "are henceforth not to be considered as subjects for future colonization by any European powers" and the United States of America will consider any European attempt "to extend their system to any portion of this hemisphere as dangerous to our peace and security." Excerpt from Message of President James Monroe at the Commencement of the first session of the 18th Congress (the Monroe Doctrine), 12/02/1823, Presidential Messages of the 18th Congress, ca. 12/02/1823–ca. 03/03/1825; Record Group 46; Records of the United States Senate, 1789–1990. Washington, DC: Center for Legislative Archives (National Archives). Available at: www.ourdocuments.gov.

2 John Edwin Fagg, *Pan Americanism* (Malabar, FL: Robert E. Krieger Publishing Company, 1982), 24. The Argentine delegate, Roque Sáenz Peña (whose name would later become synonymous with the landmark law he signed as president of Argentina in 1910 that dramatically expanded the male vote and introduced the secret ballot), rejected the idea of a customs union, "asserting that Europe was no enemy of the Americas but a friendly partner of far more significance to South America than the United States." Ibid.

3 Alonso Aguilar Monteverde, *El Panamericanismo: De la Doctrina de Monroe a la Doctrina Johnson* (México: Cuadernos Americanos, 1965), 43. The heavy commercial focus of this first inter-American conference is underscored by the fact that institutional support was provided by the Commercial Bureau of the American Republics charged with the narrow focus of collecting and disseminating commercial information. G. Pope Atkins, *Encyclopedia of the Inter-American System* (Westport, CT: Greenwood Press, 1997), 3.

4 Zuleika Arashiro, *Negotiating the Free Trade Area of the Americas* (New York: Palgrave Macmillan, 2011), 67. This development also has ironic parallels to the Free Trade Area of the Americas a century later, when the administration of George W. Bush managed to extract Trade Promotion Authority from the U.S. Congress in order to conclude the hemispheric trade negotiations. This came only after the U.S. Congress approved (and Bush signed) a Farm Bill that included trade-distorting agricultural subsidies, and safeguard tariffs detrimentally impacting Latin American steel exports.

5 John Edwin Fagg, *Pan Americanism* (Malabar, FL: Robert E. Krieger Publishing Company, 1982), 27.

6 Riordan Roett, "Brazil and the Inter-American System," in *The Future of the Inter-American System*, ed. Tom J. Farer (New York: Praeger Publishers, 1979), 241. "For much of the 20th century Brazilian foreign policy elites clung to the belief that a close working relationship with the United States and with Pan Americanism best served Brazilian interests." Ibid. Accordingly, Brazil was the only South American country to declare war on Germany in World War I and send troops to fight in Europe in World War II. Brazil adopted a more independent foreign policy in the early 1960s under the presidencies of Jânio Quadros and João Goulart, although that ended abruptly with the military coup of 1964. By the late 1970s, however, Brazil went from a policy of seeking a special relationship with the United States to one of living with unresolved tensions and a more autonomous posture, given that the Brazilian military regime disagreed with the Carter administration on human rights issues and on adherence to the Nuclear Non-Proliferation Treaty. Carlos Espinosa, "The Origins of the Union of South American Nations: A Multi-causal Account of South American Regionalism," in *Exploring the New South American Regionalism*, ed. Ernesto Vivares (Farnham, UK: Ashgate Publishing, 2014), 35. In fact, Brazil responded to the 1977 U.S. State Department's human rights report by revoking a bilateral military assistance agreement it had with the United States.

7 Carlos Gustavo Poggio Teixeira, *Brazil, the United States, and the South American Subsystem* (Lanham, MD: Lexington Books, 2012), 50. Brazilian policy-makers throughout history have consistently split the Western Hemisphere into two halves: a South American half, where Brazil would strive to exert influence, and a North American half that constituted the sphere of influence of the United States, in which Brazil would thus abstain from being seriously involved. Ibid at 36.

8 Andrew Carnegie donated most of the money to build the impressive headquarters of the Pan American Union in Washington, DC. His interest in furthering the cause of Pan Americanism is reputed to have been premised, in part, on completing the Pan American Railway, given that his great fortune rested on steel making.

9 Alan McPherson, *The Invaded* (New York: Oxford University Press, 2014), 208.

10 Mark Eric Williams, *Understanding U.S.–Latin American Relations* (New York: Routledge, 2012), 129. "Given their frustrations with the new League of Nations' inability to limit U.S. intervention, Latin American states came to the 1923 conference with a plan to replace unilateral U.S. intervention within a framework that could sanction multilateral intervention." Ibid.

11 Under the treaty, two commissions were established, one in Montevideo and the other in Washington, DC. The signatory states could submit any disputes arising among themselves that they could not resolve diplomatically for binding arbitration by either commission. John Edwin Fagg, *Pan Americanism* (Malabar, FL: Robert E. Krieger Publishing Company, 1982), 40.

12 Alan McPherson, *The Invaded* (New York: Oxford University Press, 2014), 209. While Hughes acknowledged the opinions of Latin Americans, he lectured them that the problem of Latin America was one of internal instability, and not external aggression coming from the United States. Ibid.

13 See, e.g., Mark Jeffrey Petersen, "'Vanguard of Pan Americanism': Chile and Inter-American Multilateralism in the Early Twentieth Century," in *Cooperation and Hegemony in U.S.–Latin American Relations*, ed. J.P. Scarfi et al. (Houndmills: Palgrave Macmillan, 2016), 113. "Controversy was actively avoided in second dimension issues in order to promote cooperation and nongovernmental actors were heavily involved."

14 Mark Eric Williams, *Understanding U.S.–Latin American Relations* (New York: Routledge, 2012), 130–1.

15 John Edwin Fagg, *Pan Americanism* (Malabar, FL: Robert E. Krieger Publishing Company, 1982), 50. The Calvo Doctrine, named after the Argentine jurist and diplomat Carlos Calvo (1822–1906), mandated that any disputes that might arise between a foreign investor and a government had to be resolved by the courts of the country where the investment was located and that no foreign investor could appeal to its home government for assistance. A related Drago Doctrine, named after the Argentine foreign minister who proposed it in 1902, held that a foreign government could not use armed intervention to enforce the public debt obligations incurred by another country and owed to one of its nationals.

16 Joseph S. Tulchin, *Latin America in International Politics: Challenging U.S. Hegemony* (Boulder, CO: Lynne Rienner Publishers, 2016), 71. "In the absence of an institutional framework within which to seek peace . . . countries formed ad hoc groups of 'friends' to bring the combatants to the bargaining table." Ibid. The League of Nations actually helped to resolve the Colombian–Peruvian dispute over Leticia.

17 John Edwin Fagg, *Pan Americanism* (Malabar, FL: Robert E. Krieger Publishing Company, 1982), 54.

18 G. Pope Atkins, *Encyclopedia of the Inter-American System* (Westport, CT: Greenwood Press, 1997), 2. The Meeting of Consultation of Ministers of Foreign Affairs convened in Panama in 1939, in Havana in 1940, and Rio de Janeiro in 1942, during the wartime period, when no regular inter-American conferences took place.

19 John Edwin Fagg, *Pan Americanism* (Malabar, FL: Robert E. Krieger Publishing Company, 1982), 56. The Declaration of Lima constituted another step in the process whereby the inter-American system was transforming itself into an alliance in response to coming events in Europe. Michael J. Francis, *The Limits of Hegemony* (Notre Dame, IN: University of Notre Dame Press, 1977), 25.

20 John Edwin Fagg, *Pan Americanism* (Malabar, FL: Robert E. Krieger Publishing Company, 1982), 57–8. The zone of neutral seas was an American idea intended to keep the countries who were already at war from fighting in hemispheric waters and to bar their armed ships from entering those waters.

21 "The UN Charter legitimated and sanctioned regional organizations within the UN framework and made regional action in matters of peace and security compatible with UN principles and procedures." G. Pope Atkins, *Encyclopedia of the Inter-American System* (Westport, CT: Greenwood Press, 1997), 9. While this implied that the regional organizations were subject to UN direction, "[i]n practice, however, the Inter-American System enjoyed considerable autonomy, and the UN deferred to the Inter-American System regarding peace and security" matters affecting the Western Hemisphere. Ibid. On the other hand, any peacekeeping functions of the OAS are subordinate to the UN's Security Council. See, Mônica Herz, *The Organization of American States (OAS): Global Governance Away from the Media* (New York: Routledge, 2011), 11.

22 The full text of the Inter-American Treaty of Reciprocal Assistance that entered into force in 1948 is available at: www.oas.org/juridico/english/treaties/b-29.html. The full text of the Protocol of Amendment to the Inter-American Treaty of Reciprocal Assistance that was signed in 1975 (but has not yet entered into force) is found at: www.oas.org/juridico/english/treaties/b-29(1).html.

23 Richard J. Bloomfield, "The Inter-American System: Does it Have a Future?" in *The Future of the Inter-American System*, ed. Tom J. Farer (New York: Praeger Publishers, 1979), 8. The main aim of the OAS is to "search for a consensus that will legitimize and also restrain the exercise of U.S. power in the hemisphere," thus "collective security is not the motive force for Latin American participation in the System, except when there arises a grave threat that the relatively libertarian U.S. hegemony will be replaced by one more oppressive." Ibid.

24 John Child, "The Inter-American Military System: Historical Development, Current Status, and Implications for U.S. Policy," in *The Future of the Inter-American System*, ed. Tom J. Farer (New York: Praeger Publishers, 1979), 161. The Inter-American Defense Board became an official OAS agency in March 2006 and is currently engaged in, among other things, mine-clearing as well as natural disaster mitigation.

25 John Child, "The Inter-American Military System: Historical Development, Current Status, and Implications for U.S. Policy," in *The Future of the Inter-American System*, ed. Tom J. Farer (New York: Praeger Publishers, 1979), 163.

26 John Child, "The Inter-American Military System: Historical Development, Current Status, and Implications for U.S. Policy," in *The Future of the Inter-American System*, ed. Tom J. Farer (New York: Praeger Publishers, 1979), 166.

27 Jorge Heine and Brigitte Weiffen, *21st Century Democracy Promotion in the Americas: Standing Up for the Polity* (New York: Routledge, 2015), 32.

28 David W. Dent and Larman C. Wilson, *Historical Dictionary of Inter-American Organizations, Second Edition* (Plymouth, UK: Scarecrow Press, 2014), 240. The full text of the Charter of the Organization of American States, as amended, is available at: www.oas.org/en/sla/dil/docs/inter_american_treaties_A-41_charter_OAS.pdf.

29 Tom J. Farer, ed., *The Future of the Inter-American System* (New York: Praeger Publishers, 1979), xvii. The Permanent Council, usually meeting in an emergency session, has become the *de facto* former Meetings of Consultation of Foreign Ministers inherited from the old Pan-American Union.

30 "Unlike his counterpart at the United Nations who speaks, proposes, establishes and undertakes missions on his own initiative as well as on authorization of the Security Council, the Secretary General of the OAS has little recognizable breath of competence in these areas." Christopher R. Thomas and Juliana T. Magloire, *Regionalism versus Multilateralism: The Organization of American States in a Global Changing Environment* (Boston: Kluwer Academic Publishers, 2000), 156. Although this situation has been modified somewhat by Article 18 of the Inter-American Democratic Charter, as the Secretary General can now undertake visits or other actions to assess the situation in a particular country, he or she must still receive the prior consent of that country's government before entering its national territory.

31 Mônica Herz, *The Organization of American States (OAS): Global Governance Away from the Media* (New York: Routledge, 2011), 21. One thing that has always given the U.S. the upper hand in the OAS, despite the principle of equality of states, is the cost of implementing actions called for in resolutions, as they are not budgeted items. Accordingly, if the Permanent Council is considering actions that are quite costly in terms of finances or personnel, it needs U.S. support. Carolyn M. Shaw, "Limits to Hegemonic Influence in the Organization of American States," *Latin American Politics and Society*, Vol. 45, No. 3 (2003): 64.

32 Gordon Connell-Smith, *The United States and Latin America: An Historical Analysis of Inter-America Relations* (London: Heinemann Educational Books, 1974), 213.

33 "It had been clear at the Tenth Inter-American Conference that Latin American hopes of receiving United States economic aid were an important consideration in discouraging more open support for Guatemala." Gordon Connell-Smith, *The United States and Latin America: An Historical Analysis of Inter-America Relations* (London: Heinemann Educational Books, 1974), 220. As in Bogotá in 1948, the Caracas meeting did not result in any proposals by the United States to fund a Marshall Plan for the Western Hemisphere, as many of the Latin American governments had hoped. Alonso Aguilar Monteverde, *El Panamericanismo: De la Doctrina de Monroe a la Doctrina Johnson* (México: Cuadernos Americanos, 1965), 134.

34 Long attributes Eisenhower's change of heart to the overthrow of Fulgencio Batista in Cuba and a balance of payments crisis in Brazil that the CIA suggested might result in Brazil defaulting on US$2.2 billion in debt. Tom Long, *Latin America Confronts the United States: Asymmetry and Influence* (New York: Cambridge University Press, 2015), 52–3. Equally important, according to Long, was the pressure coming from Latin American leaders for the creation of a development bank, which became too strong to ignore. "Officials in the State Department . . . referred to the near unanimous Latin American calls to insist on the bank, trumping the concerns of fiscally conservative officials in other agencies." Ibid at 71.

35 Colombian President Alberto Lleras Camargo and Argentine President Arturo Frondizi were early supporters of Kubitschek's proposal, called Operation Pan-America. Tom Long, *Latin America Confronts the United States: Asymmetry and Influence* (New York: Cambridge University Press, 2015), 30. "The principal ideas of the Alliance were contained in Operation Pan-America, and the hemispheric consensus upon which the Alliance relied was built on the diplomacy of Kubitschek and Lleras Camargo through the OAS." Ibid at 68.

36 See, e.g., David W. Dent and Larman C. Wilson, *Historical Dictionary of Inter-American Organizations, Second Edition* (Plymouth, UK: Scarecrow Press, 2014), 31. "Carried out within a democratic framework, the Alliance for Progress envisioned a peaceful revolution across the Americas that would transform the [hemisphere], diminish the enormous gap between the two Americas, and unite them more strongly on an ideological, democratic basis." Mark Eric Williams, *Understanding U.S.–Latin American Relations* (New York: Routledge, 2012), 194.

37 Gordon Connell-Smith, *The United States and Latin America: An Historical Analysis of Inter-America Relations* (London: Heinemann Educational Books, 1974), 282.

The U.S. Congress formally killed the Alliance for Progress in 1972, although the program had already atrophied following the assassination of President Kennedy in 1963 and Lyndon Johnson's decision to make a known Alliance skeptic the new Assistant Secretary of State for Inter-American Affairs. Hastening the Alliance's demise was the fact that both the CIA and the Pentagon worked to ensure that U.S. Alliance funds bypassed reform projects developed in Latin America that seemed to be too progressive or possibly infiltrated by Communists, and instead flowed to development projects controlled by local elites. Mark Eric Williams, *Understanding U.S.–Latin American Relations* (New York: Routledge, 2012), 208.

38 This was not the first time President Betancourt had appealed to the OAS. In June 1960, Betancourt had accused the Dominican dictator, Rafael Trujillo, of detonating a bomb in Caracas intended to kill him in retaliation for supporting a Dominican group that had unsuccessfully attempted to overthrow Trujillo. In response, the OAS Meeting of Consultation of Foreign Ministers held in San José, Costa Rica in August 1960 imposed diplomatic and economic sanctions on the Dominican Republic, marking the first time that the OAS had approved and applied collective sanctions. David W. Dent and Larman C. Wilson, *Historical Dictionary of Inter-American Organizations, Second Edition* (Plymouth, UK: Scarecrow Press, 2014), 122.

39 John Edwin Fagg, *Pan Americanism* (Malabar, FL: Robert E. Krieger Publishing Company, 1982), 99.

40 Mark Eric Williams, *Understanding U.S.–Latin American Relations* (New York: Routledge, 2012), 237. For Long, one important explanation as to why Panama finally succeeded in obtaining full sovereignty over the Canal Zone was its reframing of the question of the canal's security so that the canal was not a military asset best protected by U.S. bases, but a geographical resource that was impossible to defend without the engagement of the Panamanian population. Tom Long, *Latin America Confronts the United States: Asymmetry and Influence* (New York: Cambridge University Press, 2015), 146. In addition, the consistent approach followed by Panama to build a coalition of allies "helped raise the canal's profile on the U.S. agenda while increasing costs for leaving the matter unaddressed." Ibid at 127.

41 Gordon Connell-Smith, *The United States and Latin America: An Historical Analysis of Inter-America Relations* (London: Heinemann Educational Books, 1974), 246. For Carolyn Shaw, the fact that the United States provided substantial resources for the inter-American peace force gave it more influence over the actions and decisions of the OAS in the Dominican Republic. This was exacerbated by the lack of any unified Latin American alternative solution and the fact the opposing governments would have had to request that the U.S. withdraw its troops. Carolyn M. Shaw, "Limits to Hegemonic Influence in the Organization of American States," *Latin American Politics and Society*, Vol. 45, No. 3 (2003): 78.

42 Richard E. Feinberg, *Summitry in the Americas* (Washington, DC: Institute for International Economics, 1997), 32.

43 Richard E. Feinberg, *Summitry in the Americas* (Washington, DC: Institute for International Economics, 1997), 101–2. Other explanations for the failure to follow up on the initiatives coming out of Punta del Este included the wide ideological divide that existed among governments headed either by elected civilians or military dictators and the unrealistic expectation that the U.S. government would generously fund everything.

44 Because of border disputes between Belize and Guatemala and between Guyana and Venezuela, neither country became a full member of the OAS until 1989, following a concerted lobbying effort from other member states who were part of the Caribbean Community and Common Market (CARICOM).

45 David W. Dent and Larman C. Wilson, *Historical Dictionary of Inter-American Organizations, Second Edition* (Plymouth, UK: Scarecrow Press, 2014), 74. Canada had been a permanent observer at the OAS since 1972. Interestingly, the name of the

OAS had been selected in preference to the originally proposed Union of American Republics back in the 1940s, in order to facilitate Canada's full membership in the organization following WW II.

46　Tom J. Farer, ed., *The Future of the Inter-American System* (New York: Praeger Publishers, 1979), xxii. The effort to place collective economic security on a par with military security as the primary shared objectives of the inter-American system was led by Peru, at that time under a reformist-oriented military government.

47　No doubt recalling what had happened in the Dominican Republic in 1965, Latin American members rejected the U.S. proposal, fearing that it would serve as a justification for direct U.S. intervention and might not result in Somoza's giving up power. Carolyn M. Shaw, "Limits to Hegemonic Influence in the Organization of American States," *Latin American Politics and Society*, Vol. 45, No. 3 (2003): 79.

48　Mark Eric Williams, *Understanding U.S.–Latin American Relations* (New York: Routledge, 2012), 234–5.

49　See Bryce Wood, "Human Rights and the Inter-American System," in *The Future of the Inter-American System*, ed. Tom J. Farer (New York: Praeger Publishers, 1979), 142. There was actually bipartisan support for this move as Cold War warriors viewed human rights as a political instrument, a means of "ideological resistance" to Communism. Tom J. Farer, "Policy Implications of the Possible Conflict Between Capitalist Development and Human Rights in Developing Countries," in *The Future of the Inter-American System*, ed. Tom J. Farer (New York: Praeger Publishers, 1979), 115.

50　In particular, members of the U.S. Congress proposed that the OAS General Assembly be required to discuss substantive issues contained in the Inter-American Human Rights Commission's reports, including allegations of human rights in particular countries. Bryce Wood, "Human Rights and the Inter-American System," in *The Future of the Inter-American System*, ed. Tom J. Farer (New York: Praeger Publishers, 1979), 119. The United States was also a prime mover in significantly increasing the budget of the Inter-American Human Rights Commission in the mid-1970s, so that its relative standing among OAS agencies was enhanced in fiscal terms as well as in prestige. Ibid at 125. These budget increases were the result of special earmarks provided by the United States, without a previous request from the OAS. Some Latin American governments—namely those ruled at the time by brutal military dictatorships—criticized the additional money as representing "a fiscal intervention [in violation] of the principles of the OAS Charter and affecting matters that are exclusive OAS prerogatives." Ibid at 144–5.

51　Par Engstrom, "The Inter-American Human Rights System and U.S.–Latin American Relations," in *Cooperation and Hegemony in U.S.–Latin American Relations*, ed. J.P. Scarfi et al. (Houndmills: Palgrave Macmillan, 2016), 210. In the case of countries that have ratified the American Convention on Human Rights and accepted its compulsory jurisdiction (something the United States, Canada, and most of the English-speaking Caribbean have not), the Inter-American Court of Human Rights can judge states for international human rights violations and order compensation to victims, as well as pass judgment on the compatibility of national legislation with the Convention. Ibid at 225.

52　Peter J. Meyer, *Organization of American States: Background and Issues for Congress* (Washington, DC: Congressional Research Service, August 29, 2014), 10. The full text of the American Declaration of the Rights and Duties of Man is available at: www.oas.org/en/iachr/mandate/Basics/declaration.asp. The full text of the American Convention on Human Rights which entered into force on July 18, 1978 is available at: www.oas.org/dil/treaties_B-32_American_Convention_on_Human_Rights.htm.

53　Par Engstrom, "The Inter-American Human Rights System and U.S.-Latin American Relations," in *Cooperation and Hegemony in U.S.–Latin American Relations*, ed. J.P. Scarfi et al. (Houndmills: Palgrave Macmillan, 2016), 210.

54 Mark Eric Williams, *Understanding U.S.–Latin American Relations* (New York: Routledge, 2012), 279. By the late 1980s, however, the ineffectiveness of the OAS to bring an end to the civil wars in Central America because of the overwhelming influence of the United States, led a number of Latin American countries to seek alternative venues.

55 David W. Dent and Larman C. Wilson, *Historical Dictionary of Inter-American Organizations, Second Edition* (Plymouth, UK: Scarecrow Press, 2014), 145. One thing that particularly incensed the Argentine military about not receiving support from the U.S. in the Malvinas dispute was that it had provided clandestine assistance to the CIA in training the Contras in Honduras that were attempting to overthrow the Sandinista government in Nicaragua.

56 See, Remarks of U.S. Secretary of State John Kerry on U.S. Policy in the Western Hemisphere." Delivered on November 18, 2013 at the Organization of American States, Washington, DC. The full text is available at: https://2009-2017.state.gov/secretary/remarks/2013/11/217680.htm.

57 "The so-called *Esquipulas Accords* outlined a number of steps to end hostilities and promote national reconciliation, including demilitarization, free elections and democratization, a cut-off in aid to paramilitary units, refugee assistance, and arms-control talks." Mark Eric Williams, *Understanding U.S.–Latin American Relations* (New York: Routledge, 2012), 257.

58 After Aristide was elected for a second time in 2000, the OAS tried again to mediate among the different Haitian political factions, before Aristide finally fled the country in February 2004 amid rising violence. Once again, it fell to the UN and not the OAS to keep the peace in Haiti, with the establishment of a UN Mission for the Stabilization of Haiti or MINUSTAH. Heraldo Muñoz, then Chilean Ambassador to the United Nations, "maneuvered through the Security Council, on which Chile was sitting in April 2004, a mission for stabilization of Haiti, MINUSTAH, which would not include the United States." Joseph S. Tulchin, *Latin America in International Politics: Challenging U.S. Hegemony* (Boulder, CO: Lynne Rienner Publishers, 2016), 146. In order to get the buy-in of Latin America's largest country, Chile entrusted leadership of MINUSTAH to Brazil.

59 Mark Eric Williams, *Understanding U.S.–Latin American Relations* (New York: Routledge, 2012), 306–7. "Virtually every state criticized the move as a breach of international law and Panamanian sovereignty" including "Chile's pro-U.S. Pinochet dictatorship." Ibid at 307.

60 Organization of American States, "Resolution 991," adopted at the 19th Regular Session of the General Assembly in Washington, DC on November 18, 1989. *Proceedings Volume I* (Washington, DC: OAS General Secretariat, 1989), 37.

61 See Article 1 to OAS General Assembly Resolution 1080. Organization of American States, "Resolution 1080," adopted at the 21st Regular Session of the General Assembly in Santiago, Chile on June 4, 1991. *Proceedings Volume I* (Washington, DC: OAS General Secretariat, 1991), 1.

62 The power to suspend can only be exercised after diplomatic efforts to restore representative democracy have been unsuccessful and there is an affirmative two-thirds vote in favor in the General Assembly. The full text of the Protocol of Washington, which was incorporated as the new Article 9 to Chapter III of the Charter of the Organization of American States (OAS) and entered into force on September 25, 1997, is available at: www.oas.org/dil/treaties_A-56_Protocol_of_Washington.htm.

63 Richard E. Feinberg, *Summitry in the Americas* (Washington, DC: Institute for International Economics, 1997), 1. Feinberg also believes that the summit process redefined the traditional system that had governed hemispheric relations and centered on the OAS and the foreign ministries that control its agenda. Ibid at 161. In fact, the Clinton administration chose not to entrust the first Summit of the Americas in Miami to the OAS, because "[w]ith its stylized debates and culture of gaining a

consensus by accepting the least common denominator, it was feared the OAS would produce a high-sounding document with a long list of desirable ends but with few realistic goals." Ibid at 101.

64 The Convention has been criticized because it does not explicitly provide for monitoring or review by the OAS or any other body, signatories only agree to consider the applicability of important measures within their own legal and political frameworks, and there are no follow-up steps specified in the convention for encouraging or monitoring implementation of these measures. Richard E. Feinberg, *Summitry in the Americas* (Washington, DC: Institute for International Economics, 1997), 169.

65 Mark Eric Williams, *Understanding U.S.–Latin American Relations* (New York: Routledge, 2012), 39.

66 Tom J. Farer, ed., *The Future of the Inter-American System* (New York: Praeger Publishers, 1979), xviii. An example of the shared interests of the U.S. government and Latin American political elites is the Declaration on the Preservation and Defense of Democracy in the Americas, issued at the same conference in Bogotá in 1948 that launched the OAS. That declaration condemned international Communism and the threat it posed to governments in the Western Hemisphere. The declaration was influenced by allegations (never proven) that Communist agitators were involved in prolonging the rioting that engulfed the Colombian capital after the assassination of the Liberal Party candidate for the Colombian presidency, Jorge Eliécer Gaitán, that occurred while delegates from throughout the Americas gathered in the Colombian capital to sign the new OAS Charter.

67 Tom J. Farer, ed., *The Future of the Inter-American System* (New York: Praeger Publishers, 1979), xix.

Bibliography

Aguilar Monteverde, Alonso. *El Panamericanismo: De la Doctrina de Monroe a la Doctrina Johnson.* México: Cuadernos Americanos, 1965.

Arashiro, Zuleika. *Negotiating the Free Trade Area of the Americas.* New York: Palgrave Macmillan, 2011.

Atkins, G. Pope. *Encyclopedia of the Inter-American System.* Westport, CT: Greenwood Press, 1997.

Connell-Smith, Gordon. *The United States and Latin America: An Historical Analysis of Inter-America Relations.* London: Heinemann Educational Books, 1974.

Dent, David W. and Larman C. Wilson. *Historical Dictionary of Inter-American Organizations, Second Edition.* Plymouth, UK: Scarecrow Press, 2014.

Fagg, John Edwin. *Pan Americanism.* Malabar, FL: Robert E. Krieger Publishing Company, 1982.

Farer, Tom J., ed. *The Future of the Inter-American System.* New York: Praeger Publishers, 1979.

Feinberg, Richard E. *Summitry in the Americas: A Progress Report.* Washington, DC: Institute for International Economics, 1997.

Francis, Michael J. *The Limits of Hegemony.* Notre Dame, IN: University of Notre Dame Press, 1977.

Heine, Jorge and Brigitte Weiffen. *21st Century Democracy Promotion in the Americas: Standing Up for the Polity.* New York: Routledge, 2015.

Herz, Mônica. *The Organization of American States (OAS): Global Governance Away from the Media.* New York: Routledge, 2011.

Long, Tom. *Latin America Confronts the United States: Asymmetry and Influence.* New York: Cambridge University Press, 2015.

McPherson, Alan. *The Invaded*. New York: Oxford University Press, 2014.

Message of President James Monroe at the Commencement of the first session of the 18th Congress (the Monroe Doctrine), 12/02/1823, Presidential Messages of the 18th Congress, ca. 12/02/1823–ca. 03/03/1825; Record Group 46; Records of the United States Senate, 1789–1990. Washington, DC: Center for Legislative Archives (National Archives).

Meyer, Peter J. *Organization of American States: Background and Issues for Congress*. Washington, DC: Congressional Research Service, August 29, 2014.

Organization of American States. "American Convention on Human Rights (B 32) 'Pact of San Jose, Costa Rica'." Washington, DC: OAS Secretariat (Department of International Law). Entered into Force on July 18, 1978. Accessed July 27, 2017: www.oas.org/dil/treaties_B-32_American_Convention_on_Human_Rights.htm

Organization of American States. "Charter of the Organization of American States." Washington, DC: OAS Secretariat (Department of International Law). Entered into Force on December 13, 1951. Accessed July 27, 2017: www.oas.org/en/sla/dil/docs/inter_american_treaties_A-41_charter_OAS.pdf

Organization of American States. "Inter-American Democratic Charter." Washington, DC: OAS General Secretariat. Adopted at a special session of the General Assembly in Lima, Peru on September 11, 2001. Accessed July 27, 2017: www.oas.org/OASpage/eng/Documents/Democractic_Charter.htm

Organization of American States. "Inter-American Treaty of Reciprocal Assistance." Washington, DC: General OAS Secretariat (Department of International Law). Entered into Force on December 3, 1948. Accessed July 27, 2017: www.oas.org/juridico/english/treaties/b-29.html

Organization of American States. "Protocol of Amendments to the Charter of the Organization of American States (A-56) 'Protocol of Washington'." Washington, DC: OAS General Secretariat (Department of International Law). Entered into Force on September 25, 1997. Accessed July 27, 2017: www.oas.org/dil/treaties_A-56_Protocol_of_Washington.htm

Organization of American States. "Protocol of Amendment to the Inter-American Treaty of Reciprocal Assistance." Washington, DC: OAS General Secretariat (Department of International Law). Adopted by the Conference of Plenipotentiaries for the Amendment of the Inter-American Treaty of Reciprocal Assistance in San José, Costa Rica on July 26, 1975. Accessed July 27, 2017: www.oas.org/juridico/english/treaties/b-29(1).html

Organization of American States. "Resolution 991." Adopted at the 19th Regular Session of the General Assembly in Washington, DC on November 18, 1989. *Proceedings Volume I*. Washington, DC: OAS General Secretariat, 1989, 37.

Organization of American States. "Resolution 1080." Adopted at the 21st Regular Session of the General Assembly in Santiago, Chile on June 4, 1991. *Proceedings Volume I*. Washington, DC: OAS General Secretariat, 1991, 1.

Poggio Teixeira, Carlos Gustavo. *Brazil, the United States, and the South American Subsystem*. Lanham, MD: Lexington Books, 2012.

Scarfi, J.P. and Andrew R. Tillman, eds. *Cooperation and Hegemony in U.S.–Latin American Relations*. Houndmills: Palgrave Macmillan, 2016.

Shaw, Carolyn M. "Limits to Hegemonic Influence in the Organization of American States." *Latin American Politics and Society* Vol. 45, No. 3 (2003): 59–92.

Thomas, Christopher R. and Juliana T. Magloire. *Regionalism versus Multilateralism: The Organization of American States in a Global Changing Environment*. Boston: Kluwer Academic Publishers, 2000.

Tulchin, Joseph S. *Latin America in International Politics: Challenging U.S. Hegemony.* Boulder, CO: Lynne Rienner Publishers, 2016.

United States Department of State. "Remarks of U.S. Secretary of State John Kerry on U.S. Policy in the Western Hemisphere." Delivered on November 18, 2013 at the Organization of American States, Washington, DC. Accessed July 27, 2017: https://2009-2017.state.gov/secretary/remarks/2013/11/217680.htm

Vivares, Ernesto, ed. *Exploring the New South American Regionalism.* Farnham, UK: Ashgate Publishing, 2014.

Williams, Mark Eric. *Understanding U.S.–Latin American Relations.* New York: Routledge, 2012.

3 A Post-Hegemonic Inter-American System

Introduction

As the twentieth century drew to a close, the remarkable hemispheric consensus that accompanied much of the 1990s in terms of economic and political policy throughout the Americas evaporated. Alberto Fujimori's increasingly authoritarian rule in Peru and his 2000 run for a dubiously constitutional third term seriously weakened that country's democratic institutions. On the economic front, it was becoming increasingly clear that liberal economic policies in and of themselves were insufficient to overcome the serious structural barriers that prevented an equitable distribution of the gains generated by free market-based reforms in most Latin American countries. The 1998 election to the Venezuelan presidency of an army colonel who had led an unsuccessful coup attempt in 1992, and his eventual calls for a Bolivarian Alternative to the Free Trade Area of the Americas, were harbingers of things to come. In 2000, Ecuadorean President Jamil Mahuad was overthrown in a military coup supported by indigenous groups angered by his decision to substitute the U.S. dollar for the national currency, as well as his implementation of a series of unpopular market-oriented economic policies. The implosion of the Argentine economy at the end of 2001 led to the end of its dollarized economy and the rejection of the liberal macroeconomic policy it had eagerly embraced a decade earlier. In the years following the dawn of the new millennium, in a phenomenon called the Pink Tide, presidents from the left of the political spectrum were elected in Bolivia, Brazil, Chile, Ecuador, and Uruguay, oftentimes on platforms that explicitly rejected many of the so-called Washington Consensus economic reforms that, by the 1990s, all Latin American governments had so eagerly adopted.

The arrival of George W. Bush in the White House, after a contested election in 2000 in which he lost the popular vote—and perhaps even a majority of Florida's electoral vote that gave him victory in the Electoral College—initially generated cautious optimism in much of Latin America. As the former governor of Texas, Bush had been involved in a number of cross-border initiatives with Mexico. The fact that he broke with tradition and made his first overseas trip as U.S. President to Mexico instead of Canada also hinted at a heightened interest in Latin America. During his first year in office, President Bush expressed a desire to overhaul U.S. immigration policy by facilitating the legalization of millions of undocumented workers, most of them from Latin America and the Caribbean. All those initial optimistic expectations abruptly ended, however, with the terrorist attacks in the northeastern United States on September 11, 2001. Thereafter, the Bush White House became fixated on rooting out actual and perceived terrorist threats in Africa and Asia, culminating in the disastrous invasion of Iraq in 2003 and a Middle Eastern and Afghani quagmire for which there is still no end in sight.

The Diminishing Influence of the United States of America in the OAS

The terrorist attacks in the northeastern United States on September 11, 2001 coincided with a special session of the OAS General Assembly in Lima. On the agenda was a vote on whether to approve the Inter-American Democratic Charter, proposed by the host country on the heels of its recent liberation from Alberto Fujimori's authoritarian rule.[1] The Charter aimed to resolve some of the weaknesses of earlier OAS initiatives in order to support democratic governance in the Western Hemisphere. In particular, Resolution 1080 and the Washington Protocol were deemed too reactive in nature and unable to address more drawn-out deteriorations in democratic governance. By contrast, the Inter-American Democratic Charter distinguishes between the essential *elements* and the *components* of the exercise of representative democracy, and highlights other aspects of a country's political system whose development and strengthening are necessary for democratic institutions to flourish.[2] Article 17 of the Democratic Charter allows the executive branch (albeit not the legislative or judicial branches, let alone civil society groups) in any OAS member state to request the assistance of the Secretary General or the Permanent Council if its democratic political institutional process is at risk. Article 18 also authorizes the Secretary General or the Permanent Council to make their own determinations as to whether representative democracy is in peril in a particular member state. Such a declaration may lead to the preparation of reports as well as in-country visits, but the latter can only occur with the consent of that country's government. Pursuant to Article 19, an unconstitutional interruption of the democratic order or an unconstitutional alteration of the constitutional regime that seriously impairs the democratic order creates an insurmountable obstacle for participation in the OAS. Article 20 allows for collective OAS action in the event of an unconstitutional alteration of the constitutional regime that seriously impairs the democratic order in a member state. In the event that the General Assembly determines that there has been an unconstitutional interruption in the democratic order, Article 21 requires a two-thirds majority to suspend a state's membership in the OAS. Similarly, Article 22 requires a two-thirds majority vote in the General Assembly to restore a suspended government's membership in the OAS.

Given the groundswell of sympathy generated by the terrorist attacks in the United States on September 11, 2001, the OAS General Assembly unanimously approved the Inter-American Democratic Charter, following an impassioned appeal from U.S. Secretary of State Colin Powell. Days later, at the request of Brazil, the OAS Permanent Council meeting in Washington, DC activated the collective security provisions of the Inter-American Treaty of Reciprocal Assistance (aka the Rio Treaty). In response to the United States' failure to obtain UN Security Council approval for an invasion of Iraq, Mexico formally withdrew from the Rio Treaty in 2004. Bolivia, Ecuador, Nicaragua, and Venezuela followed suit in 2012. Mexican President Vicente Fox had already called for the Rio Treaty's abolition on the eve of the September 2001 terrorist attacks in the United States, labeling it an obsolete Cold War relic.

The OAS Permanent Council invoked the Inter-American Democratic Charter on April 13, 2002, following Venezuelan President Hugo Chavez's removal from power the day before by a coterie of military commanders and business leaders. Conspicuously, the U.S. was the only OAS member state not to categorically condemn the coup. In fact, the then White House press secretary, Ari Fleishman, could barely conceal his glee when discussing Chavez's overthrow during a press conference in Washington, DC. Following the intervention of mid and lower-level military officers, Chavez was quickly restored to power late in the evening of April 14, 2002. The coup, which lasted less than 48 hours, left the Bush administration in the difficult position of having to contend with the endless enmity of a victorious, and more powerful, Chavez.

The Democratic Charter was invoked again in 2004, months after an increasingly authoritarian and erratic President Jean-Bertrand Aristide had resigned the Haitian presidency and fled on a U.S.-supplied plane that initially took him to exile in the Central African Republic. In 2005, the Permanent Council used Article 18 of the Democratic Charter to approve visits by the OAS Secretary General to Ecuador, following President Lucio Gutierrez's removal from power by the Ecuadorean Congress, and to Nicaragua, in an attempt to resolve a political crisis among the different branches of government.

In 2009, the OAS Permanent Council unanimously voted to activate the collective action provisions of Article 20 to the Inter-American Democratic Charter in response to José Manuel Zelaya's June 28 removal from the Honduran presidency by that country's military and his expulsion to Costa Rica. Pursuant to Article 21 of the Inter-American Democratic Charter, a special session of the General Assembly suspended Honduras from the OAS on July 4, 2009 after the interim government refused to allow Zelaya to return to the country and reassume the presidency. In the immediate aftermath of the coup, the United States revoked the visas of various Honduran government officials, including that of interim president Roberto Micheletti, and froze its considerable military assistance program. While Brazil and other countries in South America attempted to restore Zelaya to power, the United States soon decided it was more expedient to let the clock run out on his term and recognize whoever won the presidential election scheduled for November 29, 2009. Much of this is explained by the conservative Republicans' revolt in the U.S. Senate over the Obama administration's initial response to the Honduran coup. One of the tactics used by the senators to express their displeasure was refusing to approve Arturo Valenzuela as the new Assistant Secretary of State for Western Hemisphere Affairs and to fill various ambassadorships. One of the unhappy senators—Jim DeMint of South Carolina—even flew to Tegucigalpa to express unswerving support for Micheletti. These Republicans claimed to be motivated by concerns over Zelaya's alleged sympathies for Venezuelan President Hugo Chavez.

Although Zelaya was able to sneak back into Honduras in September 2009, and immediately sought refuge in the Brazilian embassy in Tegucigalpa, he was never restored to office. He eventually left Honduras in January 2010 for exile in the Dominican Republic. Honduras was not admitted back into the OAS until June 2011, following a deal negotiated by the Colombian and Venezuelan presidents that, among other things, allowed Zelaya to return home. Zelaya's wife, Xiomora Castro, ran for the Honduran presidency in November 2013 and lost, although she challenged the results as "a fraud of incalculable proportions."[3]

The Inter-American Democratic Charter was last invoked following the September 2010 police mutiny that led to President Rafael Correa's temporary detention in a police hospital in Quito. In response, the Permanent Council authorized the OAS Secretary General to lead a fact-finding visit to Ecuador.

The Inter-American Democratic Charter has, up to now at least, never been utilized against countries whose leaders have consolidated executive power over the other branches of representative democracy, such as the cases of Rafael Correa in Ecuador, Daniel Ortega in Nicaragua, Hugo Chavez and then Nicolás Maduro in Venezuela, and Alvaro Uribe in Colombia. Nor was it invoked in 2003 when Bolivian President Gonzalo Sánchez de Lozada was forced to flee the country after massive street protests. The latter omission may have had to do with how quickly events in Bolivia transpired and the fact the Vice President quickly replaced Sánchez de Lozada—accordingly, there was no power vacuum. On the other hand, the failure of the OAS to enforce the Inter-American Democratic Charter in Ecuador, Nicaragua, and Venezuela is attributed to the complex political alliances that often develop at the OAS, thereby undermining the ability to secure the requisite two-thirds vote in the General Assembly to suspend a member state. The Chavez and Maduro governments have also consistently refused to allow OAS delegations to make on-site visits to Venezuela as sanctioned by Article 18 of the Charter.

The U.S. suffered an embarrassing defeat in 2005 at the OAS General Assembly in Fort Lauderdale, Florida, when the other member states rejected a U.S.-proposed amendment to the Inter-American Democratic Charter that would have permitted the Permanent Council, relying on civil society input, to monitor compliance with a country's commitment to representative democracy and potentially undertake preventive measures. The basic idea was that this would provide an early warning mechanism before the actual explosion of a major political crisis that caught the hemisphere off guard and left the OAS scrambling to respond. Reflecting the deep suspicion generated by the unilateralist foreign policy of the George W. Bush administration, a clear majority in the General Assembly "implicitly rejected the U.S. proposal for a 'monitoring committee,' arguing that any effort to strengthen democracy should be carried out with respect for the principle of non-intervention and the right of self-determination of citizens."[4]

In 2005, the United States' preferred candidate to become Secretary General of the OAS—Francisco Flores, the former President of El Salvador—quickly withdrew from the race as, for the first time in OAS history, a majority of the member states rejected the U.S. nominee.[5] Of the two remaining candidates, the United States preferred the Mexican Foreign Minister Luis Ernesto Derbez to the Chilean Foreign Minister José Miguel Insulza, a socialist who had spent much of the Pinochet dictatorship in exile. After five rounds of secret ballots, the vote remained tied. When it became clear that a bloc of South American and Caribbean countries would not put their votes behind anyone but Insulza, the U.S. delegation helped negotiate a deal in which Derbez withdrew his name from consideration and the U.S. threw its support behind Insulza. Insulza was re-elected for another five-year term in 2010. The current Secretary General of the OAS is the former Uruguayan Foreign Minister Luis Almargo, who ran unopposed for the position in 2015.

Insulza's period as OAS Secretary General was marked by Venezuela's decision, in September 2012, to withdraw its ratification of the American Convention on Human Rights and its acceptance of the compulsory jurisdiction of the Inter-American Court in San José, Costa Rica. The Dominican Republic threatened to do the same after the Inter-American Commission on Human Rights condemned a September 2013 decision by that country's Constitutional Tribunal to rescind the Dominican citizenship of anyone descended from people who had migrated from Haiti after 1929. For its part, Brazil rejected an interim measure of the Inter-American Commission on Human Rights in 2011 that ordered the suspension of construction activities at the Belo Monte hydroelectric complex until the government had adequately consulted with local indigenous communities. In retaliation, Brazil refused to pay its annual dues to the OAS, recalled its ambassador to the organization, and postponed for two years the proposal of its candidate to sit on the Inter-American Commission on Human Rights, the former Brazilian Minister for Human Rights, Paulo Vannuchi.

Angered by the frequent condemnations of his curtailment of press freedoms that emanated from those involved in the inter-American human rights system, in 2012 Ecuadoran President Rafael Correa spearheaded an effort, with Bolivia, Nicaragua, and Venezuela, to "reform" the inter-American human rights system. Although this not-so-disguised attempt to weaken the system was beaten back, the United States was put in an awkward position, defending the status quo despite the fact that it does not recognize the binding nature of rulings issued by the Inter-American Commission on Human Rights based in Washington, DC and has never ratified the Inter-American Convention on Human Rights. Although the U.S. signed the Convention in 1978, when Jimmy Carter was president, the U.S. Senate has never ratified it. As a result, the United States is not subject to the compulsory jurisdiction of the Inter-American Court of Human Rights in San José, Costa Rica.

The United States found itself outmaneuvered at the 2009 General Assembly meeting in San Pedro Sula, Honduras (ironically just weeks before the coup that ousted the host country's president), as all the remaining countries in the OAS voted to rescind the 1962 motion that had suspended Cuba's active membership of the OAS. The United States was able to extract a proviso, however, that Cuba's return would be in accordance with the practices, purposes, and principles of the OAS, including representative democracy and respect for human rights.[6] While Cuba has not expressed any interest in rejoining the OAS as an active member state, it did participate in the Seventh Summit of the Americas, in Panama in April 2015. This was facilitated by the Obama administration's decision at the end of 2014 to begin the process of normalizing diplomatic relations with Cuba. Many Latin American and Caribbean countries at the Sixth Summit of the Americas in Cartagena, Colombia in 2012 had already served notice on the United States that they would not attend the subsequent Summit in Panama if the Cubans were excluded. Hence, had the Obama administration not moved to normalize diplomatic relations with Havana and instead insisted on enforcing the original proviso that only countries with a representative democracy could participate, the entire Summit of the Americas mechanism might have collapsed.

The Inter-American Drug Abuse Control Commission (CICAD) was established under the auspices of the OAS in 1986 in response to concerns about the production, trafficking, and consumption of illegal narcotics and the threats this posed for societies throughout the Western Hemisphere. Mexico took the lead in creating CICAD as a way to end the U.S. Congress's humiliating annual certification of the foreign countries that actively cooperated in the U.S. "War on Drugs" and those that did not, the latter therefore being ineligible for U.S. aid and preferential market access programs.[7] CICAD's primary mission has been to develop a comprehensive anti-drug policy for the entire hemisphere. A criticism leveled at CICAD in the past was that it often served to reinforce Washington's then hardline approach to dealing with the illicit narcotics problem.[8] Accordingly, many heads of state attending the Sixth Summit of the Americas in Cartagena in April 2012 called on the OAS to prepare a comprehensive report examining the effectiveness of some four decades of anti-drug policies in the Western Hemisphere and to propose new approaches. In response, the Office of the Secretary General of the OAS (with technical and administrative support from CICAD) issued two, separate but interconnected, reports on the drug problem in the Americas in May 2013.[9] The first, analytical part of the report implicitly criticized the four-decade-long "War on Drugs" waged by the United States as a failure. The second part, labeled "Scenarios," suggested a number of policy options and potential outcomes. The report emphasized the need to: (1) address the drug problem from a public health perspective; (2) enact judicial reforms to provide alternatives to incarceration (including the decriminalization of drug use); (3) acknowledge that transnational organized crime is a major aspect of the drug problem; and (4) strengthen the judiciary and public security institutions in order to effectively combat criminal organizations.

The War on Drugs

The Richard M. Nixon administration launched the "War on Drugs" in the 1970s in response to widespread domestic use of marijuana and heroin, particularly among poor minority groups concentrated in urban centers of the United States. By the late 1980s, with rising public concern over drug abuse—particularly the media blitz surrounding the "crack epidemic"—coinciding with the drawdown of Cold War hostilities and the resulting search for a mission within the Defense Department, U.S. officials declared that drugs were a national security threat, linking narcotics trafficking with international terrorism.[10] By this time the drug of widespread concern had become cocaine, which is a derivative of a plant only grown at certain altitudes in the Andean foothills. First as Vice-President under Ronald Reagan and then as President, George H.W. Bush played a key role in forging the link between drugs and terrorism.[11]

> [W]hile the concept of narcoterrorism in the United States initially served as a rhetorical weapon with which to bludgeon Marxist-Leninist regimes in the Western Hemisphere, it evolved as a devise to link the interests of the United States in the drug war with those of the Andean cocaine producing countries battling guerilla insurgencies.[12]

Congress passed the Anti-Drug Abuse Act in 1986 (subsequently modified in 1998), which required the White House to annually certify which countries were cooperating with U.S. anti-narcotics efforts, and to cut off aid and trade to those who did not.

The U.S. "War on Drugs" targeted the most vulnerable people in some of the world's poorest nations by focusing on eradication at the source. To a lesser degree, it also focused on interdiction, although this produced a so-called "balloon effect," whereby drug-trafficking routes interrupted in one part of the hemisphere were easily replaced by new trade routes through other regions. The balloon effect was also a phenomenon of the eradication initiative, as disrupting production in one country simply led to it popping up in another. Little effort was made to address the problem's root cause, namely the socio-pathological peculiarities of American society that contribute to a voracious appetite for narcotics consumption. One reason is that this is the most complicated and expensive part of the drug abuse phenomenon to resolve. By focusing on eradication, the bulk of the violence and huge numbers of deaths wrought by these policies occurred beyond the hegemon's border. At the same time, through lax enforcement of anti-corruption and money-laundering statutes, the U.S. financial services and real estate sectors benefitted from the fabulous wealth generated by the illegal narcotics industry.

The OAS is today an organization in perpetual financial crisis, as it has no monetary reserve to respond to contingencies. Part of the problem is that the OAS has spread itself thin, accepting too many mandates from its member states without a rigorous assessment of the costs and benefits. The OAS currently supports programs and activities in four principal areas: (1) democracy promotion; (2) human rights protection; (3) regional security cooperation; and (4) economic and social development. In addition, high-salaried employees at the OAS are often appointed or promoted in less-than-transparent circumstances. Another important factor contributing to the budget shortfalls is countries not paying their dues (as Brazil did for a number of years, angered by the interim measure issued by the Inter-American Commission on Human Rights in 2011) or doing so late. In May 2016, for example, the severely backlogged Inter-American Commission on Human Rights warned it might have to dismiss 40 percent of its staff in response to the severe financial difficulties at the OAS, and was forced to suspend hearings.

The United States currently contributes approximately 60 percent of the annual budget of the OAS, collected from member state dues. The U.S. government also makes additional, voluntary contributions to support special OAS initiatives. In October 2013, the U.S. Congress approved, with bipartisan support, the Organization of American States Revitalization and Reform Act of 2013, which called for a move to a new membership dues structure in which no member state pays more than 50 percent of the organization's assessed fee.[13] The Act also called on the OAS to annually review and reduce the number of mandates not directly related to its core functions, ensure that any new mandates should be accompanied by an analysis of how they will be funded, and implement a transparent and merit-based system for hiring, firing, and promoting staff. The Act followed years of growing frustration, particularly among Republican members of the U.S. Congress, about an OAS which they viewed as advancing policies counter to U.S. interests. Even bureaucrats within the Obama administration were heard to complain that a group of Latin American nations had "hijacked" the OAS General Assembly for their own purposes without giving due consideration to U.S. interests, thereby leading to the administration's decision to lower the profile of the OAS and the role of the United States within it.[14] Paradoxically, one explanation for U.S. frustration with the OAS is the success of the market-oriented economic reforms promoted by the U.S. government in the 1990s. This development, coupled with the Chinese-fueled commodities boom, contributed to more affluent societies throughout Latin America. These countries are no longer dependent on U.S. financial assistance and now feel emboldened to assert foreign policies more independent of Washington, DC.

The Appearance of Potential Rival Institutions to the OAS

The creation of new organizations, such as the Union of South American Nations (UNASUR) and the Community of Latin American and Caribbean

States (CELAC), that purposefully exclude the United States is yet another manifestation of the decline of U.S. hegemony in the Western Hemisphere. Such a development would once have been deemed unwise, as it would have undermined a system designed—particularly with the creation of the OAS in 1948—"to make the exercise of American power less arbitrary and more benevolent, or, at the very least, less malevolent."[15] The fact that so many Latin American and Caribbean states now feel comfortable to create alternative regional institutions without a U.S. presence indicates a degree of confidence that U.S. hegemony is no longer in need of as much restraint as was the case in the past.

The Union of South American Nations (UNASUR)

At a meeting in Cuzco, Peru in December 2004, the South American presidents launched the Community of South American Nations. In 2008, this entity was transformed into the Union of South American Nations (*Unión de Naciones Suramericanas*) or UNASUR.[16] The 12 member states of UNASUR are Argentina, Bolivia, Brazil, Chile, Colombia, Ecuador, Guyana, Paraguay, Peru, Suriname, Uruguay, and Venezuela. UNASUR seeks to integrate the entire South American continent politically, socially, culturally, economically, financially, and environmentally, as well as in terms of physical infrastructure. The inclusion of two member states of the Caribbean Community and Common Market, or CARICOM (Guyana and Suriname), has the potential to facilitate deeper cooperation between South America and the 15-member CARICOM on issues of mutual interest. Brazil is UNASUR's intellectual author, and views the continental entity as a vehicle to secure its leadership in South America and allow it to choose when and where to involve the United States in managing regional crises.[17] There is a strategic orientation to forging a South American identity through common policies, aiming, as a first step, at the containment of external interference in regional affairs.[18]

In 2000, then Brazilian President Fernando Henrique Cardoso hosted a meeting in Brasilia of all the South American presidents, which resulted in the Initiative for the Integration of South American Infrastructure (*Iniciativa para la Integración de la Infraestructura Sudamericana*), or IIRSA. When launched, IIRSA included proposals for expanding and modernizing the physical infrastructure of South America over an initial ten-year period, particularly in the energy, transportation, and telecommunication sectors. By the end of the first decade, however, only two projects were completed, and 19 remained in the execution phase.[19] Despite its lackluster results, some commentators have emphasized the symbolic importance of IIRSA as a concrete sign of the realization that South America was in fact a distinct regional subsystem, one in which Brazil played a central role.[20] By gathering all the South American heads of state at a meeting in Brasilia, the Brazilian government officially signaled its attempt to rally the South American states around Brazil's political project of organizing a South American space as a means of inserting the region into the post-Cold War international system.[21] IIRSA is now closely linked to UNASUR because of the 2009 creation of UNASUR's South American Infrastructure and Planning Council (COSIPLAN), which incorporated IIRSA's Executive Committee as its technical advisory body. Many of UNASUR's current infrastructure projects are focused on creating bi-oceanic transportation corridors that link the Atlantic coast of the continent with ports on the Pacific by rail, road, and/or riverboats and barges to facilitate trade with Asia.

One of the most tangible achievements of UNASUR, which to date has had a direct impact on the citizens of all Spanish and Portuguese-speaking member nations, was the lifting of all passport and visa requirements for intra-South American travel. South American citizens need only show a national identity card to enter another South American country and remain for up to 90 days as a tourist. (Guyana and Suriname have yet to be incorporated into this mechanism.) Because they are now all either full or associate members of MERCOSUR, the Spanish and Portuguese-speaking countries of UNASUR also adopted its procedures for facilitating the acquisition of temporary and then permanent residency status for nationals in a country without requiring that they return to their country of origin. The ability of UNASUR to resolve migration issues contrasts with the situation in the OAS, where Article 1, paragraph 2 of the OAS Charter explicitly states that the OAS is not authorized to intervene in matters that are within the internal jurisdiction of member states. In the United States, in particular, immigration matters fall within the exclusive jurisdiction of the Department of Homeland Security. Other than the actual issuance of visas, the U.S. Department of State plays no other role in terms of immigration (even though the issue has major foreign policy ramifications within the Americas). Hence, with the exception of issues directly related to the human rights treatment of migrants, how the United States or other member states handle the migration issue has traditionally not been a topic of deliberation at the OAS.

UNASUR has been active on the issue of energy security, including the need to expand the use of renewable or alternative energy resources as well as to enhance energy efficiency and conservation. In fact, even before the formal launch of UNASUR, the first South American Energy Summit was held in Venezuela in April 2007, attended by all the South American presidents. The summit led to the creation of a South American Energy Council. The Energy Council is made up of the ministers of energy from all 12 UNASUR member states, and since its launch has issued guiding principles for a South American energy strategy, a Plan of Action on Regional Energy Integration, and the general parameters for negotiating a South American Treaty on Energy Integration.

Another area in which UNASUR has been very active is that of enhancing civic–military relations and regional security through a South American Defense Council consisting of the ministers of defense from each member state. Brazil first proposed the Council's creation in 2008, in response to Colombian soldiers' incursion into Ecuador in March of that year to attack a FARC guerilla encampment, leading to the death of an important FARC commander. In response to that incursion, Venezuela had sent troops to the Colombian border and Ecuador broke off diplomatic relations with Colombia. The creation of a South American Defense Council was supported by Argentina and Chile, both of which emphasized they did not want it to turn into a NATO-like alliance. Instead, the goal was a cooperative defense arrangement to enhance multilateral military cooperation, promote confidence and security-building measures, and foster the intra-continental trade of weaponry manufactured in South America.[22] Accordingly, the UNASUR defense arrangements do not include any references to collective security or to joint command structures. In an effort to avoid an arms race erupting between the South American countries, all the UNASUR governments are now required to make public their expenditures on national defense as part of a South American Registry of Defense Spending.[23] In addition, a South American Registry of Military Inventory was created in 2014.

The establishment of the South American Defense Council reflects the limitations of the inter-American defense system, historically perceived as serving the U.S. national interest rather than South American defense priorities.[24] The shortcomings of the inter-American system were evident in the 2008 Colombian incursion into Ecuador that almost led to a war between Colombia and Venezuela. The Defense Council offers a tool for promoting autonomy in defining defense priorities, developing appropriate defense technology, and eliminating opportunities for intervention by external agents by deactivating and preventing intraregional conflicts that the United States had traditionally exploited to bolster its own objectives.[25] The Lula government, in particular, promoted the South American Defense Council as a vehicle for Brazil to enhance its role as regional stabilizer, thereby avoiding the need for any U.S. involvement.[26] A concrete manifestation of South America's quest for autonomy in defense matters has been the continued rejection by many South American nations of post-Cold War efforts by the United States to convince them to utilize their armed forces to fight organized crime, or to equate domestic guerilla movements with terrorism. A notable exception was Colombia under President Álvaro Uribe Vélez.

A UNASUR Center for Strategic Defense Studies opened in Buenos Aires in May 2011. Among other things, it examines threats to regional security posed by transnational criminal networks and offers human rights courses to military personnel. It is also responsible for collecting, verifying, and disseminating the data collected for the South American Registry of Defense Spending and the new South American Registry of Military Inventory. A South American Defense School located in Ecuador opened its doors in 2014. It provides online training for both civilians and military personnel on matters related to regional defense and security, as well as for participation in international peacekeeping missions.[27]

In October 2010, the UNASUR countries adopted a democracy clause that called for the imposition of sanctions on any member government that comes to power because of a break in the democratic order, such as a coup. The measure was a direct response to the September 2010 police-led mutiny against President Rafael Correa in Ecuador (which also resulted in a fact-finding trip to Ecuador, led by the OAS Secretary General, pursuant to the Inter-American Democratic Charter). UNASUR invoked this provision and suspended Paraguay from the organization following the impeachment of the Paraguayan president, Fernando Lugo, after a "trial" in Congress in June 2012 that lasted less than 48 hours. In addition, Lugo had only been notified of the charges against him a few hours before the impeachment proceedings actually began. Although the technical requirements for impeachment found in Paraguay's Constitution were followed, the majority of UNASUR countries deemed the impeachment a farce that constituted a break in the democratic order. The core member states of the MERCOSUR also adopted a similar position with respect to Paraguay's non-compliance with the Protocol of Ushuaia on the Commitment to Democracy, and suspended the country's participation in MERCOSUR's institutional bodies.[28] Paraguay's suspension from UNASUR was finally lifted in August 2013 following the inauguration of a new democratically elected president, Horacio Cartes Jara.

UNASUR's democracy clause was formalized into the Additional Protocol to the Treaty Establishing UNASUR on the Commitment to Democracy, which came into force on March 19, 2014.[29] Pursuant to Article 1, the Protocol is applicable in all cases of a break or threat of a break in the democratic order, of a violation of the constitutional order, or of any situation that puts at risk the legitimate exercise of power or the maintenance of democratic values and principles. The UNASUR countries can respond by imposing sanctions on the non-compliant country. At its most extreme, these sanctions may include suspending the country's participation in UNASUR's institutions and a partial or complete trade, transportation, communication, and/or energy embargo until representative democracy is restored.

There is a concerted effort to meld the existing MERCOSUR with UNASUR in order to achieve UNASUR's ultimate goal of creating a South American common market. Originally, when it began in 1991, MERCOSUR included only Argentina, Brazil, Paraguay, and Uruguay. Venezuela was brought into the customs union in 2012, as part of a controversial back-door maneuver while Paraguay was temporarily suspended from participating in MERCOSUR's institutional framework due to the impeachment of President Fernando Lugo. Venezuela's ability to participate in MERCOSUR's institutional bodies was suspended on December 2, 2016, however, following repeated failures to implement its trade obligations and concerns over the state of the country's representative democracy. The other Spanish-speaking countries in South America have free-trade agreements with the MERCOSUR countries and are now deemed associate members of the MERCOSUR. Guyana and Suriname have official observer status in MERCOSUR. As part of an effort at convergence with UNASUR, spearheaded by Chile, MERCOSUR's highest governing body (the Common Market Council) adopted Decision 32 in 2014, which allows initiatives pursued by either MERCOSUR or UNASUR to be deemed as binding on both if they arise from a set of goals and objectives common to both integration schemes.

MERCOSUR's Common Market Council Decision 32/14 was put into practice when the Ministers of Health of all the South American nations met in Montevideo on September 11, 2015 and launched an *ad hoc* committee for negotiations with pharmaceutical companies over the prices paid for public-sector purchases of certain high-cost medications. Although currently operating under the auspices of MERCOSUR, the *ad hoc* committee utilizes a data bank housed at the UNASUR General Secretariat in Quito that includes the prices charged by the pharmaceutical companies for specified medicines in each member state. The data bank was supposed to have been up and running in conjunction with the launch of the *ad hoc* committee in 2015, but did not in fact become operational until 2017.[30] By the end of 2015, the UNASUR/MERCOSUR and an Indian pharmaceutical company had negotiated a significant price reduction in the cost of an anti-retroviral medication to treat HIV.

UNASUR's deep interest in health issues stems from the social objectives found in the treaty that established UNASUR, including that found in Article 3(j) calling for universal access to health services. UNASUR's highest institutional body, the Council of the Heads of State and Government, created a permanent South American Health Council made up of the Ministers of Health from each member state shortly after UNASUR's launch in 2008. Article 6(a) of the actual Decision creating the South American Health Council states that one of its principal objectives is to promote common policies, coordinated activities, and cooperation among the member states.[31] Of the five technical groups that operate under the Health Council, one of them is denominated "Universal Access to Medications" and is tasked with, among other things, the formulation of proposals for the creation of a policy on prices. In 2009, UNASUR's Health Council approved a Five Year Plan for the period 2010–15 which outlined actions in five key areas, including universal access to medications.[32] Among the specific actions to guarantee universal access to medicines is one calling for the promotion of new price negotiations and joint purchase of medications by UNASUR member governments.

In order to provide the requisite technical assistance in implementing UNASUR health-related programs, UNASUR's Health Council created the *Instituto Sudamericano de Gobierno en Salud*, or ISAGS (the South American Institute of Health Governance).[33] Based in Rio de Janeiro, ISAGS opened its doors in 2011. Pursuant to Article 1 of its by-laws, ISAGS is an intergovernmental body that falls under the jurisdiction of the South American Health Council.[34] ISAGS is statutorily able to enter into legally binding contracts and agreements (although these would normally be for operational matters such as entering into leases, hiring personnel, etc.). The main purpose of ISAGS is to serve as a center for study and investigation as well as a forum for debate on all matters related to health policy in South America. ISAGS also coordinates an extensive training network of public health-care professionals throughout South America. It is affiliated with the *movimento sanitarista* and the Oswaldo

Cruz Foundation (a Brazilian health institute), which was instrumental in setting up ISAGS.[35] The core philosophy of ISAGS is that health cannot be left to the market or commodified, and it believes that health-care users are pivotal is shaping UNASUR's health policies.[36] In addition to providing technical support for UNASUR's data bank on pharmaceutical prices, which is housed in UNASUR's General Secretariat in Quito, ISAGS is currently engaged in mapping private- and public-sector capacity in each of the UNASUR member states to manufacture pharmaceutical products. In 2012, UNASUR was instrumental in getting a resolution approved by the World Health Organization's World Health Assembly that replaced the International Medical Products Anti-Counterfeiting Task Force (IMPACT) with an inter-governmental body, due to concerns that private-sector interests dominated IMPACT and were using it, among other things, to thwart developing countries' access to generic medications.

UNASUR effectively displaced the OAS as the preferred institution to resolve the political crises that erupted in Bolivia in 2008 following the uncovering of a plot against President Evo Morales, as well as to respond to the impeachment of President Fernando Lugo in Paraguay in 2012. It also played a much more visible role than the OAS in resolving the crisis in Ecuador following the police uprising that led to President Rafael Correa's temporary detention, and in responding to the political instability and violence that has plagued Venezuela since February 2014. Although the OAS initially responded forcefully to President José Manuel Zelaya's removal from the Honduran presidency in 2009, UNASUR actually facilitated Zelaya's return home from exile and the lifting of Honduras's suspension from the OAS. Furthermore, Colombia was pressured by the other UNASUR countries in March 2009 to release details of its previously secret deal with the United States to allow the latter access to several bases in Colombian territory, a disclosure that helped de-escalate rising regional tensions over the matter. UNASUR, and not the OAS, also helped defuse rising military tension between Colombia and Venezuela in 2010 when Hugo Chavez was accused of providing asylum to Colombian guerilla fighters in Venezuelan territory.

In April 2010, UNASUR created a South American Council to Combat Drug Trafficking, in an attempt to harmonize policies to combat drug production and trafficking and related crimes such as money laundering. In devising a continental strategy, the original intent was to limit the type of outside intervention exemplified by the 2009 U.S.–Colombia agreement to establish a military presence at a number of bases throughout that country to better monitor efforts at containing drug trafficking. The heightened U.S. military presence in Colombia was, in turn, the result of Ecuadorian President Rafael Correa's decision not to renew the lease for the U.S. drug-monitoring facility at Manta in Ecuador. Although Colombia's Supreme Constitutional Court eventually scuttled the base agreement with the U.S., finding it an unconstitutional overreach on the part of President Álvaro Uribe, the attempt raised alarm in many neighboring countries. There were concerns that U.S. military activities would not be confined to Colombia and would spill over into their territories. The Council's creation also provided a convenient forum for coordinating a unified position on a new drug policy in anticipation of the VI Summit of the Americas in Cartagena in 2012. As previously discussed, it was as a result of that Summit meeting that the OAS came to release two, separate but interconnected, reports on the drug problem in the Americas, in May 2013. UNASUR's Council to Combat Drug Trafficking has also been used to coordinate efforts led by Bolivia to remove the designation of the coca leaf, which has been used for centuries by indigenous peoples in the Andes for religious and medicinal purposes, as a narcotic, subject to international treaties that prohibit its exportation and commercialization.

Following the creation of a Technical Election Unit in 2014, UNASUR has fielded election observer missions in various national and municipal elections, as well as plebiscites, where similar types of mission from the OAS have occasionally been excluded. Among the recent elections monitored by UNASUR observers are the 2016 constitutional plebiscite in Bolivia; the 2015 municipal and regional elections and the 2014 general election in the Dominican Republic; the 2016 general election in Guyana; the 2015 general and municipal elections in Paraguay; the 2016 general election and the 2014 municipal and regional elections in Peru; and the 2015 general election in Suriname. Election monitors from UNASUR were also invited to observe the Venezuelan legislative elections in December 2015; a similar OAS team was specifically excluded. UNASUR is fast approaching a regional function that had since 1962 been the exclusive prerogative of the OAS.

The Community of Latin American and Caribbean States (CELAC)

In December 2008, then Brazilian President Luiz Inácio Lula da Silva hosted a meeting at the resort town of Sauípe in northeastern Brazil for the heads of state of all the countries of Latin America and the Caribbean. The Brazilian government even sent planes from its air force to ferry leaders from poorer countries in Central and South America to the meeting, to ensure they could attend.[37] Cuba was present; the United States and Canada were purposely excluded. At the three-day summit, the decades-long U.S. trade embargo against Cuba was roundly condemned, as were U.S. and European economic policies that had allegedly caused the global economic instability whose negative effects were being felt in the region at the time. The meeting underscored the growing economic and geo-political power of Brazil, and served as a warning to the United States to expect an emboldened Latin American bloc at the next Summit of the Americas, scheduled for Trinidad and Tobago in April 2009. The meeting in Sauípe was the precursor to what eventually became the Community of Latin American and Caribbean States (*Comunidad de Estados Latinoamericanos y Caribeños*), or CELAC—which, in turn, was the latest manifestation of a movement with roots in the 1980s responding to the inability of the OAS to facilitate a peace agreement in Central America.

The Permanent Mechanism of Political Consultation and Coordination, or Rio Group, was created in 1986 and reflected Latin American interest in devising a political solution to end the civil wars in El Salvador, Guatemala, and Nicaragua. Specifically, it was an attempt to circumvent the Reagan administration's bellicose preferences that were seen as thwarting efforts to achieve a peaceful resolution through the OAS.[38] Formally launched following the issuance of the Declaration of Rio de Janeiro, the Rio Group was itself an outgrowth of the Contadora Group established by Colombia, Mexico, Panama, and Venezuela in 1983, which also sought to bring an end to the violence in Central America. In July 1985, Argentina, Brazil, Peru, and Uruguay established the Support Group to the Contadora Group. The Reagan administration was initially very hostile to both the original Contadora Group and its Support Group, which it viewed as hindering its efforts to overthrow the Nicaraguan government. Bolivia, Chile, Ecuador, and Paraguay, as well as CARICOM, became part of the Rio Group in 1990. Costa Rica, El Salvador, Guatemala, Honduras, Nicaragua, and the Dominican Republic soon followed. Belize joined in 2005, while Cuba, Guyana, and Haiti became members in 2008. The last countries to associate themselves with the Rio Group were Suriname and Jamaica in 2009. Between its first meeting in Rio de Janeiro in 1986 and its last in Venezuela at the end of 2011, the Rio Group met every year in a different member state.

President Felipe Calderón of Mexico used a 2008 meeting of the Rio Group in Santo Domingo to propose the creation of a Union of Latin American and Caribbean Nations. Calderón viewed this initiative as a way to strengthen Mexico's ties with Latin American neighbors, which had been strained by Mexico's membership in the North American Free Trade Agreement, or NAFTA. Mexico, as a member of the Latin American Trade Association (ALADI), was obligated by ALADI's Most Favored Nation clause to extend the same preferential tariff arrangements to other member states that it had granted Canada and the United States under NAFTA. Mexico never did so. Initially this did not raise concerns, as all the other ALADI countries were also engaged in negotiations to create a Free Trade Area of the Americas (FTAA) that would eventually give them the same duty-free access that Canadian and U.S. goods received in the Mexican market and, vice versa, through NAFTA. However, the collapse of the FTAA negotiations in 2005 reawakened Latin American sentiment that Mexico had turned its back on its neighbors to the south by hitching its economic wagon to North America. In February 2010, in Cancun, Mexico hosted a meeting of the Rio Group that also served as a second summit of all the Latin American and Caribbean heads of state, following President Lula's hosting of a first in northeastern Brazil in 2008. It was at this meeting that CELAC was formally launched, although it would not become operational until after what turned out to be the last meeting of the Rio Group, in Caracas, Venezuela in December 2011.[39]

Despite the key role Mexico played in CELAC's founding, Venezuela and its allies in the Bolivarian Alliance for Our America (ALBA) soon captured the bloc. As a result, it quickly morphed into an alternative to the OAS without the bothersome presence of the United States. The fact that CELAC excludes Canada, a country seen by radical Latin American elements as subservient to U.S. dictates, is particularly ironic given that Canada had long resisted joining the OAS, in order to preserve a foreign policy independent of Washington, DC *vis-à-vis* Latin America. Canada and Mexico were the only countries in the Western Hemisphere never to break diplomatic and economic relations with Castro's Cuba.

All the sovereign states of Latin America and the Caribbean are currently members of CELAC. However, its institutional framework is weak and it does not even have its own website. The presidency of CELAC rotates annually among each member state (which is then responsible for posting information on the last CELAC Summit on a temporary website usually linked to the official website of that country's Ministry of Foreign Affairs). Up to now, CELAC has been little more than a talk shop, providing another excuse for the region's heads of state to travel to another regional conference for yet another photo opportunity. However, that has not prevented the European Union from utilizing CELAC as a means of facilitating a dialogue between both regions. At least two CELAC–EU Summits have taken place (the first in Santiago, Chile in January 2013, and the second in Brussels in June 2015). The Chinese have also been keen on using CELAC as a way to channel discussions and negotiations with Latin America and the Caribbean through a single institution, just as they have done with sub-Saharan Africa since 2000 through the Forum of China–Africa Cooperation.

In January 2015, the People's Republic of China hosted a summit in Beijing. All CELAC member states attended. The summit concluded with the announcement of a five-year cooperation plan and promises of billions of dollars in new Chinese loans and investments, as well as a pledge by Chinese President Xi Jinping to provide 6,000 scholarships and 6,000 training opportunities for citizens from the member states of CELAC to come to China. Chile will host the next CELAC–China summit in 2018. Given CELAC's current weak institutional framework, however, it is difficult to see how it can serve as an effective interlocutor for directing investment between China and Latin America and the Caribbean. On the other hand, CELAC does provide an indirect way for China to deal with countries in Latin America and the Caribbean with which it does not have bilateral diplomatic relations.

Conclusion

In many ways, the United States only has itself to blame for the current debilitation of the inter-American system. Over the course of a century, the United States has swung wildly from utilizing the system to achieve narrow realist security objectives, whether under Dollar Diplomacy or during the Cold War, to using it in pursuit of liberal goals, as exemplified by FDR's Good Neighbor Policy and the human rights advocacy of the Carter era. There were also periods in which the United States utilized its hegemonic position within the inter-American system to provide public goods, such as during the Clinton administration and, arguably, Kennedy's Alliance for Progress. The predominant U.S. position within the inter-American system has historically been decidedly realist in character, however. At the same time, the United States has long resisted entertaining neo-realist notions of balance of power and security demanded by the Latin Americans premised on non-intervention and a strict respect for national sovereignty as well as adequate funding for economic development. For that matter, the United States frequently ignored the decidedly liberal objectives of the inter-American system favored by its neighbors to the south. Accordingly, the inter-American system failed to move beyond the role of a facilitator of continuous bargaining among the competing objectives of Latin America on the one hand, and the United States on the other, into a solid, regional political institution built on a congruence of interests.[40]

The United States' role with regard to what is probably the most effective aspect of the inter-American system, namely the promotion and protection of human rights, is inapposite to the ancient Greek conception or contemporary international relations notions of hegemony synonymous with the exercise of leadership. In particular, the United States resists recognizing the Inter-American Commission on Human Rights' authority to issue legally binding findings of violations of the American Declaration of the Rights and Duties of Man, whose provisions are applicable to all OAS member states. The United States has also failed to ratify the American Convention on Human Rights, which means, *ipso facto*, it does not recognize the compulsory jurisdiction of the Inter-American Court of Human Rights in San José, Costa Rica. Although there may be some genuine constitutional justification that, in part, explains some of this equivocation, the practical effect has been to undermine the legitimacy of the inter-American human rights process. This explains the calls in recent years to remove the Inter-American Commission on Human Rights from Washington, DC to a South American capital. It also served as the pretext for Venezuela's decision in 2012 to rescind its ratification of the American Convention of Human Rights and withdraw from the compulsory jurisdiction of the Inter-American Court of Human Rights.

The June 2009 coup in Honduras provides the most notorious recent example of the United States' failure to exercise leadership or provide a necessary public good in the context of the inter-American system. Although the United States initially joined the hemispheric community in condemning President Zelaya's overthrow and in imposing sanctions authorized by the Inter-American Democratic Charter, the Obama administration soon succumbed to a rebellion by a group of Republican senators and unilaterally sought an expedient solution to the crisis. In particular, the U.S. never used its significant economic and political clout to boost Latin American efforts to restore Zelaya to power. Instead, the Obama administration preferred to wait out the clock until what would have been the end of Zelaya's term in office, and then accept the results of the November 29, 2009 elections. While that may have ended the immediate political crisis as far as the Americans were concerned, it did nothing to overcome the intense political polarization within Honduras. That deep polarization is one factor contributing to Honduras's dubious distinction of having among the highest per capita homicide rates in the world today.

The dwindling influence of the United States in the Western Hemisphere, and the growing autonomy of Latin America, are reflected in the OAS, an organization once synonymous with U.S. hegemony. This has been most apparent in the Americans' inability to utilize the OAS to address the unfolding political, economic, and humanitarian crisis in Venezuela. In February 2014, the government of Nicolás Maduro violently repressed student-led demonstrations and other mass mobilizations, leading to numerous deaths and the imprisonment of major opposition figures. The Obama administration could only drum up support from Canada and Panama to support an OAS resolution condemning the actions as a threat to Venezuelan democracy. Another resolution with respect to Venezuela in June 2017, sponsored by the United States, Canada, and a now much larger contingent of Latin American countries, could not pass because it lacked the support of a bloc of Caribbean nations plus Caracas's Bolivarian Alliance (ALBA) allies. The resolution had called on President Maduro to, *inter alia*, permit mediation by a group of OAS member states to try to find an end to the most recent bout of political violence, which had claimed the lives of at least 75 people after weeks of street protests.

During the past decade, UNASUR has increasingly displaced the OAS as the preferred forum for resolving internal political disputes in member states that are related to actual or perceived interruptions in representative democracy, and in fielding electoral observer missions. UNASUR has proved more dynamic in handling defense-related issues as well, while the inter-American defense system has been marginalized as an irrelevant Cold War relic. Some Latin American governments have even withdrawn from the Rio Treaty and its collective security mechanism. They believe there is no longer a credible threat from outside the Western Hemisphere to justify its continued existence. UNASUR has also proven to be more adept in resolving sensitive cross-border migration issues and enhancing citizens' access to high-cost medications.

Currently, neither UNASUR and CELAC can realistically substitute for the OAS or serve as an effective counter-hegemonic force to the United States.[41] Both organizations have very weak institutional frameworks that lack any type of supranational authority. They also do not have any mechanism equivalent to the OAS to promote and defend human rights. There are also major issues that can be effectively resolved only with the participation of all the nations of the Western Hemisphere, such as suppression of the illicit drug trade or illegal immigration to the United States. Accordingly, the OAS remains a relevant institution, even if under a changed set of circumstances wherein the United States is unable or incapable of providing effective leadership or public goods to entice other countries to support its objectives. The survival of the OAS without the domineering presence of the self-centered hegemon that was most responsible for its creation, and that once wielded effective control over its agenda, is a plausible outcome under international regime theory.

In the future, CELAC's fortunes could be boosted by a Chinese decision to use it as the primary forum for engaging in discussions on investment projects and resolving contentious trade disputes with countries in Latin America and the Caribbean. CELAC might also be able to play a more effective role than the OAS in ensuring a smooth transition from authoritarian rule to representative democracy in Cuba. For now, UNASUR and CELAC provide alternative fora for discussing issues that countries do not feel comfortable raising in the presence of the country that still enjoys military predominance in the Western Hemisphere. Both organizations also play an important "soft balancing" role. Soft balancing accepts the existing balance of power but seeks to obtain better outcomes within it, by assembling countervailing coalitions designed to thwart or impede specific policies of the hegemon.[42] Mark Eric Williams notes that "as American unilateralism increased during the Bush administration, other states began to balance the United States 'softly', through shrewd diplomacy, more subtle policy coordination, and limited or tacit ententes" in order "to check U.S. hegemonic influence non-militarily, frustrate or delay disagreeable U.S. policy designs, and on certain issues, undermine Washington's ability to realize its preferred outcomes."[43] Soft balancing, he says, has the added virtue that it is unlikely to generate a security dilemma, because it does not threaten the hegemon's security directly as would a neo-realist conception of balancing. Rather than try to balance U.S. hard power, soft-balancing strategies seek to limit its influence and freedom to act unilaterally.[44]

Notes

1 The full text of the Inter-American Democratic Charter is available at: www.oas.org/ OASpage/eng/Documents/Democractic_Charter.htm. There is a certain irony to the Inter-American Democratic Charter's adoption on what was also the 28th anniversary of the overthrow of Salvador Allende's democratically elected government in Chile on September 11, 1973. The Nixon administration's contributions to further polarizing the Chilean political climate that eventually led to that military coup have been amply demonstrated in books such as Peter Kornbluh's *The Pinochet Files: A Declassified Dossier of Atrocity and Accountability* (New York: New Press, 2004), which relies extensively on materials sourced from the U.S. National Security Archives.

2 Jorge Heine and Brigitte Weiffen, *21st Century Democracy Promotion in the Americas: Standing up for the Polity* (New York: Routledge, 2015), 55. Despite marked improvements on Resolution 1080 and the Washington Protocol, Heine and Weiffen identify at least three major limitations of the Inter-American Democratic Charter. First, it is a political agreement and not a legally binding treaty. Second, its invocation is dependent on the political will of the governments (particularly the executive branch). Third, it lacks a clear threshold determining precisely at what point the OAS should intervene, because of the uncertain meaning of key terms and the lack of precision in the criteria for defining when and to what extent a country's democratic institutions have been altered. Ibid at 61–3. The third critique encompasses "insufficient provisions to anticipate democratic crises and take preventive action in their early stages." Ibid at 164.

3 Nicholas Phillips and Elizabeth Malkin, "Honduras Election Results Challenged," *New York Times*, November 30, 2013. Accessed July 27, 2017: www.nytimes. com/2013/12/01/world/americas/honduras-election-results-challenged.html. Electoral Observer missions from the OAS and EU expressed concerns about the voter rolls and the transparency of campaign financing, but concluded the results were reasonably transparent.

4 David W. Dent and Larman C. Wilson, *Historical Dictionary of Inter-American Organizations, Second Edition* (Plymouth, UK: Scarecrow Press, 2014), 116.

5 Mark Eric Williams, *Understanding U.S.–Latin American Relations* (New York: Routledge, 2012), 338.

6 Peter J. Meyer, *Organization of American States: Background and Issues for Congress* (Washington, DC: Congressional Research Service, August 29, 2014), 16. Impatience at U.S. policy and its continued trade embargo against Cuba was already evident in 1996 when, in response to President Clinton's signing the Cuban Liberty and Democratic Solidarity Act, aka the Helm–Burton Bill, the OAS condemned the legislation as a violation of international law, primarily because of its extraterritorial scope. In particular, most OAS member states expressed concerns over provisions that prohibited the local subsidiaries of U.S. companies based in foreign countries from trading with Cuba, as well as the revocation of the U.S. visas of the employees of foreign companies utilizing assets in Cuba nationalized by the Castro government after the revolution.

7 Joseph S. Tulchin, *Latin America in International Politics: Challenging U.S. Hegemony* (Boulder, CO: Lynne Rienner Publishers, 2016), 118. The tactic worked, according to Tulchin, as the U.S. Congress came to view CICAD as a viable alternative to its own work and eventually eliminated the annual certification requirement in 2002.

8 Peter J. Meyer, *Organization of American States: Background and Issues for Congress* (Washington, DC: Congressional Research Service, August 29, 2014), 14. The counter-argument is that CICAD and its multilateral evaluation mechanisms have been instrumental in building trust and establishing common ground for cooperation between the United States and other nations in the Western Hemisphere. Among other things, this helped to end the annual certification process by the U.S. government in 2002 as to which countries cooperated in the U.S. War on Drugs and which did not.

9 The full report, entitled *The Drug Problem in the Americas*, is available at: www. cicad.oas.org/Main/Template.asp?File=/drogas/elinforme/default_eng.asp.

10 Michelle Denise Reeves, "The Evolution of 'Narcoterrorism': From the Cold War to the War on Drugs," in *Beyond the Eagle's Shadow: New Histories of Latin America's Cold War*, ed. Virginia Garrard-Burnett et al. (Albuquerque: University of New Mexico Press, 2013), 282.

11 Within half a year of the Colombian military's November 1985 disastrous storming of the Palace of Justice in Bogotá following its capture by M-19 guerillas, which resulted in the death of some 60 hostages (including many judges), National Security Decision Directive 221 was issued at then Vice-President Bush's directive. It declared drugs a national security threat, widening the scope of military involvement in the drug war and linking counter-insurgency and counter-narcotics in official U.S. policy for the first time. Michelle Denise Reeves, "The Evolution of 'Narcoterrorism': From the Cold War to the War on Drugs," in *Beyond the Eagle's Shadow: New Histories of Latin America's Cold War*, ed. Virginia Garrard-Burnett et al. (Albuquerque: University of New Mexico Press, 2013), 283.

12 Michelle Denise Reeves, "The Evolution of 'Narcoterrorism': From the Cold War to the War on Drugs," in *Beyond the Eagle's Shadow: New Histories of Latin America's Cold War*, ed. Virginia Garrard-Burnett et al. (Albuquerque: University of New Mexico Press, 2013), 284. One of the wilder accusations made by Reagan administration officials was that Cuba and the Sandinista government in Nicaragua had

cultivated extensive ties with leftist guerilla groups in the northern Andes, in order to use profits from drug trafficking to finance Marxist revolution in the Western Hemisphere and, as a bonus, to destabilize U.S. society by exacerbating the problem of drug addiction. Ibid at 285–6.

13 Public Law 113-41-Oct. 2, 2013 at 22 USC 290q. The full text of the OAS Revital-ization and Reform Act of 2013 is available at: www.congress.gov/113/plaws/publ41/PLAW-113publ41.pdf.

14 Jorge Heine and Brigitte Weiffin, *2lst Century Democracy Promotion in the Americas: Standing Up for the Polity* (New York: Routledge, 2015), 139–140.

15 Richard J. Bloomfield, "The Inter-American System: Does It Have a Future?" in *The Future of the Inter-American System*, ed. Tom J. Farer (New York: Praeger Publishers, 1979), 6.

16 Because the Community of South American Nations had no international legal standing, the 12 countries of South America signed the Treaty Establishing UNASUR on May 23, 2008 in Brasilia. The Treaty entered into force on March 11, 2011. The full text, in Spanish, of the Treaty Establishing UNASUR is available at: www.unasursg.org/images/descargas/DOCUMENTOS%20CONSTITUTIVOS%20DE%20UNASUR/Tratado-UNASUR-solo.pdf. The General Secretariat of UNASUR is located in Quito, Ecuador.

17 Harold Trinkunas, "Reordering Regional Security in Latin America," *Journal of International Affairs*, Vol. 66, No. 2 (2013): 83. Brazil envisions itself as the axis of a subcontinental region receptive to Brazilian investment and industrial exports that is strategic not only economically but also geopolitically, thereby boosting the country's status in the eyes of the international community. Carlos Espinosa, "The Origins of the Union of South American Nations: A Multicausal Account of South American Regionalism," in *Exploring the New South American Regionalism*, ed. Ernesto Viva-res (Farnham, UK: Ashgate Publishing, 2014), 38. For Brazil, which seeks to erode established powers' stranglehold on international multilateral institutions, this is important because if it can credibly present itself as the interlocutor of the subconti-nent *vis-à-vis* the UN Security Council, its chances of being granted a seat at the Security Council would be bolstered. Ibid.

18 Kharchik DerGhougassian, "The Post-Washington Consensus Regional Integration in South America: Convergence and Divergence in ALBA and UNASUR: A Com-parative Perspective," in *Decline of U.S. Hegemony? A Challenge of ALBA and a New Latin American Integration of the Twenty-First Century*, ed. Bruce M. Bagley et al. (Lanham, MD: Lexington Books, 2015), 175.

19 Marcela Ganem, "UNASUR: Constructing the South American Identity," in *Decline of U.S. Hegemony? A Challenge of ALBA and a New Latin American Integration of the Twenty-First Century*, ed. Bruce M. Bagley et al. (Lanham, MD: Lexington Books, 2015), 206. Among the reasons offered for such slow progress are a tripling in the original estimates for what it would take to complete the projects, and political disputes among countries (e.g., Colombia and Venezuela) hindering cross-border cooperation.

20 See, e.g., Carlos Gustavo Poggio Teixeira, *Brazil, the United States, and the South American Subsystem* (Lanham, MD: Lexington Books, 2012), 126.

21 Carlos Gustavo Poggio Teixeira, *Brazil, the United States, and the South American Subsystem* (Lanham, MD: Lexington Books, 2012), 126.

22 Jorge Battaglino, "Defense in a Post-Hegemonic Regional Agenda: The Case of the South American Defense Council," in *The Rise of Post-Hegemonic Regionalism: The Case of Latin America*, ed. Pia Riggirozzi et al. (Dordrecht, NL: Springer, 2012), 82. At a time in which Brazil was upgrading its military, Brasilia viewed the South American Defense Council as a way of unifying the military industries of the region, presumably around joint ventures with Brazilian firms. Carlos Espinosa, "The Origins of the Union of South American Nations: A Multicausal Account of

South American Regionalism," in *Exploring the New South American Regionalism*, ed. Ernesto Vivares (Farnham, UK: Ashgate Publishing, 2014), 46.

23 The information is provided on an annual basis by the Ministry of Defense of each UNASUR member state and covers money paid on salaries, arms purchases, research and development, and operational costs actually expended by the defense ministries and the different branches of the Armed Forces. It includes foreign military assistance for national defense (although it excludes monies directed to strictly domestic security forces such as the police). The published reports are available to the public online at http://ceed.unasursg.org/Espanol/02-Lineas/02.1-Gastos-Def. html. The reports use common definitions and a standardized methodology approved in 2011 and include cumulative data for all 12 UNASUR countries during the period from 2006 through 2015. Interestingly, the UNASUR initiative appears to be the outgrowth of an effort that was originally proposed in the OAS in the 1990s but ultimately ran into bottlenecks, which had sought to place an emphasis on confidence and security-building measures by guaranteeing transparency of military procedures and the availability of information. Mônica Herz, *The Organization of American States (OAS): Global Governance Away from the Media* (New York: Routledge, 2011), 42.

24 Jorge Battaglino, "Defense in a Post-Hegemonic Regional Agenda: The Case of the South American Defense Council," in *The Rise of Post-Hegemonic Regionalism: The Case of Latin America*, ed. Pia Riggirozzi et al. (Dordrecht, NL: Springer, 2012), 82. The South American Defense Council "represents a counter-hegemonic impulse of South America, led by Brazil, which tends to counteract the virtual relative disengagement of the United States with respect to South America." Raúl Benítez Manaut and Rit Diamint, "The South American Defense Council vis-à-vis ALBA: Dilemmas and Contradictions of the New Security Diplomacy," in *Decline of U.S. Hegemony? A Challenge of ALBA and a New Latin American Integration of the Twenty-First Century*, ed. Bruce M. Bagley et al. (Lanham, MD: Lexington Books, 2015), 225.

25 Francisco Carrión Mena, "Washington and the New South American Regionalism," in *Exploring the New South American Regionalism*, ed. Ernesto Vivares (Farnham, UK: Ashgate Publishing, 2014), 62.

26 Carlos Espinosa, "The Origins of the Union of South American Nations: A Multicausal Account of South American Regionalism," in *Exploring the New South American Regionalism*, ed. Ernesto Vivares (Farnham, UK: Ashgate Publishing, 2014), 46.

27 Interestingly, Bolivia first proposed a regional defense school within the realm of the *Alianza Bolivariana para los Pueblos de Nuestra América* (ALBA). A School of Defense of the Armed Forces—with Iranian financial support—opened its doors in the Bolivian city of Santa Cruz in June 2011. "[T]his initiative seems to indicate, at least on this issue, of an institution parallel to UNASUR that denotes differences in terms of the conceptual perspectives in topics such as security and defense." Francine Jácome, "Political and Ideological Aspects of the Alianza Bolivariana Para Los Pueblos De Nuestra América—Tratado de Comercio De Los Pueblos (ALBA-TCP): Viability and Sustainability?" in *Decline of U.S. Hegemony? A Challenge of ALBA and a New Latin American Integration of the Twenty-First Century*, ed. Bruce M. Bagley et al. (Lanham, MD: Lexington Books, 2015), 50. The decision to establish the defense school based in Bolivia also created a rift with the English-speaking Caribbean members of ALBA, who reportedly refused to participate, utilizing the excuse that they are already participants in a Caribbean Regional Security System.

28 The UNASUR and MERCOSUR responses contrast with the situation in the OAS, where several special meetings of the Permanent Council were called to discuss the possibility of invoking the Inter-American Democratic Charter against Paraguay. "Although critical of the haste that marked the impeachment process, the OAS

ultimately decided to take a more cautious approach and refrained from second-guessing the interpretation of a member state's constitution." Jorge Heine and Brigitte Weiffen, *21st Century Democracy Promotion in the Americas: Standing Up for the Polity* (New York: Routledge, 2015), 95. Another factor, no doubt, was the experience of the Honduran coup in 2009, where the OAS responded quickly in imposing sanctions but was never able to restore the ousted president to power.

29 The full text, in Spanish, of the Additional Protocol to the Treaty Establishing UNASUR on the Commitment to Democracy is available at: http://unasursg.org/ images/descargas/DOCUMENTOS%20CONSTITUTIVOS%20DE%20UNASUR/ Protocolo-Adicional-al-Tratado-Constitutivo-de-UNASUR-sobre-Compromiso-con-la-Democracia-opt.pdf. The full text, in English, of the Protocol of Ushuaia on the Commitment to Democracy in the MERCOSUR, Bolivia, and Chile signed on July 24, 1998 can be found in Appendix 43 of Thomas Andrew O'Keefe, *Latin American Trade Agreements* (Ardsley, NY: Transnational Publishers, 1997–).

30 While it waited for UNASUR's data bank to come online, MERCOSUR's *ad hoc* committee used one developed by Brazil nearly two decades earlier. One reason for the delay in bringing the UNASUR data bank online quickly was that some governments (Venezuela, in particular) claimed to have confidentiality agreements with multinational pharmaceutical companies on pricing arrangements that prevented them from sharing this information. Still others had no national systems in place to collect this data at the domestic level. Accordingly, there are serious concerns as to the reliability and accuracy of the information found in the UNASUR data bank of pharmaceutical prices.

31 The full text, in Spanish, of the Decision of the UNASUR Council of Heads of State and Government of December 16, 2008 authorizing the creation of the UNASUR Health Council is available at: www.unasursg.org/images/descargas/ESTATUTOS%20 CONSEJOS%20MINISTERIALES%20SECTORIALES/ESTATUTO%20 CONSEJO%20DE%20SALUD.pdf.

32 The full text, in Spanish, of the ISAGS Five Year Plan for 2010–2015 is available at: www.isags-unasur.org/uploads/biblioteca/1/bb[67]ling[2]anx[147].pdf.

33 The full text, in Spanish, of Resolution 05/2009 adopted by the South American Health Council of the UNASUR on November 24, 2009 approving the creation of ISAGS is available at: www.isags-unasur.org/uploads/biblioteca/1/bb[18]ling[2] anx[28].pdf.

34 The full text, in English, of the ISAGS By-Laws adopted by the South American Council of Health of the UNASUR as Resolution 02/2011 on April 14, 2011 is available at: www.isags-unasur.org/uploads/biblioteca/1/bb[14]ling[2]anx[2110].pdf.

35 Pia Riggirozzi, "Comparing SADC and UNASUR Regional Health Governance and Policy," Poverty Reduction and Regional Integration Working Paper 15-2 (2015), 14. Available at: www.academia.edu/12902796/COMPARING_SADC_AND_UNA-SUR_REGIONAL_HEALTH_GOVERNANCE_AND_POLICY. The *movimento sanitarista* was founded in Brazil by health professionals in the early twentieth century in response to various epidemics and outbreaks of disease in Rio de Janeiro as a result of poor sanitary conditions. It has traditionally favored a strong, centralized role for the federal government in the provision of health services in Brazil (as opposed to what it views as ineffective and uncoordinated state or municipal initiatives). Osvaldo Cruz was a bacteriologist who led a successful campaign to end the conditions that facilitated the spread of yellow fever and bubonic plague in Rio.

36 Pia Riggirozzi, "Comparing SADC and UNASUR Regional Health Governance and Policy," Poverty Reduction and Regional Integration Working Paper 15-2 (2015), 15. Available at: www.academia.edu/12902796/COMPARING_SADC_AND_UNA-SUR_REGIONAL_HEALTH_GOVERNANCE_AND_POLICY.

37 Alexi Barrionuevo, "At Meeting in Brazil, Washington is Scorned," *New York Times*, December 18, 2008: 10.
38 Rodrigo Tavares, *Security in South America: The Role of States and Regional Organizations* (Boulder, CO: First Forum Press, 2014), 243.
39 The name of CELAC came about after an intense debate in which Venezuela preferred to include the term "Organization" instead of "Community" (thereby emphasizing CELAC was in opposition to the OAS). Mexico suggested "Union," while Brazil proposed the more palatable "Community" that was eventually adopted. Rodrigo Tavares, *Security in South America: The Role of States and Regional Organizations* (Boulder, CO: First Forum Press, 2014), 245. The text in Spanish of the Declaration of the Latin American and Caribbean Unity Summit, held in Cancun, Mexico in February 2010, that launched CELAC is available at: http://walk.sela.org/attach/258/default/Declaracion_delaCumbre_de_la_Unidad_de_America_Latina_23_02_2010.pdf. Other declarations, plans of action, and related documents concerning CELAC are available through the website of the Latin American Economic System (SELA) at: www.sela.org/celac/quienes-somos/que-es-la-celac/otras-declaraciones/.
40 Peter J. Katzenstein, *A World of Regions* (Ithaca, NY: Cornell University Press, 2005), 227.
41 One reason why UNASUR or CELAC do not provide a counter-hegemonic alternative to the United States is that both entities retain the traditional inter-American emphasis, for example, on encouraging and defending representative democracy. Hence, UNASUR and CELAC accept the long-standing U.S. ideological viewpoint that representative democracy is the ideal form of governance (as opposed to the Bolivarian Republic of Venezuela's preference for participatory democracy).
42 Stephen M. Walt, "Alliances in a Unipolar World," in *International Relations Theory and the Consequences of Unipolarity*, ed. G. John Ikenberry et al. (New York: Cambridge University Press, 2011), 120. "In the current era of US dominance, therefore, soft balancing is the conscious coordination of diplomatic action in order to obtain outcomes contrary to US preferences, outcomes that could not be gained if the balancers did not give each other some degree of mutual support." Ibid.
43 Mark Eric Williams, *Understanding U.S.–Latin American Relations* (New York: Routledge, 2012), 335. "Historically, states in the anarchic system have sought to preserve their independence and security through 'internal' or 'external' hard balancing, manifest in domestic defense build-ups or formal military alliances with other states. Their main objective has been to protect the interests of the weak against the strong and potentially threatening. But these defensive moves are impractical in situations where one state's power exceeds that of a weaker state (or coalition of states) by orders of magnitude." Ibid.
44 Mark Eric Williams, *Understanding U.S.–Latin American Relations* (New York: Routledge, 2012), 336. "In the current era of US dominance, therefore, soft balancing is the conscious coordination of diplomatic action in order to obtain outcomes contrary to US preferences, outcomes that could not be gained if the balancers did not give each other some degree of mutual support." Stephen M. Walt, "Alliances in a Unipolar World," in *International Relations Theory and the Consequences of Unipolarity*, ed. G. John Ikenberry et al. (New York: Cambridge University Press, 2011), 120.

Bibliography

Bagley, Bruce M. and Magdalena Defort, eds. *Decline of U.S. Hegemony? A Challenge of ALBA and a New Latin American Integration of the Twenty-First Century*. Lanham, MD: Lexington Books, 2015.

Barrionuevo, Alexi. "At Meeting in Brazil, Washington is Scorned." *New York Times*, December 18, 2008: 10.

CELAC. "Declaración de la Cumbre de la Unidad de América Latina y el Caribe." Issued by the Heads of State and Government of the Countries of Latin America and the Caribbean Gathered for the Latin America and Caribbean Unity Summit in Cancun, Mexico on February 23, 2010. Accessed July 27, 2017: http://walk.sela.org/attach/258/default/Declaracion_delaCumbre_de_la_Unidad_de_America_Latina_23_02_2010.pdf

Dent, David W. and Larman C. Wilson. *Historical Dictionary of Inter-American Organizations, Second Edition.* Plymouth, UK: Scarecrow Press, 2014.

Farer, Tom J., ed. *The Future of the Inter-American System.* New York: Praeger Publishers, 1979.

Garrard-Burnett, Virginia, Mark Atwood Lawrence, and Julio E. Moreno, eds. *Beyond the Eagle's Shadow: New Histories of Latin America's Cold War.* Albuquerque: University of New Mexico Press, 2013.

Heine, Jorge and Brigitte Weiffen. *21st Century Democracy Promotion in the Americas: Standing Up for the Polity.* New York: Routledge, 2015.

Herz, Mônica. *The Organization of American States (OAS): Global Governance Away from the Media.* New York: Routledge, 2011.

Ikenberry, G. John, Michael Mastanduno, and William C. Wohlforth, eds. *International Relations Theory and the Consequences of Unipolarity.* New York: Cambridge University Press, 2011.

Katzenstein, Peter J. *A World of Regions.* Ithaca, NY: Cornell University Press, 2005.

MERCOSUR. "Consejo del Mercado Común Decisión 32/14: Complementación y Articulación MERCOSUR-UNASUR." Adopted at the XLVII Session of the Common Market Council in the City of Paraná, Argentina on December 16, 2014. Accessed July 27, 2017: www.mercosur.int/innovaportal/v/5798/2/innova.front/2014

Meyer, Peter J. *Organization of American States: Background and Issues for Congress.* Washington, DC: Congressional Research Service, August 29, 2014.

O'Keefe, Thomas Andrew. *Latin American Trade Agreements.* Ardsley, NY: Transnational Publishers, 1997–.

Organization of American States. *The Drug Problem in the Americas.* Washington, DC: OAS General Secretariat, 2013. Accessed July 27, 2017: www.cicad.oas.org/Main/Template.asp?File=/drogas/elinforme/default_eng.asp

Organization of American States. *Inter-American Democratic Charter.* Washington, DC: OAS General Secretariat. Adopted at a Special Session of the General Assembly in Lima, Peru on September 11, 2001. Accessed July 27, 2017: www.oas.org/OASpage/eng/Documents/Democractic_Charter.htm

Phillips, Nicholas and Elizabeth Malkin. "Honduras Election Results Challenged." *New York Times*, November 30, 2013. Accessed July 27, 2017: www.nytimes.com/2013/12/01/world/americas/honduras-election-results-challenged.html

Poggio Teixeira, Carlos Gustavo. *Brazil, the United States, and the South American Subsystem.* Lanham, MD: Lexington Books, 2012.

Riggirozzi, Pia. "Comparing SADC and UNASUR Regional Health Governance and Policy." Poverty Reduction and Regional Integration Working Paper 15-2, 2015. Accessed July 27, 2017: www.academia.edu/12902796/COMPARING_SADC_AND_UNASUR_REGIONAL_HEALTH_GOVERNANCE_AND_POLICY

Riggirozzi, Pía and Diana Tussie, eds. *The Rise of Post-Hegemonic Regionalism: The Case of Latin America.* Dordrecht, NL: Springer, 2012.

Tavares, Rodrigo. *Security in South America: The Role of States and Regional Organizations*. Boulder, CO: First Forum Press, 2014.

Trinkunas, Harold. "Reordering Regional Security in Latin America." *Journal of International Affairs* Vol. 66, No. 2 (2013): 83–99.

Tulchin, Joseph S. *Latin America in International Politics: Challenging U.S. Hegemony*. Boulder, CO: Lynne Rienner Publishers, 2016.

UNASUR. *Bylaw of the South American Institute of Government in Health*. Rio de Janeiro: UNASUR-ISAGS. Adopted by the South American Council of Health of the UNASUR as Resolution 02/2011 in Montevideo, Uruguay on April 14, 2011. Accessed July 27, 2017: www.isags-unasur.org/uploads/biblioteca/1/bb[14]ling[2]anx[2110].pdf

UNASUR. *Decisión para el Establecimiento del Consejo de Salud Suramericano de la UNASUR*. Quito: Secretaría General de UNASUR. Adopted by the Heads of State and Governments of the UNASUR in Salvador do Bahia, Brazil on December 16, 2008. Accessed July 27, 2017: www.unasursg.org/images/descargas/ESTATUTOS%20CONSEJOS%20MINISTERIALES%20SECTORIALES/ESTATUTO%20CONSEJO%20DE%20SALUD.pdf

UNASUR. *Plan Quinquenal: 2010–2015*. Quito: Secretaría General de UNASUR. Approved by the South American Health Council of the UNASUR in Cuenca, Ecuador on April 30, 2010. Accessed July 27, 2017: www.isags-unasur.org/uploads/biblioteca/1/bb[67]ling[2]anx[147].pdf

UNASUR. *Protocolo adicional al Tratado Constitutivo de UNASUR sobre Compromiso con la Democracia*. Quito: Secretaría General de UNASUR. Entered into Force on March 19, 2014. Accessed July 27, 2017: http://unasursg.org/images/descargas/DOCUMENTOS%20CONSTITUTIVOS%20DE%20UNASUR/Protocolo-Adicional-al-Tratado-Constitutivo-de-UNASUR-sobre-Compromiso-con-la-Democracia-opt.pdf

UNASUR. *Resolución 05/2009 sobre la Creación del Instituto de Gobierno en Salud*. Quito: Secretaría General de UNASUR. Adopted by the South American Health Council of the UNASUR in Guayaqùil, Ecuador on November 24, 2009. Accessed July 27, 2017: www.isags-unasur.org/uploads/biblioteca/1/bb[18]ling[2]anx[28].pdf

UNASUR. *Tratado Constitutivo de la Unión de Naciones Suramericanas*. Quito: Secretaría General de UNASUR. Entered into Force on March 11, 2011. Accessed July 27, 2017: www.unasursg.org/images/descargas/DOCUMENTOS%20CONSTITUTIVOS%20DE%20UNASUR/Tratado-UNASUR-solo.pdf

United States Senate and House of Representatives. "Organization of American States Revitalization and Reform Act of 2013." Public Law 113–41–Oct. 2 2013 at 22 USC 290q. Accessed July 27, 2017: www.congress.gov/113/plaws/publ41/PLAW-113publ41.pdf

Vivares, Ernesto, ed. *Exploring the New South American Regionalism*. Farnham, UK: Ashgate Publishing, 2014.

Williams, Mark Eric. *Understanding U.S.–Latin American Relations*. New York: Routledge, 2012.

4 The Emergence and Collapse of the Free Trade Area of the Americas

Introduction

The Free Trade Area of the Americas (FTAA) had the potential to rival the European Union as the most ambitious trade initiative of the immediate post-Cold War period. The FTAA arose within the context of an unusual set of coincidences, including the fact that for the first time in history, all the countries in the Western Hemisphere (but one) had democratically elected civilian heads of state. In addition, with varying degrees of ambition, almost all of the governments were now pursuing market-based liberal economic policies. The one exception was Cuba, which explains why it was not invited to participate. For many of the participating governments, "the FTAA seemed as though it was an inevitability, given the triumph of capitalism and democracy augured by the collapse of the Soviet Union and the growing awareness of the concept of globalization."[1] Had it succeeded, the FTAA would have created the largest trade bloc in the world and reinforced the structural and ideological underpinnings of U.S. hegemony in the Western Hemisphere.

What follows is a detailed description of the major events that characterized the FTAA negotiations, from the time that the association was proposed at the first Summit of the Americas in 1994. In particular, there is an examination of the different negotiating strategies and goals sought by the hemisphere's major economies and emerging trade blocs. It is important to keep in mind that the FTAA negotiations coincided with the revival of various older attempts at regional economic integration throughout Latin America and the Caribbean.[2] These included the Andean Pact (later the Andean Community); the Caribbean Common Market and Community, or CARICOM; and the Central American Common Market, which became the Central American Integration System, or SICA. It was also a period marked by the appearance of a new integration initiative called the Common Market of the South, or MERCOSUR. Chile, the Dominican Republic, and Panama were outliers, as they were never full members of any of these trade blocs. In addition, these blocs varied in terms of the level of trade conducted among themselves in comparison to extra-regional trade, and in terms of their dependence on the United States as an export market and a source of imports and foreign investment. As a general rule, the further south one went, the weaker the dependence on the United States was, to the point that the MERCOSUR countries had closer commercial links to the European Union and with each other than with the United States.

Preparing the Stage for the Negotiations

At the First Summit of the Americas, celebrated in Miami in December 1994, the elected heads of state of all countries in the Western Hemisphere but Cuba met to discuss issues of mutual concern. It was the first gathering of hemispheric leaders since a conference in Punta del Este, Uruguay in 1967, which was infamous for its failure to produce anything of substance or sustainability. The Miami gathering concluded with a plan of action that contained dozens of initiatives related to, *inter alia*, respect for human rights, promotion of representative democracy, improvements to educational systems, and protection of the environment. Without a doubt the topic that drew the most attention, however, was the issue of free trade. At the conclusion of the Summit, all 34 leaders pledged to have an agreement to create an FTAA ready for signature by 2005. A Tripartite Committee made up of the UN's Economic Commission for Latin America and the Caribbean (ECLAC), the Inter-American Development Bank (IADB), and a special trade unit staffed by a team of professional trade experts at the Organization of American States (OAS) was established. The goal was to assist member states in preparing for the negotiations by drafting specialized research reports and setting up a comprehensive data bank of trade-related statistics.

Although this is conveniently overlooked by many of its critics, particularly in Latin America, the FTAA was a project initially pushed by the Latin American countries—albeit that Brazil was always ambivalent—and not the United States.[3] Having just emerged from a divisive political debate seeking to get NAFTA ratified by the U.S. Congress in 1993, a move that alienated many important Democratic constituencies, the Clinton administration was reluctant to engage in another bruising political battle to ratify a new free trade agreement.[4] For many Latin American governments, however, securing duty-free access to the affluent U.S. market was crucial in order to support the new export-led development strategies that most had recently adopted in response to the failed import substitution model of earlier decades. Those older policies had left them heavily indebted and contributed to the severe economic contraction seen in the "lost decade" of the 1980s. By Clinton's second term, however, the FTAA emerged as the centerpiece of U.S. foreign policy toward Latin America and the Caribbean, as its goal of economic liberalization was seen as supporting other important U.S. objectives such as poverty reduction, strengthening democracy, and supporting alternatives to narcotics production.

The First Summit of the Americas, in December 1994, was followed by four other meetings of the trade ministers from each of the 34 countries present in Miami. At the first so-called Trade Ministerial, held in Denver in June 1995, it was agreed that all the countries participating in the FTAA process would be required to accept all of its obligations and no country could opt out of certain provisions (although it was also agreed to take into consideration the adjustment concerns of the smaller economies in the Caribbean). In addition, the FTAA would have to be compatible with obligations created under the General Agreement on Tariffs and Trade (GATT) and World Trade Organization (WTO). In particular, duties could not be raised to higher levels than existed prior to the creation of the FTAA, and new, non-tariff barriers could not be imposed *vis-à-vis* other WTO member states not participating in the FTAA.

In the Cartagena Trade Ministerial, held in March of 1996, the ministers agreed to establish four more working subgroups to add to the seven already established in Denver the year before. The trade ministers' meeting in Colombia also received recommendations developed by the newly created Americas Business Forum, a group representing mostly large and medium-sized business interests that formally provided input into the FTAA process until 1999.

The third Trade Ministerial, held in Belo Horizonte in May 1997, ended without what was supposed to have been a definitive agreement for how and when to begin formal negotiations to create the FTAA. A major reason for this was that the host government, Brazil, sought to delay the negotiations as much as possible, in order to allow vulnerable sectors of its own national economy—particularly the industrial sector—to better adapt to increased competition.[5] Running in parallel to the third Trade Ministerial was a forum named "Our America," organized by agrarian, social, and environmental groups, that eventually coalesced into a Hemispheric Social Alliance agitating for greater grassroots influence over the course of the FTAA negotiations.[6]

The fourth and final Trade Ministerial was held in San José, Costa Rica on March 19, 1998. The meeting produced a definitive negotiating framework for the FTAA and specific dates and venues were set for launching key aspects of the negotiations. It was also agreed that decisions in the FTAA negotiating process would be based on consensus and would be part of a "single undertaking" (i.e., there could be no final agreement until every issue had been agreed to). In addition, the San José meeting produced a declaration of understanding that the various sub-regional economic integration projects would not disappear or be subsumed into the FTAA, but would continue to coexist so long as their rules and regulations did not conflict with FTAA obligations, or provided for a deeper form of integration. In addition, it was acknowledged that countries could negotiate and accept the obligations of the FTAA individually or as members of a sub-regional bloc. This marked an important concession on the part of the United States, which for a long time had visualized the FTAA as the steady expansion southwards of the North American Free Trade Agreement, or NAFTA, as individual countries would accede to the tripartite agreement between Canada, Mexico, and the United States. One important area where no consensus was achieved, however, was determination of the point during the negotiating process at which countries would be prohibited from imposing new trade restrictions. The United States advocated that the "stand-still" date should be the day negotiations actually launched, while other countries argued it should come at the end of the negotiating process. In a victory for the U.S.

position that the FTAA was a "WTO plus" agreement, however, all 34 countries at the San José meeting agreed that the FTAA should improve upon WTO rules and disciplines whenever possible.

It was also agreed in San José that for the following 18 months, the chair of the overall FTAA process, which oversaw both the Trade Ministerial Meetings and the Trade Negotiations Committee, would be Canada. After that the chairmanship would go to Argentina (November 1, 1999–April 30, 2001), and Ecuador (May 1, 2001–October 31, 2002), with the United States and Brazil serving as co-chairs for the last two years of the negotiations. The country chairing the FTAA process would also be the host of the Trade Ministerial Meetings and would chair the Trade Negotiations Committee (TNC). Both the Trade Ministerial Meetings and the TNC (made up of the vice-ministers from the 34 participating countries) were given the authority to provide overall direction and management to the FTAA negotiations. A Consultative Group on Smaller Economies was also approved to review the concerns and interests of the smaller economies in the FTAA process, as well as to alert the TNC to issues of concern and make recommendations on how best to resolve them.

Nine initial negotiating groups were established and chairs from specific countries were selected, to be replaced every 18 months. The idea behind the alternations was to allow wide participation and a dispersion of leadership among the different countries. The nine negotiating groups consisted of: (1) market access; (2) investment; (3) services; (4) government procurement; (5) dispute settlement; (6) agriculture; (7) intellectual property rights; (8) subsidies, anti-dumping, and countervailing duties; (9) competition policy.

The fact that a negotiating group on agriculture was accepted at the last minute marked a significant victory for the MERCOSUR countries. In the weeks leading up to the San José Ministerial, the Office of the United States Trade Representative (USTR) had insisted that such a committee was unnecessary and that agricultural issues should be addressed by the market access group. The MERCOSUR countries argued in favor of the creation of a separate negotiating group, given the importance of agricultural exports to their economies and the high tariff and non-tariff barriers (including those created indirectly by generous subsidy programs) their exporters had to overcome in order to access the U.S. market. One important factor that contributed to MERCOSUR getting its way was the Clinton administration's inability to secure fast-track authority from Congress. Under fast-track authority, the legislative branch cedes to the White House its authority to amend or modify any trade agreement that has been negotiated by the executive branch. Fast-track authority also requires that Congress vote to approve or reject a trade agreement within a 90-day period.

The delegates to the San José Trade Ministerial also authorized the establishment of a roving FTAA Administrative Secretariat to be located in the sites where the actual negotiations by the nine working groups would also be taking place. The Administrative Secretariat had the task of providing logistical support for the negotiating groups, translating documents, and disseminating as well as serving as a repository of official documents. For the first three years (i.e., through February 28, 2001), the Secretariat was housed in Miami, then for two years in Panama City, with Puebla, Mexico serving as the final site from March 1, 2003 until the negotiations were formally suspended in 2006.

A special Committee of Government Representatives on the Participation of Civil Society was created to accept recommendations and suggestions from a broad range of interest groups from throughout the Western Hemisphere, including the business sector, labor unions, environmental groups, consumer associations, and academics. The Committee was supposed to evaluate the recommendations and refer those (if any) deemed particularly worthy to the trade ministers of the 34 participating countries. The creation of this new Committee was intended to phase out the Americas Business Forum, which had been held in conjunction with every Trade Ministerial, up to and including San José. Although business groups were not particularly happy with this outcome, since they now had to share the stage with civil society groups, they claimed to have alternative ways of influencing the process. The creation of the committee dealing with civil society matters was an alternative to the two study groups the Clinton administration had originally proposed to investigate the links between trade and labor and trade and the environment. Most Latin American governments viewed these two study groups suspiciously as they felt they could open the door to the inclusion of labor and environmental provisions in the FTAA that the United States could then abuse for protectionist ends.[7]

The Trade Ministerial in Costa Rica in March 1998 further agreed to achieve substantive business facilitation measures that were supposed to be in place by the 2005 deadline for ending the FTAA negotiations. These measures included such things as harmonizing customs valuation codes and making greater use of electronic filing systems. These measures fell far short of the "early harvest" interim-type agreements the U.S. private sector had hoped to achieve by 2000 on matters such as early adoption of intellectual property protections mandated by the WTO, liberalization of certain sectors of the economy, and transparency in the awarding of government procurement contracts.

The Growing Rift Between U.S. and Brazilian Objectives

The heads of state from all the nations of the Western Hemisphere (but for Cuba) met in Santiago, Chile on April 18–19, 1998 and officially launched the FTAA negotiations, reaffirming their determination to conclude them no later than 2005. The leaders also agreed to ensure that the negotiating process would be transparent and take into account the different levels of development and size of the economies in the Americas. In conjunction with the Second Summit of the Americas, an alternative People's Summit of the Americas took place, representing the first massive mobilization of social movements—a phenomenon that would repeat itself at all subsequent major FTAA meetings.[8]

Interestingly, the centerpiece issue at the Second Summit of the Americas was education and not trade. One reason for this was that U.S. President Clinton still had not secured fast-track authority from the U.S. Congress. Accordingly, the United States was not interested in focusing attention on trade, given its inability to begin serious negotiations on a trade agreement. The emphasis on education, however, was also the result of a realization by many governments that the human capacity skills of their citizens needed significant improvement if they were ever going to benefit from the opportunities promised by an economically integrated hemisphere.

In addition to educational goals, the leaders of the Western Hemisphere created a Special Rapporteur on Freedom of Expression linked to the Inter-American Human Rights Commission of the OAS. On November 2, 1998, the Commission appointed Alejandro Canton, a well-known Argentine human rights lawyer, as the first Special Rapporteur for Freedom of Expression. A decade later, Ecuadorean president Rafael Correa attempted, unsuccessfully, to abolish this particular rapporteur position after it strongly criticized his attempts to muzzle the press in Ecuador.

The Fifth Trade Ministerial was held in Toronto, Canada on November 3–4, 1999. The event was rather low-key, since most governments' attention was on the WTO meeting scheduled for later that month in Seattle that was supposed to have launched the so-called Millennium Round of multilateral trade negotiations. As it turned out, these negotiations never got off the ground, following a revolt by developing countries against efforts by the major trading powers to engage in closed-door wheeling and dealing among themselves. At the same time, anti-globalization rioting erupted in the streets outside the meeting hall. The trade ministers' meeting in Toronto instructed the nine negotiating groups to prepare a draft of their respective chapters for the proposed FTAA so as to have it ready before the next Trade Ministerial meeting scheduled for Buenos Aires, Argentina in April 2001. These instructions came despite initial opposition from the MERCOSUR countries, who felt preparing a draft would be a meaningless exercise given the U.S. president's inability to secure "fast-track" negotiating authority. The trade ministers in Toronto also agreed to implement eight specific business facilitation measures that dealt exclusively with customs-related issues by January 1, 2000. Finally, the ministers agreed to a series of measures to make the FTAA process more transparent and accessible to the public. This included posting on the FTAA home page various reports prepared by the former working groups, statistical data compiled by ECLAC, and information on government regulations, procedures, and agency contacts in those subject areas handled by each of the nine negotiating groups.

During a March 2001 meeting in Washington, DC between Brazilian President Fernando Henrique Cardoso and his newly elected U.S. counterpart, George W. Bush, Brazil proposed that the United States negotiate a separate free trade agreement with the four core MERCOSUR member states in parallel with or even in lieu of an FTAA.[9] Although President Bush promised to look into the Brazilian proposal, it never went anywhere.[10] The thought was that negotiating with the United States as part of a smaller group would enhance Brazil's negotiating position. Even if the 4+1 negotiations floundered, it would at least tease out the areas in which the United States was willing to offer concessions on issues of most interest to Brasilia in the context of the FTAA negotiations.[11]

The sixth Trade Ministerial was held in Buenos Aires on April 7, 2001. Among the trade ministers' most important acts here was approving the first draft of the FTAA agreement. On those issues where agreement had not been achieved, the different proposals were included in brackets and left for future negotiations.

The Third Summit of the Americas was held in Quebec City on April 20–22, 2001. The Summit focused heavily on maintaining and strengthening the rule of law and the democratic system throughout the Western Hemisphere. As a result, the heads of state issued a strongly worded declaration that "any unconstitutional alteration or interruption of the democratic order in a state of the Hemisphere constitutes an insurmountable obstacle to the participation of that state's government in the Summit of the Americas process."[12] In addition, the foreign ministers of the 34 countries negotiating the FTAA were instructed to prepare within the OAS framework an Inter-American Democratic Charter to defend against threats to representative democracy. The Inter-American Democratic Charter was eventually approved at a special meeting of the OAS in Lima, Peru on September 11, 2001.

The Quebec City Summit resulted in a consensus to have the heavily bracketed draft text of the FTAA in its four official languages (i.e., English, French, Portuguese, and Spanish), which had been approved two weeks earlier in Buenos Aires by the trade ministers, posted on the official FTAA website. This development had initially been proposed by Canada in response to complaints from some non-governmental organizations (NGOs) and civil society groups that the FTAA negotiation process lacked transparency and failed to take into consideration the concerns of the full spectrum of civil society. The heads of state meeting in Quebec also made a firm commitment to conclude the FTAA negotiations no later than January 2005 and to make all efforts to have it ratified so that it could enter into force by the end of that year. Venezuela, however, made an explicit reservation not to be bound by the 2005 deadline. The new January 2005 deadline put an end to a controversial proposal put forward by the U.S. government (with Canadian and Chilean support) to push forward the conclusion date of the FTAA negotiations to 2003.

At a July 2001 meeting of the FTAA negotiating group on subsidies, anti-dumping, and countervailing duties, the United States re-tabled a proposal to eliminate a separate chapter in the FTAA text on unfair trade remedy laws and replace it with a simple statement that each country retained the right to apply current domestic anti-dumping and countervailing duty laws. Chile and the MERCOSUR countries strongly opposed the proposal. The U.S. proposal was a response to strong opposition emanating from the U.S. Congress and certain U.S. manufacturers (especially in the steel and semiconductor industries) that opposed any attempt to restrict the continued use of unfair trade legislation against even future FTAA partner states.

In January 2002, the USTR announced the Bush administration's intention to begin negotiating a free trade agreement with Central America. This marked a reversal of the originally cool reception the idea had received from Washington, DC when first proposed by the Central Americans, led by Costa Rica, in September 2001. However, actual negotiations for a U.S.–Central America Free Trade Agreement, or CAFTA, did not get underway until January 2003. In the meantime, negotiations for a free trade agreement between the United States and Chile, which had begun in the final days of the Clinton administration (following promises made in 1994 to make the country the fourth member of NAFTA), ended in December 2002. That bilateral agreement came into effect on January 1, 2004, following its ratification in the U.S. and then the Chilean Congress.

In August 2002, U.S. President George W. Bush was finally able to obtain Trade Promotion Authority, or TPA—previously known as "fast-track" authority—from the U.S. Congress. The original grant of TPA (which grandfathered the free trade agreement negotiations that had started with Chile in 2000) was valid through July 1, 2005. It could, however, be extended through July 1, 2007 if the White House requested an extension from Congress and certified that all the conditions included in the initial authorization were met. TPA passed the United States Senate on August 1, 2002 in a 64–34 bipartisan vote. The U.S. House of Representatives approved TPA on July 27, 2002 by a narrow 215–212 vote, split heavily along Republican and Democratic party lines. In the TPA bill were a number of Trade Adjustment Assistance initiatives, including a tax credit for the purchase of health insurance by workers losing their jobs as a result of increased imports or factories moving abroad, and an increase in Labor Department cash assistance and job retraining benefits. The Republican-controlled Congress had long denied renewal of this authority to the Clinton administration after it expired at the end of 1994. The fact that President Bush now had it meant that countries negotiating trade agreements with the United States could rest assured that they would not have to negotiate twice—once with the executive branch and the second time with Congress.

Although approval of TPA should have re-energized the FTAA negotiations, this was undermined by the compromises the White House had been forced to make in order to obtain TPA. For example, the Bush administration acquiesced to an expansion of trade-distorting agricultural subsidy programs in the 2002 Farm Bill approved by the U.S. Congress. The Bush administration also imposed safeguard measures on imported steel that had a particularly negative impact on Argentina and Brazil. Both measures raised concerns regarding the level of the United States' commitment to the free trade agenda. The Brazilian government also expressed apprehension over language in the TPA that required the White House to consult with Congress on tariff negotiations affecting import-sensitive products.

At the seventh Trade Ministerial, held in Quito, Ecuador on November 1, 2002, a second draft of the heavily bracketed FTAA agreement was approved and immediately posted on the FTAA's official website. The ministers also established a timetable for the exchange of offers in services, investment, agriculture, government procurement, and non-agricultural market access. Furthermore, the trade ministers endorsed an earlier agreement to have tariff reduction negotiations be based on actual applied duty rates rather than the generally higher tariff rate ceilings that are bound at the WTO. Earlier intransigence over this issue from the CARICOM countries led to a compromise in which smaller economies could use WTO bound rates as the starting point for tariff cuts on certain—predominately agricultural—products deemed "sensitive."

Other results coming out of the Quito Trade Ministerial included a strongly worded declaration rejecting the abuse of environmental and labor standards for protectionist purposes, whether as a pre-condition for participating in the FTAA or as the basis for imposing trade restrictions or sanctions for alleged non-compliance with internationally recognized labor and environmental standards. Perhaps the most noteworthy development, however, was the establishment of a Hemispheric Cooperation Program (HCP) designed to assist less developed and smaller economies to participate in the FTAA negotiating process, implement FTAA obligations, and make the necessary economic adjustments to benefit from free trade. Although the United States proposed the HCP, it made no commitment to fund it. Instead, money was expected to be provided by existing USAID and the Inter-American Development Bank programs, as well as the private sector, academic institutions, and foundations. Interestingly, as Venezuela tried to organize opposition to the FTAA, particularly from smaller Caribbean countries, by offering a more radical alternative, the HCP would become that country's principal target of attack at subsequent FTAA meetings. Venezuela would eventually propose a Structural Convergence Fund to reduce the asymmetries among the different countries in the Americas by financing infrastructure and social welfare programs.[13]

In January 2003, Brazil announced that it would delay tabling offers in services, investment, and government procurement beyond the February 15, 2003 deadline agreed to in Quito. The official excuse was that the government needed time to put together an offer in view of the recent inauguration of President Luiz Inácio Lula da Silva. Undoubtedly, the new government's concerns as to whether it was in Brazil's interests to continue participating in the negotiations also played a major part in this announcement. During the presidential campaign, Lula had presented himself as a vociferous opponent of the FTAA. Perhaps not coincidentally, a consensus had still not yet been achieved as to the modalities or bases from which offers in these sectors would commence (i.e., negative vs. positive lists with respect to services, etc.). By the April 2003 TNC meeting in Puebla, Mexico, neither Argentina, Brazil, the Bahamas, nor Haiti had submitted offers in services, investment, and government procurement. For its part, Venezuela proposed a number of measures of a political nature that challenged the underlying ideological premises of the FTAA.

Following USTR Robert Zoellick's visit to Brasilia on May 27, 2003, the Brazilian and U.S. governments announced that a mini-ministerial would take place at the Wye River Conference Center in Maryland on June 12–13, 2003, attended by a limited number of FTAA countries: in addition to Brazil and the United States, Argentina, Canada, Chile, Colombia, the Dominican Republic, El Salvador, Jamaica, Mexico, Panama, Peru, Trinidad and Tobago, and Uruguay. Although invited, Costa Rica did not attend. As initially reported in the press, the objective of the meeting was to explore ways to reduce the FTAA's ambitious scope in order to make the January 2005 deadline.[14] In particular, Brazilian officials indicated that the mini-ministerial would decide which issues would remain in the FTAA and which would be relegated to the WTO or to bilateral negotiations. The actual discussion that took place at Wye River, however, centered more on exploring the possibility of negotiating lesser obligations in sensitive sectors in order to meet the January 2005 target.

By the time of the July 7–11, 2003 TNC meeting in San Salvador, the Argentine, Brazilian, and Haitian governments still had not tabled their offers on services, investment, and government procurement. Argentina and Brazil refused to submit offers, piqued at the continuing inability to achieve consensus among all the participating states as to the exact scope of the FTAA. The inability to reach consensus on utilizing a positive or negative list approach in terms of services further hampered progress. In San Salvador, MERCOSUR formally submitted a three-track proposal for resolving certain issues it deemed contentious by leaving some to be negotiated within the FTAA, relegating others to the WTO, and leaving any remaining issues for direct negotiations between MERCOSUR and the United States.

The disarray at the WTO Ministerial in Cancun, Mexico on September 14, 2003, and the failure to reach any consensus, had repercussions for the FTAA negotiations as well, since it undercut the feasibility of relegating certain contentious issues within the FTAA context to the multilateral arena for resolution. Since at least 2001, the United States had been suggesting that anti-dumping and agricultural support payments to U.S. farmers could only be resolved at the WTO. On the agricultural subsidies issues, the United States argued that if it were to concede to disciplines on agriculture in the FTAA, it would spend the only negotiating capital it had to pressure the EU and Japan in the WTO negotiations to make reductions in their respective subsidy programs. The U.S. anti-dumping position was less logical, given that competition policy was being negotiated in the FTAA, and it can be argued that competition laws are a substitute for anti-dumping legislation. In response to the U.S. position on subsidies and antidumping, the MERCOSUR countries proposed in May 2003 to relegate government procurement, intellectual property, investment, and services to the WTO as well. The rationale was that if the United States did not want to include politically sensitive issues on which the MERCOSUR governments needed concessions in order to sell the hemispheric trade pact to skeptical publics at home, then MERCOSUR should be able to make the same choice. Not surprisingly, this hardening of positions led to a TNC meeting in Port of Spain, Trinidad on September 30–October 2, 2003 that, by all accounts, achieved nothing of substance.[15]

The acrimony that developed between the United States and Brazil following Cancun, as each tried to blame the other for the failure to make any progress in the WTO talks, did not bode well for the eighth FTAA Trade Ministerial, scheduled for Miami on November 20–21, 2003. In order to prevent the Trade Ministerial from degenerating into another round of finger-pointing and in turn burying the FTAA, the Bush administration was eager to punt any contentious issues over to the next TNC, scheduled for Puebla, Mexico in February 2004. The ambiguously worded declaration that emerged from the Miami Trade Ministerial appeared to endorse the concept of a two-tiered "FTAA Lite" by the original target date of January 2005.[16] Although all 34 participating countries would be bound to "a common set of rights and obligations" within each of the nine negotiating categories established in San José in March 1998, countries were also free to negotiate within the FTAA context "additional obligations and benefits" on a plurilateral basis. For the U.S. negotiators, language in the Miami Trade Ministerial Declaration that "countries [will] reap the benefits of their respective commitments" meant that market access would be contingent on the level of overall liberalization undertaken within the FTAA context. Brazil, on the other hand, argued that other language in the same Declaration recognized, *inter alia*, "that negotiations must aim at a balanced agreement that addresses the issue of differences in the levels of development and size of economies." Accordingly, there could not be penalties for opting out of the presumably more demanding plurilateral commitments. In addition, the Brazilians pointed out that the Most Favored Nation clause in either the WTO's General Agreement on Tariffs and Trade or in a future FTAA agreement itself would eventually obligate all the FTAA countries to extend to everyone else the same generous market access concessions that had been provided to one set of countries under a plurilateral agreement.

Among other commitments included in the Miami Ministerial Declaration was one to conclude the negotiations on market access by September 30, 2004. Establishment of the "common set of rights and obligations" for market access (as well as the eight other negotiating sectors) was left for the scheduled February 2004 TNC in Puebla to resolve. The trade ministers also approved posting the third draft of the trade agreement's text on the official FTAA website, but in light of the new mandates that emerged from Miami, this would require extensive new edits.

In a move reflecting U.S. frustration regarding its attempts to overcome MERCOSUR's tough negotiating stance, at the conclusion of the Miami Trade Ministerial the USTR announced plans to negotiate free trade agreements with four of the five members of the Andean Community (Bolivia, Colombia, Ecuador, and Peru) as well as Panama. The announcement appeared to be part of a strategy to pressure the MERCOSUR governments into concluding the FTAA on U.S. terms or risk being the only countries in the Western Hemisphere (along with Cuba and Venezuela) not to enjoy some type of preferential access to the U.S. market. The U.S. negotiators also seemed to hope that this strategy might undermine internal MERCOSUR solidarity and entice the smaller states to seek a free trade agreement with the United States and thereby isolate Brazil. Whatever the precise motivations, Brazil remained unfazed, confident that its huge and potentially lucrative internal market would eventually cause the U.S. private sector to lobby its government to conclude a more balanced FTAA, or even a bilateral Brazil–U.S. free trade agreement. For a variety of reasons, the other MERCOSUR countries followed Brazil's lead and stood their ground. In the case of Argentina, the inability to resolve the agricultural subsidies issue would make any bilateral deal with the U.S. not only economically but also politically unpalatable. Paraguay, mired in economic and political instability, feared alienating Argentina and Brazil (its two largest trading partners) if it pursued a bilateral deal with the United States. Only Uruguay appeared ready to take the leap, but the eventual election of the leftist *Frente Amplio* government in 2004 made a bilateral free trade deal with the U.S. ideologically unpalatable to many in the governing coalition.

On January 12–13, 2004, the elected heads of state of all the countries in the Western Hemisphere (but for Cuba; also, Guatemala, Dominica, and Guyana only sent special representatives) met in Monterrey, Mexico for a Special Summit of the Americas. This was actually the second time that such a Special Summit had been held: the first was in 1996, in Santa Cruz, Bolivia, on sustainable development. The idea for a second Special Summit was originally proposed in July 2002 by then President Fernando Henrique Cardoso of Brazil, who wanted it to focus on job creation. The Canadian government then made a strong push for a Special Summit in early 2004, arguing that the Hemisphere had gone through a number of crises and new leaders had been elected since the Quebec Summit of April 2001. It therefore felt that too long a period would elapse before the next Summit, scheduled for Argentina in late 2005.

Although trade did not figure prominently on the agenda of the Special Summit of the Americas in Monterrey, a reference to concluding the negotiations for the FTAA within the established timetable was included in the Declaration issued by the Hemisphere's leaders. Prior to the Summit, Brazil had demanded that trade not be included at all on the Special Summit's agenda and had initially refused to allow any mention of the FTAA in the Declaration. In the end, though, the only dissenting voice in the actual Declaration with respect to the FTAA came from Venezuelan President Hugo Chavez.[17]

The Negotiations become Hopelessly Deadlocked

As had been widely expected, the TNC meeting held in Puebla, Mexico on February 2–6, 2004 was unable to come up with negotiating modalities for the two-tiered approach to the FTAA proposed at the November 2003 Trade Ministerial in Miami. That proposal would have moved the FTAA away from a comprehensive trade agreement whose disciplines would be obligatory for all the signatory states to being one in which all 34 countries would agree to a set of core obligations, while other disciplines would be the subject of plurilateral agreements involving a smaller group of interested countries. The major stumbling block that developed at Puebla was an inability to decide what should be included among the core obligations and the procedures for negotiating the voluntary plurilateral agreements. The MERCOSUR countries insisted that no industrial or agricultural goods could be excluded from the market access provisions of any FTAA. The MERCOSUR countries also pressed for including the elimination of export subsidies, as well as the trade-distorting effects of state-trading enterprises, food aid, and domestic price support systems for agricultural products, in the core obligations. On the other hand, the MERCOSUR countries refused to go beyond WTO commitments on government procurement, intellectual property, investment, and trade in services, and advocated relegating further concessions in those areas to the plurilateral agreements. While the United States did reiterate a previously made commitment to eliminate the use of agricultural export subsidies within the Western Hemisphere, it again insisted that domestic agricultural support payments could only be handled at the WTO. The United States also insisted that government procurement, intellectual property, investment, and services had to be included within the set of core obligations for all 34 countries.

A series of bilateral talks between the co-chairs of the FTAA process, Brazil and the United States, throughout 2004 and early 2005 failed to produce a consensus on what to include in the set of common obligations under the two-tiered "FTAA Lite" approach. The inability of the G-20 group of developing countries led by Brazil, China, and India to make any headway in the WTO Doha Development Round and obtain meaningful concessions, particularly from the EU, on agricultural subsidies also negatively impacted the FTAA negotiations. Perhaps not surprisingly, the January 1, 2005 date for concluding the FTAA negotiations came and went. An August 2005 effort by Mexico and CARICOM to push for a new TNC meeting before the next scheduled Summit of the Americas in November 2005 was rebuffed by Brazil and the United States. There had been no formal FTAA meetings since the last TNC in Puebla in February 2004 had ended in discord.

The Fourth Summit of the Americas was held in the seaside resort city of Mar del Plata, Argentina on November 4–5, 2005. In the months leading up to the Summit there were doubts that U.S. President George W. Bush would even appear, given the impasse that had developed between the United States and the MERCOSUR countries. Although Bush did show up, he became the focal point of mass demonstrations protesting against the FTAA and U.S. foreign policy in general. At an alternative People's Summit of the Americas held in a huge soccer stadium in Mar del Plata, Venezuelan President Hugo Chavez delighted the crowds with fiery denunciations of the FTAA as a project designed to make Latin America and the Caribbean economic vassals of U.S. imperialism, ripe for exploitation.

By the end of the Summit in Mar del Plata it was clear that the FTAA process was dead. Although 28 of the 34 countries in the Western Hemisphere supported a U.S. proposal to reinitiate the FTAA negotiations in early 2006, the four MERCOSUR countries and Venezuela refused on the basis that the necessary conditions for achieving a balanced and equitable free trade agreement were not in place. The Declaration of the Heads of State that emerged from the Fourth Summit of the Americas underscored this division by including two conflicting statements on the FTAA process.[18] The only thing all 34 countries could agree to include in the Declaration was a statement to explore both positions in light of the outcomes of the next WTO ministerial meeting. Furthermore, the government of Colombia was entrusted with hosting a meeting of all 34 countries to examine the outcome of the WTO negotiations—something that never happened, as the WTO talks dragged on inconclusively for years. A WTO Ministerial Conference in Nairobi at the end of 2015 finally made clear what had long been obvious. The Millennium Development Round, launched at Doha in November 2001, was also dead. About the only other concrete thing that could be agreed upon in Mar del Plata with respect to the FTAA was for the Inter-American Development Bank to continue funding the FTAA Secretariat in Puebla, Mexico beyond December 2005. That funding came to an abrupt halt in 2006 (parenthetically, the last year the official FTAA website was updated).

In response to the demise of the FTAA, the Bush administration did move forward and pursue bilateral free trade agreements—negotiated under highly asymmetrical conditions—with Colombia, Peru, and Panama.[19] Following the expiration of the last extensions to the Andean Trade Preference and Drug Eradication Act (ATPDEA) on July 31, 2013, Bolivia and Ecuador officially joined MERCOSUR and Venezuela in the position of having no kind of preferential access to the U.S. market (although Bolivia had already lost eligibility under the ATPDEA in 2008). While the Peru–U.S. free trade agreement was signed in 2006, it actually did not come into force until President Bush's last days in office, in 2009. Bush was required by the Democratic-controlled Congress to certify that Peru had made the necessary changes to its national legislation that facilitated enforcement of five basic internationally recognized labor principles plus acceptable conditions with respect to minimum wages, hours of work, and occupational safety and health. Peru was also forced to accept foreign inspection of tropical rainforests to prevent illegal logging, on pain of suffering trade sanctions if it refused. The U.S. free trade agreements with Colombia and Panama were signed in 2006 and 2007, respectively, but did not come into force until 2012, as Barack H. Obama's first term in office was about to end. The Colombian trade accord included a Labor Action Plan under which Bogotá was obligated to make a whole series of legal and institutional modifications to beef up enforcement of labor rights, better protect union members, and permit enhanced oversight by the International Labor Organization.

The Bolivarian Alternative for the Peoples of Our America and the Peoples' Trade Treaty

In April 2006, the Presidents of Bolivia, the Bolivarian Republic of Venezuela, and Cuba met in Havana to sign what they denominated an Agreement to

Implement the Bolivarian Alternative for the Peoples of Our America and the Peoples' Trade Treaty.[20] This initiative was the result of a declaration issued by Cuban President Fidel Castro and his Venezuelan counterpart Hugo Chavez in December 2004 that sought to create an *Alternativa Bolivariana para los Pueblos de Nuestra América*, or Bolivarian Alternative for the Peoples of Our America (ALBA) in opposition to an FTAA. Castro and Chavez viewed the FTAA as a project to consolidate U.S. economic and political hegemony in the Western Hemisphere.[21] Although the Chavez government had been critical of the FTAA from the time it took office in 1999, "[i]t was from the radicalization of political conflict in Venezuela between 2002 and 2004 and allegations of U.S. support to the Venezuelan opposition that a critical position vis-à-vis FTAA was radicalized."[22] ALBA emphasized the need to fight against social exclusion and poverty, with the FTAA depicted as a process that prioritized the interests of international capital and would not improve the lives of the average Latin American. ALBA further sought to encourage "endogenous" economic development and promised to provide compensatory or structural readjustment funds to overcome asymmetries in economic development among participating countries. Finally, ALBA envisioned a heightened role of the state in overcoming the structural failures of the market at the national level. "[W]ith the growing mobilization of the hemisphere's social movements in mind, [ALBA] sought to demonstrate that another type of regional integration was possible that was not based on neoliberal [economic] policies."[23]

The April 2006 trilateral agreement included a Peoples' Trade Treaty designed to encourage the exchange of goods among Bolivia, Cuba, and Venezuela. The commitments either were limited to bartered trade arrangements, or called on Cuba and Venezuela to open up their respective markets, on a non-reciprocal basis, to imports from Bolivia. What was most remarkable about the Peoples' Trade Treaty is that it was devoid of any rules of origin to establish the eligibility of the products that could enjoy preferential market access. Presumably just declaring a good to originate in one of the three signatory states would suffice.

Apart from promises on trade, Cuba also committed itself to providing free and high-quality ophthalmology care for poor Bolivians by sending Cuban doctors to Bolivia and building new eye clinics in major population centers in Bolivia. In addition, Cuba agreed to provide up to 5,000 scholarships over a two-year period for Bolivians wishing to study medicine in Cuba. Furthermore, the Cuban government agreed to provide educational materials to support Aymara, Quechua, Guaraní, and Spanish literacy programs in Bolivia. For its part, Venezuela established a US$100 million fund to finance projects to improve infrastructure and the petrochemical, steel-making, and industrial chemical sectors in Bolivia. An additional US$30 million of Venezuelan money was also made available to the Bolivian government to use at its discretion for social and productive needs. Furthermore, Venezuela agreed to donate an asphalt plant that could be used to maintain existing as well as build new roads in Bolivia. In addition, Venezuela offered 5,000 scholarships for Bolivians to study in Venezuelan universities.

In 2009, the Bolivarian Alternative for the Peoples of Our America formally changed its name to the Bolivarian Alliance for the Peoples of Our America. In addition to the original three member states of Bolivia, Cuba, and Venzuala, ALBA expanded to include Nicaragua (2007), Saint Vincent and the Grenadines (2007), Dominica (2008), Honduras (2008, although it withdrew in 2010), Antigua and Barbuda (2009), Ecuador (2009), Suriname (2012), Saint Lucia (2013), Grenada (2014), and Saint Kitts and Nevis (2014).

Included under ALBA's umbrella early on was an agreement to establish a financial entity called the ALBA Bank to provide capital for economic and social development projects. The basic concept later morphed into the proposal to create a *Banco del Sur* or Bank of the South that was supposed to serve as an alternative to the World Bank, the Inter-American Development Bank, and even the Andean Community's Development Bank, the *Corporación Andina de Fomento* or CAF. The *Banco del Sur* reflected not only a search for autonomy but also an alternative financial architecture that would not operate based on conditional loans and would be more democratic in its decision-making process.[24] The world never got to see how this would work in practice, however: after the initial pledges of paid-in capital (with Venezuela committing itself to providing some 85 percent of that), the *Banco del Sur* soon fell off the radar. Similarly, a proposed Unified System for Regional Compensation, or SUCRE, that would have created a new Latin American monetary unit and facilitated intraregional trade without the need to effectuate cash transfers for each transaction, stalled after a relatively small number of mostly symbolic transfers. That may have been because SUCRE was directly competing with the decades-old central clearinghouse mechanism administered by the Latin American Integration Association, or ALADI, that allows participating countries to trade among themselves without utilizing hard currency reserves.

One concrete development, however, was large Venezuelan grants of money to other ALBA nations. These primarily went toward funding infrastructure projects and electoral campaigns, and bailing governments out of fiscal crises through the forgiveness of debts owed to Caracas. Although this aid reputedly totaled billions of dollars over the years, the precise number is difficult to ascertain due to murky and non-transparent accounting practices. In any event, with the sharp drop in oil prices that began in 2014, Venezuelan generosity began to disappear.

One ALBA project that had a highly visible impact was the creation of *Telesur*, a regional TV station designed to be an alternative to the perceived biased reporting of Atlanta-based *CNN en Español*. Argentina, Bolivia, Cuba, Ecuador, Nicaragua, and Venezuela all contributed financially (although the election of Mauricio Macri caused Buenos Aires to pull its support for *Telesur* in 2016). Little of substance came out of ALBA's Grand National Projects involving two or more member states engaged in specific activities to overcome shortcomings in food security, environmental protection, research and development, literacy, public health services, telecommunications, and transportation. The record was even scantier with respect to concrete achievements provided by the Grand

National Companies (i.e., multi-state-run entities that were supposed to facilitate an integrated chain of production involving two or more countries). The latter is not surprising given that a similar scheme in the Andean Pact in the 1970s was a dismal failure despite oversight by a regional decision-making entity with supranational authority; by contrast, ALBA has a weak institutional framework and no delegated authority, as all decisions require the approval of the presidents.

Among the most significant programs falling under the ALBA umbrella are those targeting the energy sector. Since 2004, Venezuela has sold petroleum to Cuba in exchange for Cuban doctors and public health professionals working primarily with the poor in Venezuela's urban slums.[25] Cuba has also sent intelligence operatives to assist the Bolivarian government in Caracas in detecting dissent and squashing any potential coup attempts. There have also been bartered trade arrangements whereby Argentina under the Kirchners exported cows and buses in exchange for Venezuelan fuel oil (or at least fuel oil purchased by the Venezuelan state petroleum company PDVSA on the open market), energy cooperation agreements with Brazil and Uruguay to build refineries, and technical assistance agreements with Bolivia focused on the hydrocarbon industry.

Although technically not an ALBA program, the energy initiative most associated with ALBA is PetroCaribe. Under this initiative, Venezuela sells petroleum to most Caribbean island nations, as well as Belize, El Salvador, Guatemala (until 2013), Guyana, Honduras, Nicaragua, and Suriname, with one- or two-year grace periods and long repayment schedules ranging from 15 to 25 years at 1 or 2 percent interest. Participating countries can even pay with products or services in lieu of hard currency. The generous terms offered under PetroCaribe made it almost impossible for Caribbean Basin countries to resist signing up, as they are among the most heavily indebted countries in the world, primarily because of the need to finance energy imports. The only two English-speaking Caribbean countries that have never participated in PetroCaribe are Trinidad and Tobago (already self-sufficient in oil and natural gas) and Barbados (which was hesitant to put at risk a potential natural gas pipeline project to Trinidad and Tobago).

The death of Hugo Chavez in March 2013 raised numerous questions about the ALBA's sustainability, given its weak institutional framework and a tendency to depend on the whims of the personalities governing the key member states. By 2015, the future of PetroCaribe and even the bilateral Cuban–Venezuelan energy pact was in question, as the worsening economic turmoil in Venezuela raised serious concerns about that country's ability to continue offering such generous repayment terms for oil purchases.[26] Many Venezuelans openly question the wisdom of generously offering subsidized petroleum to other countries as a projection of Bolivarian Venezuela soft power while supermarket shelves at home are devoid of foodstuffs and basic household items such as toilet paper and there are severe medicine shortages. In response to threats from the Maduro government in Caracas to shorten repayment periods and increase interest rates under PetroCaribe agreements, the Dominican Republic and Jamaica used funds raised on international capital markets in 2015 to reduce their debt overhang with Venezuela.

Conclusion

By the time the Fourth Summit of the Americas took place in Mar del Plata, Argentina in November 2005, the hemispheric consensus to build an FTAA that had accompanied the proposal made at the First Summit in Miami in 1994 had evaporated. The reasons for this were many, including market-based economic policies' failure, in many of those countries that had enthusiastically pursued them in the 1990s, to provide for a more equitable distribution of wealth and a significant reduction in poverty. Although the blame for this failure is, in some cases, attributable to the way these policies were implemented—Argentina being the most egregious example—the result was a decided shift in favor of enhanced government intervention in the economy. The changes in economic orientation at the start of the twenty-first century in a sufficient number of countries made the goals sought through an FTAA incompatible and often in direct conflict with policies actually pursued at the domestic level. Equally important, neither of the two main players in the negotiations—Brazil and the United States—provided the requisite leadership, and seemed to prefer bilateral negotiations among themselves rather than a hemisphere-wide trade agreement.[27]

Given that the FTAA was linked to a set of market-oriented economic reforms advocated by the United States that came to be known as the "Washington Consensus," the United States' inability to conclude the FTAA negotiations seriously undermined both its prestige and its influence in the region, especially in South America. Hence, for Marcel Nelson, the effort to institutionalize U.S. hegemony along the lines of the Washington Consensus that emerged at the end of the Cold War failed.[28] Among the numerous factors that contributed to that failure was the appearance of the ALBA, which, at least rhetorically, provided an alternative vision of how to construct a community of nations in the Western Hemisphere. Although Venezuela could never hope to match the military or economic strength of the United States, through the ALBA it creatively devised "strategies to undercut the credibility and integrity of the unipole and to concoct alternative values or political visions that other states may find more attractive."[29] Brazil's role, at the helm of MERCOSUR, in putting a halt to the FTAA as conceived by Washington, DC was, however, crucial.

According to Carlos Gustavo Poggio Teixeira, Brazil's strategy throughout the entire FTAA process was one of securing and reinforcing its position within South America in order to avoid its absorption by an all-encompassing hemispheric subsystem, and it used MERCOSUR to build an alternative pole of attraction to create obstacles for greater U.S. penetration in South America.[30] For Zuleika Arashiro, Brazil's strategy is better understood as deriving from decision makers' efforts to construct Brazil's international identity as a middle power, which in turn required the preservation of its margin of autonomy in the international system in order to implement its own vision of how to achieve economic development.[31]

From a classical realist perspective, the collapse of the FTAA is a reflection of a declining U.S. hegemon having to confront—at least in the South American context—an emerging Brazil acting in what it perceived to be in its own best interests. A neo-realist would argue that the strong position Brazil and its MERCOSUR allies eventually adopted in opposition to the type of FTAA which Washington, DC was trying to impose reflected resistance to a unipolar world order with the United States at the helm, and their preference for a new global balance of power. This viewpoint predominated in Argentina under the Kirchners and in Lula's Brazil, as both governments viewed the post-Cold War world order to be highly inequitable and undemocratic.

From the perspective of hegemonic stability theory, the United States' refusal to eliminate the use of anti-dumping duties in the FTAA fatally undermined its position as the upholder of the global liberal economic order and exposed it to charges of gross hypocrisy. As a result, the United States was unable to entice key players in South America to engage in an economic project under which the Americans were likely to emerge as the biggest beneficiaries. Instead of pursuing the interests of the system as a whole, the Bush White House succumbed to the narrow, parochial interests of a few influential members of the U.S. Congress and helped bring down the entire FTAA.

Liberals and even proponents of international regime theory would see in the collapse of the FTAA a failure on the part of the United States to exercise leadership and make the requisite sacrifices that would have facilitated buy-in from Brazil and its MERCOSUR allies, as well as the ALBA countries. For example, the U.S. never offered to ensure that interest rate policies set by the Federal Reserve Bank would not have negative repercussions for its FTAA partners. Similarly, there was never any discussion of any significant economic development program to accompany the FTAA's implementation—such as the generous assistance provided by the European Union to new member states—in order to create even a modicum of a level playing field. The ballyhooed Hemispheric Cooperation Program proposed by the United States turned out to be nothing more than rhetorical hot air. The United States never made any significant financial contributions to the HCP to encourage others to take it seriously and make their own contributions. The Venezuelan counterproposal, a Structural Convergence Fund, was much more in line with what was actually required to reduce the deep asymmetries among the different countries in the Americas, by targeting funding for infrastructure and social welfare programs.

Notes

1 Marcel Nelson, *A History of the FTAA: From Hegemony to Fragmentation in the Americas* (New York: Palgrave Macmillan, 2015), 4. In many Latin American nations following the end of the Cold War, "policymaking elites were increasingly

convinced of the need to adopt market economy practices and political pragmatism" which "altered their perceptions of how to engage with the United States, from a previous attitude of suspicion to one that assumed the possibilities of advantages in an asymmetrical association." Zuleika Arashiro, *Negotiating the Free Trade Area of the Americas* (New York: Palgrave Macmillan, 2011), 63.

2 For a more detailed description of the various regional economic integration schemes in the Americas, see Thomas Andrew O'Keefe, *Latin American and Caribbean Trade Agreements: Keys to a Prosperous Community of the Americas* (Leiden, NL: Martinus Nijhoff (Brill), 2009).

3 Brazil's reticence was premised, in part, on fears that the FTAA would further enhance the economic predominance of the United States in South America and threaten the country's perceived natural leadership role in the continent. Carlos Gustavo Poggio Teixeira, *Brazil, the United States, and the South American Subsystem* (Lanham, MD: Lexington Books, 2012), 115. There were also those who argued that an FTAA would create disincentives for new U.S. investment and any accompanying technology transfer in Brazil, as U.S. companies would simply export products from their home base or from wherever in the Western Hemisphere it was cheapest to produce. Luciano G. Coutinho and João Furtado, "A Integracão Continental Assimétrica e Acelerada: Riscos e Oportunidades da ALCA," in *ALCA e MERCOSUL: Riscos e Oportunidades para o Brasil,* ed. Samuel Pinheiro Guimarães (Brasilia: IPRI, FUNAG, 1999), 115–6, 136, and 141. Similarly, there were fears the FTAA would divert European and Asian investment away from Brazil and the other MERCOSUR countries in favor of the United States or at least North America, in order to be within or near the largest market in the Americas.

4 Officials from the U.S. Treasury Department and the Office of the United States Trade Representative were also concerned that including discussions about a free trade agreement for the Western Hemisphere in the Summit of the Americas agenda could complicate efforts to complete the multilateral Uruguay Round trade talks. David Scott Palmer, *U.S. Relations with Latin America during the Clinton Years* (Gainesville, FL: University Press of Florida, 2006), 55. Still others felt that if the U.S. was going to pursue regionalism, it should do so with the fast-growing newly industrialized economies in Asia rather than with Latin America and the Caribbean. Richard E. Feinberg, *Summitry in the Americas: A Progress Report* (Washington, DC: Institute for International Economics, 1997), 69. The actual decision to proceed with an FTAA was not made by U.S. government officials until just weeks before the First Summit in Miami. Ibid at 71.

5 Marcel Nelson, *A History of the FTAA: From Hegemony to Fragmentation in the Americas* (New York: Palgrave Macmillan, 2015), 87. Brazilian manufacturers were often quick to point out that the process of opening up the economy to global competition had only just begun in the 1990s and Brazil still required massive reforms in terms of tax policy and getting rid of excessive bureaucratic red tape, as well as major infrastructure investments.

6 Marcel Nelson, *A History of the FTAA: From Hegemony to Fragmentation in the Americas* (New York: Palgrave Macmillan, 2015), 88. The Belo Horizonte trade ministerial also saw the important Inter-American Regional Organization of Workers or ORIT demand official inclusion of labor within the FTAA negotiating process. This proposal was vetoed by most Latin American governments, although it did result in a new alliance, composed of the hemisphere's major labor organizations, that vowed to organize a "People's Summit of the Americas" to parallel the second Summit of the Americas scheduled for Santiago in 1998. Ibid at p. 89.

7 Marcel Nelson, *A History of the FTAA: From Hegemony to Fragmentation in the Americas* (New York: Palgrave Macmillan, 2015), 85–6. The Clinton administration felt that the creation of study groups examining labor and environmental issues would facilitate eventual ratification of any FTAA by the U.S. Congress, just as the

side agreements to the NAFTA on both issues had been crucial to securing sufficient votes, particularly from wary Democratic Congresspersons, to ratify the trilateral trade accord in 1993.

8　Marcel Nelson, *A History of the FTAA: From Hegemony to Fragmentation in the Americas* (New York: Palgrave Macmillan, 2015), 93. For Nelson, the People's Summit and the election of Hugo Chavez in Venezuela later that year, which set off an electoral wave of left-wing governments throughout Latin America often called the Pink Tide, meant that the ideology underlying the content of the FTAA would increasingly come under attack, reflecting a rising challenge to U.S. hegemony.

9　Rubens Barbosa, *The Washington Dissensus* (Nashville, TN: Vanderbilt University Press, 2014), 67.

10　Rubens Barbosa, *The Washington Dissensus* (Nashville, TN: Vanderbilt University Press, 2014), 69 and 124. Brazilian President-Elect Luiz Inácio Lula da Silva and high-ranking advisers from his Worker's Party visited Washington, DC in December 2002 and again "raised the possibility of Brazil signing a free trade agreement with the U.S., something they said the Lula government could propose after consultation with its MERCOSUR partners." Ibid at 82. This reflected a remarkable shift given that, during the presidential race Lula had just run, the Worker's Party had organized a non-binding referendum in which those voting overwhelmingly rejected the FTAA. In fact, on the campaign trail, Lula himself often spoke out against the FTAA as a tool for the economic annexation of Latin America by the United States.

11　Rubens Barbosa, *The Washington Dissensus* (Nashville, TN: Vanderbilt University Press, 2014), 125–6. The desire to enhance Brazil's bargaining power also explains why in 1994 the Brazilian government had proposed consolidating a South American Free Trade Area, or SAFTA, before actually sitting down to begin the negotiations for an FTAA.

12　The full text of the Declaration of Quebec City is available at: www.summit-americas.org/iii_summit/iii_summit_dec_en.pdf.

13　Marcel Nelson, *A History of the FTAA: From Hegemony to Fragmentation in the Americas* (New York: Palgrave Macmillan, 2015), 105. At the Quito Trade Ministerial, Venezuela also proposed pushing the deadline for concluding the FTAA negotiations back to 2010 and served notice that any FTAA would have to be submitted for approval in a plebiscite as a result of the country's new Bolivarian constitution approved in 1999.

14　See, e.g., "U.S., Brazil Begin Process that Could Scale Back Scope of the FTAA," Vol. 21 *Inside U.S. Trade* (May 30, 2003): 1 and "U.S., Brazilian Decisions Emerge Over Agenda at FTAA Mini-Ministerial," Vol. 21 *Inside U.S. Trade* (June 6, 2003): 1.

15　The Port of Spain TNC meeting also exposed growing fissures within MERCOSUR. Uruguay submitted a separate document that contained its own view of the FTAA, while Argentina, whose acute economic crisis was consuming all its political attention, favored the Brazilian position in terms of offers on investment, services, and government procurement. Zuleika Arashiro, *Negotiating the Free Trade Area of the Americas* (New York: Palgrave Macmillan, 2011), 44. In truth, fissures were also present in 1994 when the idea of the FTAA first surfaced. At that time, Argentina expressed the most enthusiasm for the project, while Brazil and Uruguay favored a slower, more measured approach.

16　The full text of the Ministerial Declaration from the Eighth Ministerial Meeting held in Miami and dated November 20, 2003 is available at: www.ftaa-alca.org/Ministerials/Miami/Miami_e.asp.

17　That dissent noted: "Venezuela enters a reservation with respect to the paragraph on the Free Trade Area of the Americas (FTAA) because of questions of principle and profound differences regarding the concept and philosophy of the proposed model and because of the manner in which specific aspects and established timeframes are addressed. We ratify our commitment to the consolidation of a regional fair trade bloc as a basis for strengthening levels of integration. This process must consider each country's particular cultural, social, and political characteristics; sovereignty and constitutionality; and the level and size of its economy, in order to guarantee fair treatment." The full text of the Declaration of Nueva León issued in conjunction with the Special Summit of the Americas dated January 13, 2004 is available at: www. summit-americas.org/sp_summit/sp_summit_dec_en.pdf.

18 The full text of the Declaration of Mar del Plata dated November 5, 2005 is available at: www.summit-americas.org/iv_summit/iv_summit_dec_en.pdf.

19 The already existing asymmetry in negotiating power in terms of material and human resources was exacerbated by the fact that most partners were not very relevant to the United States from a trade viewpoint, whereas the United States constituted a key market for many of the countries joining the agreements. Zuleika Arashiro, *Negotiating the Free Trade Area of the Americas* (New York: Palgrave Macmillan, 2011), 104.

20 The full text in English of the Agreement to Implement the Bolivarian Alternative for the Peoples of Our America and the Peoples' Trade Treaty can be found in Appendix 44 in Thomas Andrew O'Keefe, *Latin American Trade Agreements* (Ardsley, NY: Transnational Publishers, 1997–).

21 Various Latin American commentators, particularly on the Left, were quick to point out that the FTAA was a continuation of the Monroe Doctrine, except this time the goal was to make the Americas a strategic reserve for United States business interests and keep out economic competitors from beyond the Western Hemisphere. See, e.g., Marco Aurélio Garcia, "O Brasil e a ALCA: Regionalizacão e Projeto Nacional de Desevolvimento," in *ALCA e MERCOSUL: Riscos e Oportunidades para o Brasil*, ed. Samuel Pinheiro Guimarães (Brasilia: IPRI, FUNAG, 1999), 253.

22 Josette Altmann Borbón, "ALBA: Ideology Overcomes Integration?" in *Decline of U.S. Hegemony? A Challenge of ALBA and a New Latin American Integration of the Twenty-First Century*, ed. Bruce M. Bagley et al. (Lanham, MD: Lexington Books, 2015), 70. The ALBA incorporates many concepts of Chavez's Socialism for the Twenty-First Century, which is based on four pillars: regional democratic development, the economy of equivalences (to set a target value for goods and services so that they are not subject to the laws of supply and demand), participatory democracy, and community organizations. Ibid.

23 Marcel Nelson, *A History of the FTAA: From Hegemony to Fragmentation in the Americas* (New York: Palgrave Macmillan, 2015), 137. Nelson acknowledges that while ALBA did not lead to concrete measures resulting in regional integration, it did play an important symbolic role in garnering opposition to the FTAA.

24 Pia Riggirozzi, "Reconstructing Regionalism: What does Development Have to Do with It?" in *The Rise of Post-Hegemonic Regionalism: The Case of Latin America*, ed. Pia Riggirozzi et al. (Dordrecht, NL: Springer, 2012), 28.

25 By 2008, Cuba had sent to Venezuela approximately 13,000 physicians, 3,000 dentists, 4,100 nurses, and 10,000 technical experts in different fields of medicine. Magdalena Defort, "Neo-Bolivarian Challenges: Cuba and Venezuela and Their Foreign Policies," in *Decline of U.S. Hegemony? A Challenge of ALBA and a New Latin American Integration of the Twenty-First Century*, ed. Bruce M. Bagley et al. (Lanham, MD: Lexington Books, 2015), 100. Cuba also offered some 2,000 scholarships to Venezuelans to study in Cuban universities, and in 2005 alone provided 122,000 free surgeries to needy Venezuelans.

26 Raul Castro's decision to pursue discussions with the Obama administration, which led to the resumption of diplomatic relations in July 2015, is attributed to concerns in Havana about future oil shipments and other economic largesse provided by Venezuela. By 2011, imports of crude oil from Venezuela made up 61 percent of Cuba's total oil supply. Magdalena Defort, "Neo-Bolivarian Challenges: Cuba and Venezuela and Their Foreign Policies," in *Decline of U.S. Hegemony? A Challenge*

of ALBA and a New Latin American Integration of the Twenty-First Century, ed. Bruce M. Bagley et al. (Lanham, MD: Lexington Books, 2015), 102.

27 Zuleika Arashiro, *Negotiating the Free Trade Area of the Americas* (New York: Palgrave Macmillan, 2011), 3. Arashiro believes that U.S. foreign trade policy decision-makers' dominant view that the Western Hemisphere, beyond neighboring Canada and Mexico, was not sufficiently relevant to the United States to warrant specific attention meant that if engagement were required, it should take place through bilateral mechanisms. Ibid at 108. For the Brazilian foreign policy-making elite, a successful bilateral negotiation with the United States, which occurred through the prevalence of Brazil's idea of fragmenting the FTAA, was an indication of the country's position as a special player and U.S. recognition of Brazil as a distinct power in South America. Ibid at 46–7.

28 Marcel Nelson, *A History of the FTAA: From Hegemony to Fragmentation in the Americas* (New York: Palgrave Macmillan, 2015), 16. British economist John Williamson was the first to coin the expression "Washington Consensus" in 1989. It consisted of ten reforms that would facilitate Latin American countries escaping the deep recessions most experienced in the 1980s: 1) fiscal discipline; 2) reordering public expenditure priorities; 3) tax reform; 4) liberalizing interest rates; 5) a competitive exchange rate; 6) trade liberalization; 7) liberalization of inward foreign direct investment; 8) privatization; 9) deregulation; 10) property rights. See John Williamson, *A Short History of the Washington Consensus* (Washington, DC: Institute for International Economics, 2004). Available at: https://piie.com/sites/default/files/publications/papers/williamson0904-2.pdf.

29 Martha Finnemore, "Legitimacy, Hypocrisy, and the Social Structure of Unipolarity: Why Being a Unipole Isn't All It's Cracked Up to Be," in *International Relations Theory and the Consequences of Unipolarity*, ed. G. John Ikenberry et al. (New York: Cambridge University Press, 2011), 76.

30 Carlos Gustavo Poggio Teixeira, *Brazil, the United States, and the South American Subsystem* (Lanham, MD: Lexington Books, 2012), 116. One noted Brazilian foreign policy expert viewed MERCOSUR as contributing to the creation of a multipolar world. In the event that this multipolar world failed to materialize, MERCOSUR would better position its member states politically and economically in a unipolar system under United States domination. Helio Jaguaribe, "MERCOSUL e as Alternativas para a Ordem Mundial," in *ALCA e MERCOSUL: Riscos e Oportunidades para o Brasil*, ed. Samuel Pinheiro Guimarães (Brasilia: IPRI, FUNAG, 1999), 36.

31 Zuleika Arashiro, *Negotiating the Free Trade Area of the Americas* (New York: Palgrave Macmillan, 2011), 110. Ambassador Samuel Pinheiro Guimarães, who was dismissed from the Brazilian Foreign Ministry under President Cardoso due to vocal criticism of the FTAA and then brought back by Lula, summed up this sentiment when he stated that "[t]he participation of Brazil in an eventual FTAA would destroy its economic autonomy and rob it of an independent foreign policy." Samuel Pinheiro Guimarães, "Brazil, MERCOSUR, the FTAA and Europe," in *Free Trade for the Americas?*, ed. Paulo Vizentini et al. (London: Zed Books, 2004), 117–8.

Bibliography

Arashiro, Zuleika. *Negotiating the Free Trade Area of the Americas*. New York: Palgrave Macmillan, 2011.

Bagley, Bruce M. and Magdalena Defort, eds. *Decline of U.S. Hegemony? A Challenge of ALBA and a New Latin American Integration of the Twenty-First Century*. Lanham, MD: Lexington Books, 2015.

Barbosa, Rubens. *The Washington Dissensus*. Nashville, TN: Vanderbilt University Press, 2014.

Feinberg, Richard E. *Summitry in the Americas: A Progress Report*. Washington, DC: Institute for International Economics, 1997.

FTAA Secretariat. "Ministerial Declaration." Declaration of the Eighth Ministerial Meeting of the Free Trade Area of the Americas. Issued in Miami, Florida on November 20, 2003. Accessed July 27, 2017: www.ftaa-alca.org/Ministerials/Miami/Miami_e.asp

Ikenberry, G. John, Michael Mastanduno, and William C. Wohlforth, eds. *International Relations Theory and the Consequences of Unipolarity*. New York: Cambridge University Press, 2011.

Inside U.S. Trade, "U.S., Brazil Begin Process that Could Scale Back Scope of the FTAA." Vol. 21 *Inside U.S. Trade* (May 30, 2003): 1.

Inside U.S. Trade, "U.S., Brazilian Decisions Emerge Over Agenda at FTAA Mini-Ministerial." Vol. 21 *Inside U.S. Trade* (June 6, 2003): 1.

Nelson, Marcel. *A History of the FTAA: From Hegemony to Fragmentation in the Americas*. New York: Palgrave Macmillan, 2015.

O'Keefe, Thomas Andrew. *Latin American Trade Agreements*. Ardsley, NY: Transnational Publishers, 1997–.

O'Keefe, Thomas Andrew. *Latin American and Caribbean Trade Agreements: Keys to a Prosperous Community of the Americas*. Leiden, NL: Martinus Nijhoff (Brill), 2009.

Organization of American States, "Declaration of Mar del Plata." Washington, DC: OAS (Summit of the Americas Secretariat). Signed in Mar del Plata, Argentina on November 5, 2005. Accessed July 27, 2017: www.summit-americas.org/iv_summit/iv_summit_dec_en.pdf

Organization of American States. "Declaration of Nueva León." Washington, DC: OAS (Summit of the Americas Secretariat). Signed in Monterrey, Mexico on January 13, 2004. Accessed July 27, 2017: www.summit-americas.org/sp_summit/sp_summit_dec_en.pdf

Organization of American States. "Declaration of Quebec City." Washington, DC: OAS (Summit of the Americas Secretariat). Signed in Quebec City, Canada on April 22, 2001. Accessed July 27, 2017: www.summit-americas.org/iii_summit/iii_summit_dec_en.pdf

Palmer, David Scott. *U.S. Relations with Latin America during the Clinton Years*. Gainesville, FL: University Press of Florida, 2006.

Pinheiro Guimarães, Samuel, ed. *ALCA e MERCOSUL: Riscos e Oportunidades para o Brasil*. Brasilia: IPRI, FUNAG, 1999.

Poggio Teixeira, Carlos Gustavo. *Brazil, the United States, and the South American Subsystem*. Lanham, MD: Lexington Books, 2012.

Riggirozzi, Pia and Diana Tussie, eds. *The Rise of Post-Hegemonic Regionalism: The Case of Latin America*. Dordrecht, NL: Springer, 2012.

Vizentini, Paulo and Marianne Wiesebron, eds. *Free Trade for the Americas?* London: Zed Books, 2004.

Williamson, John. *A Short History of the Washington Consensus*. Washington, DC: Institute for International Economics, 2004. Accessed July 27, 2017: https://piie.com/sites/default/files/publications/papers/williamson0904-2.pdf

5 The Energy and Climate Partnership of the Americas

Introduction

Energy had been on the agenda of almost every Summit of the Americas going back to the first one in Miami in 1994, when a Partnership for Sustainable Energy Use was proposed. That initial proposal sought to:

(1) promote sustainable economic growth;
(2) facilitate financing by the multilateral lending agencies (such as the Inter-American Development Bank) in energy projects, particularly those related to enhancing efficiency and the development of non-conventional renewable energy resources;
(3) enhance the use of efficient and non-polluting conventional and renewable energy technologies;
(4) encourage market-oriented pricing to discourage wasteful energy use;
(5) promote, in cooperation with the private sector and isolated communities, rural electrification projects (including ones that, where appropriate, utilized renewable energy resources).

Although the Partnership for Sustainable Energy Use soon fell by the wayside, energy was a major topic of discussion at the Special Summit of the Americas on Sustainable Development held in Santa Cruz, Bolivia in 1996.[1] A Hemispheric Energy Steering Committee was also launched in Santa Cruz to coordinate efforts at increasing investment in the energy sector, promoting cleaner energy technologies in electrical power markets, advancing regulatory cooperation and training, increasing the economic and environmental sustainability of the petroleum sector, creating new opportunities for natural gas, and promoting energy efficiency. These same goals were also objectives of the Hemispheric Energy Initiative launched at the Second Summit of the Americas in Santiago, Chile in 1998. The Third Summit of the Americas in Quebec City in 2001 referred to the Hemispheric Energy Initiative as promoting policies and practices to advance the regional integration of energy markets. By the time of the Fourth Summit of the Americas in Mar del Plata, Argentina in 2005, however, the Hemispheric Energy Initiative had (as was true of its predecessor, the Partnership for Sustainable Energy Use) faded into oblivion.

While not as prominent on the hemispheric agenda as energy, past Summits of the Americas also discussed climate change, albeit oftentimes under a broader environmental umbrella. For example, at the first Summit in Miami in 1994, the governments of the Western Hemisphere pledged to ratify and begin implementing the provisions of the UN Framework Convention on Climate Change that had entered into force earlier that same year. A similar pledge was repeated in Santiago in 1998, as well as another urging ratification of the Kyoto Protocol (something the United States, alone among all the countries in the Americas, never did). At the Third Summit of the Americas in Quebec City in 2001, the 34 heads of state agreed

> to address the issue of climate change as a priority of action, working constructively through international processes in order to make necessary progress to ensure a sound and effective response to climate change; recognize the vulnerabilities in all our countries, in particular of Small Developing States and low lying coastal states, and the need to support the conduct of vulnerability assessments, the development and implementation of adaptation strategies, capacity building and technology transfer.[2]

Eight years later, all the heads of state from throughout the Americas (but for Cuba) gathered in Port of Spain for the Fifth Summit of the Americas, and acknowledged the need to make deep cuts in greenhouse gas emissions "on the basis of equity, and in accordance with our common but differentiated responsibilities and respective capabilities."[3]

In a May 2008 speech in Miami, where he outlined his policy vision for Latin America and the Caribbean if he were to win the election that November, then Senator Barack H. Obama raised the idea of an energy and climate partnership encompassing all the nations of the Western Hemisphere. Although his speech focused on U.S. relations with Cuba, Obama did mention a proposal to create an "Energy Partnership *for* the Americas." In particular, Obama stated that he would allow industrial emitters of greenhouse gases in the U.S. to offset a portion of their emissions by investing in low-carbon energy projects in Latin America and the Caribbean. He also pledged to increase research to develop clean coal technology as well as the next generation of sustainable bio-fuels not taken from food crops, and to expand the use of wind, solar, and nuclear energy throughout the Western Hemisphere.

Given the importance of the hydrocarbons sector to Trinidad and Tobago and the fact that the country was then the most important source of imported LNG in the United States, it is not surprising that energy security was a central theme of the Fifth Summit of the Americas in Port of Spain in 2009. The by now familiar pledges to promote cleaner, more affordable and sustainable energy systems, as well as to foster energy efficiency and conservation, were again iterated. Also apparent at the Trinidad Summit, however, was the resurgence of resource nationalism in many Latin American countries, as well as a collapse of the market-oriented economic consensus that had been characteristic of prior Summits during the 1990s. For example, the Declaration issued at the close of the Trinidad Summit "reaffirm[ed] the sovereign right of each country to the conservation, development and sustainable use of its energy resources." Another pledge to encourage the sustainable development, production, and use of both current and next-generation biofuels elicited a lengthy footnote from the government of Bolivia that proposed "an alternative vision based on living well and in harmony with nature, [and] developing public policies aimed to promote safe, alternative energies that guarantee the preservation of our planet, our 'Mother Earth'."[4] Interestingly, the leaders gathered in Port of Spain broached the usually controversial subject of expanding the use of nuclear energy and proposed interconnecting regional energy networks. Additional commitments arose "to improve and enhance the collection and reporting of market data on oil and other energy sources in all countries to ensure smooth functioning of energy markets at the regional and global levels" as well as "to support the development and implementation of voluntary corporate social responsibility best practices in the energy sector."[5]

Launching the Energy and Climate Partnership of the Americas (ECPA)

At the Fifth Summit of the Americas in Port of Spain in April 2009, the U.S. delegation proposed creating an Energy and Climate Partnership of the Americas or ECPA. According to a press release put out by the White House in conjunction with the Summit in Trinidad,

> President Obama invited countries of the region to participate in an Energy and Climate Partnership of the Americas; a voluntary and flexible frame-work for advancing energy security and combating climate change. Countries will be encouraged to suggest tangible ideas for cooperation, including on energy efficiency, renewable energy, cleaner fossil fuels, and energy infrastructure.[6]

By the time of the Trinidad Summit, the word "for" that candidate Obama had used in his Miami address the previous year had now been substituted with the word "of," to downplay any dominant leadership role for the United States. The change in terminology reflected the image the Obama administration wished to project at this Summit: that the United States was meeting with partners on an equal level and that "[t]here is no senior partner and junior partner in our relations; there is simply engagement based on mutual respect and common interests and shared values."[7] More cynical observers have pointed out that the emphasis on an "equal partnership" served to mask the fact that the recently inaugurated Obama appeared unable to offer anything of substance in Port of Spain. Given the collapsing economy he inherited from the outgoing administration of George W. Bush, as well as two major foreign wars and a financial services sector teetering on bankruptcy, Obama was in no position to propose any type of initiative that would involve significant contributions of capital. Regardless of the precise explanation for the new American approach, the emphasis on "partnership" was popular and welcome in a region long accustomed to bowing to the dictates of the United States, and even elicited an effusive embrace of Obama at the Summit by Venezuelan President Hugo Chavez.

ECPA was a particularly relevant proposal for a region of the world blessed with a wide variety and abundance of energy resources. Roughly a third of the planet's proven reserves of oil are found in the Western Hemisphere.[8] Venezuela alone has the largest oil reserves of any country in the world (followed by Saudi Arabia and Canada). Even today, Latin America still produces more petroleum than it consumes (and that remains true despite the contraction in Venezuelan output in recent years due to the country's political and economic mismanagement).[9] Around the time of ECPA's launch, Brazil had begun drilling down into vast reserves of oil found under miles of salt and rock formations in deep off-shore waters. At around the same time, Canada's oil sands industry, centered in the province of Alberta, was poised to emerge as a major global supplier of unconventional heavy crude oil. In addition, large shale rock formations with presumably vast reserves of natural gas accessible through hydraulic fracturing ("fracking") were known to exist throughout Argentina, Brazil, Canada, Mexico, and the United States. In less than a decade, the extensive exploitation of natural gas from shale rock in the United States has already transformed the country from a net natural gas importer to an exporter of liquefied natural gas (LNG). In fact, by 2009 the United States had already surpassed Russia to become the world's largest producer of natural gas.[10]

The Western Hemisphere energy surplus is not just in fossil fuels, however, with all the attendant problems this contributes to exacerbating climate change. Bolivia has more than half the world's supply of lithium, an essential input for making the batteries to power electric cars. Chile is currently the world's biggest commercial supplier of lithium, and Argentina has the potential to become a major supplier as well. With more than a quarter of the world's fresh water supplies, South America is still in a position to comfortably expand its already high electricity-generating capacity through hydropower (albeit that there are medium to long-term sustainability issues related to the climate change-induced melting of mountain glaciers, where much of this water originates). Equally as important, huge expanses of tropical rainforests in South and Central America offer a natural carbon sink for sequestering global greenhouse gas emissions. For example, the Amazon Basin stores an estimated 20 times the carbon content of the world's annual greenhouse gas emissions, or 49 billion metric tons of carbon, in the biomass of its tropical forest.[11]

Not all of the Western Hemisphere's abundant and diverse energy resources are evenly distributed. ECPA, however, offered the prospect of facilitating trade in energy resources from those countries that have such resources to those, such as nations in the Caribbean and Central America, that are net energy importers. The inclusion of a hemispheric cap-and-trade program in ECPA also offered the possibility of providing funding for renewable energy projects to harness power generated by the sun, wind, and ocean currents, as well as geothermal sources. Under such a scheme, U.S.-based utility companies seeking an offset for their carbon emissions would have had an incentive to invest in renewable energy projects on small Caribbean islands that would otherwise not be built because of the high initial investment costs and the long lag time needed to recoup a profit. The inclusion in any hemispheric cap-and-trade program of the concept embodied in the UN's Programme on Reducing Emissions from Deforestation and Forest Degradation (REDD) as an alternative means for obtaining greenhouse gas emission credits would have further incentivized protection of natural carbon sinks such as extensive tropical rainforests in Central and South America. REDD creates a financial value for the carbon stored in forests, offering incentives for developing countries to reduce emissions from forested lands and to invest in low-carbon paths to sustainable development. REDD-plus subsequently added the role of conservation, sustainable management of forests, and enhancement of carbon stocks as a way to incentivize the flow of capital from the developed world to developing countries.

The first Energy and Climate Ministerial of the Americas, which formally launched ECPA, took place in Washington, DC on April 15–16, 2010, with representatives from 32 of the 35 Western Hemisphere governments. EPCA was built around seven pillars (the last two of which were added by then U.S. Secretary of State Hillary Clinton just before the April 2010 Ministerial itself):

(1) *Energy efficiency* (i.e., promoting best policy practices through assistance in developing building codes and other standards in the industrial and residential sectors, as well as training for energy audits);

(2) *Renewable energy* (i.e., accelerating clean energy deployment via project support, policy dialogues, scientific collaboration, and the clean energy technology network);

(3) *Cleaner and more efficient use of fossil fuels* (i.e., promoting clean energy technologies to reduce both conventional pollution and the carbon footprint of fossil fuels, as well as best practices on land use management);

(4) *Energy infrastructure* (i.e., fostering modernized, integrated, and more resilient energy infrastructure, particularly electrical grids and gas pipelines);

(5) *Energy poverty* (i.e., targeting urban and rural energy poverty with strategies to promote sustainable urban development and improve access to modern clean energy services and appropriate technologies in rural areas that can improve public health and reduce fuel wood use, benefiting forest management);

(6) *Sustainable forestry and land use* (i.e., reducing emissions from deforestation and forest degradation, and enhancing carbon sequestration in the land use sector, including through the conservation and sustainable management of forests);

(7) *Adaptation assistance to developing countries impacted by climate change.*

At the first Energy and Climate Ministerial, the U.S. Department of Energy announced that it would provide technical support to explore the potential for building a Caribbean-wide system using submarine sea cables to transmit electricity generated from renewable energy sources. The U.S. Department of Energy and the Inter-American Development Bank (IADB) also signed an agreement creating an Energy Innovation Center permitting the coordination of resources to support regional projects and activities through the use, *inter alia*, of the IADB's US$1.5 billion special fund for financing energy-related projects.[12] In addition, the U.S. Department of Energy and the U.S. National Energy Laboratory in Golden, Colorado announced a partnership with scientists and technology experts in Colombia to identify, evaluate, and promote technologies for sustainable biomass use in that country. Furthermore, three U.S. scientists were appointed to serve as Senior ECPA Fellows to provide advice, share experiences, and consult with counterparts from throughout the Americas on clean energy, sustainable landscapes, and adaptation to climate change.[13] Finally, the U.S. Department of Agriculture was selected to serve as the lead agency to coordinate U.S. government technical assistance to countries interested in sharing information in order to expand the production and usage of sustainable, renewable biomass energy.

ECPA Initiatives

Following the April 2010 Energy and Climate Ministerial of the Americas in Washington, DC, a number of new initiatives emerged under the ECPA umbrella, often led by countries other than the United States. One such initiative was a working group on heavy oil, chaired by Canada but with representation from Brazil, Colombia, Mexico, the U.S., and Venezuela, to facilitate the exchange of information on best practices and technological innovation to reduce the environmental footprint of heavy oil extraction and development. For its part, Mexico led a working group on energy efficiency that included all the countries of the Western Hemisphere but Cuba and which, *inter alia*, shared best practices and experiences to develop regional partnerships promoting efficiency and conservation. By contrast, Brazil chaired an initiative focused on building environmentally sustainable low-income housing across Latin America and the Caribbean and reducing greenhouse gas emissions from solid waste. The American Planning Association agreed to provide technical assistance for the Brazilian housing initiative, with limited funding provided by the U.S. State Department. Brazil also teamed up with the United States to assist seven countries in Central America and the Caribbean nations to develop their own biofuels industry, focusing on sugar-based ethanol through a program already under development by the Department of Sustainable Development at the Organization of American States (OAS) prior to ECPA. In fact, the OAS program was a result of the U.S.–Brazil Memorandum of Understanding to Advance Cooperation on Biofuels, signed in March 2007 during the Bush administration. That MOU included a proposal to support the establishment of sustainable bioenergy programs and projects in Latin American and Caribbean nations, thereby helping to diversify the energy production mix, improve economic sustainability and competitiveness, and improve air quality.[14]

Chile aggressively used ECPA to address energy-related matters affecting the country and its neighbors. For example, Chile became the host of a regional Renewable Energy Center that received technical assistance from the U.S. Department of Energy and operated an open-access website portal called "Open Energy Information" to facilitate the regional exchange of information on renewable resources. Along with Argentina, Colombia, Peru, the United States, and Uruguay, Chile also participated in an ECPA shale gas initiative to exchange information on how to safely exploit shale gas reserves and minimize negative environmental impacts. Chile also joined Colombia, Ecuador, Panama, Peru, and the United States in an initiative called "Connecting the Americas 2022" that sought to interconnect all the national electric grids from Panama to Chile, beginning with harmonizing the respective regulatory frameworks of each country (something originally proposed within the UNASUR framework, but without Panama's participation).

Other ECPA projects included the U.S.-based electricity generator Southern Company working with a Colombian non-governmental organization to train disadvantaged secondary students for future careers in the energy sector. The U.S. Department of Energy and the Ecuadorean Ministry for Coordination in Production, Employment and Competitiveness worked together on a project to convert industrial waste into valuable commodities or inputs. For its part, the OAS oversaw implementation of the Caribbean Sustainable Energy Program (CESP), funded primarily by the EU (with some contributions from the U.S. Department of Energy). The goal was to reduce carbon emissions in the Eastern Caribbean and the Bahamas generated by the energy sector through the development and use of renewable energy, as well as to enhance the efficiency of existing energy systems. The OAS also oversaw implementation of a Caribbean-wide program funded by the U.S. Department of Energy to facilitate regional dialogue on long-term sustainable energy solutions and assist national governments to promote and implement sustainable energy policies and programs through short-term legal and technical assistance. Overall, the OAS became an important clearinghouse for disseminating information on ECPA initiatives and bringing together potential public- and private-sector partners.

Finally, the U.S. Peace Corps had an ECPA initiative that supported energy-efficient practices and the use of alternative energy technologies, including small-scale home or school solar solutions, cook stoves, small wind turbines, and other energy-efficiency solutions in Costa Rica, the Dominican Republic, Guyana, Honduras, Nicaragua, Panama, Peru, and Suriname. In Paraguay, the Peace Corps trained a group of small farmers to use a device called a bio-digester to properly treat organic waste and provide renewable energy and organic fertilizer.

With the exception of the IADB's US$1.5 billion line of credit for energy and climate related projects, the money provided to fund ECPA projects was negligible. U.S. government agencies often piggybacked onto projects already developed and financed by the IADB or the OAS, for example, and promoted them as ECPA-related. At other times, ECPA claimed ownership over programs that began years before it had even come into existence and which enjoyed independent sources of funding.[15] For its part, the U.S. Trade Development Agency modestly funded a Clean Energy Exchange Program for the Americas, designed to familiarize leading Latin American and Caribbean energy sector officials with U.S. clean energy technologies through a series of trade missions to the United States. As the Obama administration ended, the U.S. government had spent a paltry US$150 million on stand-alone projects exclusively attributed to ECPA.

A Missed Opportunity to Establish a Hemispheric Cap-and-Trade Program

In addition to being blessed with an abundance of diverse energy resources, the Americas is home to a vast expanse of tropical rainforests that serve as a natural carbon sink for sequestering greenhouse gas emissions. At the same time, some of the world's largest contributors to global greenhouse gas emissions are found in the Western Hemisphere, including the United States (now ranked number two after being dethroned by China around the time that ECPA was first proposed by candidate Obama in 2008). Canada's emissions, while only one tenth of those from the United States, are expected to increase as it further develops its oil sand reserves in Alberta and Saskatchewan. Mexico has traditionally also been another major contributor to greenhouse gas emissions because of widespread natural gas flaring as well as heavy dependency on fossil fuels (historically oil, but more natural gas in recent years) to generate electricity. Brazil is a major contributor to global carbon emissions from the burning of tropical rainforests.[16] The Western Hemisphere therefore offered the perfect opportunity to establish the type of cap-and-trade initiative advocated by then Senator Obama in 2008, whereby industrial emitters of greenhouse gases in North America could offset a portion of their emissions by investing in low-carbon energy projects in Latin America and the Caribbean. By limiting such a program to the Americas, many of the shortcomings of the UN-administered Clean Development Mechanism, or CDM, established by the Kyoto Protocol could be avoided.

Under the multilateral CDM, credits are issued to a developed country and its companies in return for financing cleaner energy projects in the developing world (e.g., building a more expensive thermal plant fueled by natural gas or a hydro dam to generate electricity instead of a cheaper coal-powered generator), thus contributing to reducing global greenhouse gas emissions. This is premised on the understanding that these cleaner energy facilities would not have been built but for the funding emanating from the rich-country donor. The credits received through the CDM are then used to offset mandated emission reduction targets at home. The CDM was originally set to expire at the end of

2012, but received a reprieve until 2020.[17] The United States never ratified the Kyoto Protocol and therefore did not participate in the CDM.

One big advantage offered by a CDM limited to the Western Hemisphere was that it would be less susceptible to the type of fraud that plagued the UN-administered CDM system.[18] This was not only because of the smaller number of countries involved, but also because of the plethora of institutions in the Western Hemisphere with the potential to administer a hemispheric carbon offset program more effectively than the UN. For example, the Andean Development Corporation (CAF) already oversees a Latin American carbon market through the registration and issuance of certified reductions in the transportation sector. The CAF has also signed contracts for carbon emission sales with public and private agencies (including Spain's Ibero-American Carbon Initiative) and investment funds resulting in new energy generation facilities using renewable resources, forestry-related activities, and an expansion of biofuel production. While the CAF on its own might not have had the resources and personnel to administer a CDM for the entire Western Hemisphere, this task could have been divided among different sub-regional entities with a proven record of reliability. Accordingly, the CAF might have been assigned the Andean region of South America (including Chile), for example, while a similar role could have been entrusted to the Central American Bank for Economic Integration, the North American Development Bank, and the Caribbean Development Bank in those three sub-regions. Similarly, the task of monitoring a hemispheric carbon offset program for the core MERCOSUR countries (i.e., Argentina, Brazil, Paraguay, and Uruguay) could have been assigned to the Financial Fund for the Development of the Rio de la Plata Basin (FONPLATA).

A CDM limited to the Western Hemisphere would likely have neutralized Brazil's refusal—premised on historical sovereignty concerns about "internationalizing" the Amazon—to permit the multilateral CDM under the Kyoto Protocol to fund any type of forest conservation or reforestation projects in the Amazon. Brazil would have been more amenable to utilizing rainforest preservation projects in the Amazon to gain carbon offsets under a CDM limited to the Western Hemisphere, and administered by regional institutions where it enjoyed greater influence. Evidence of this can be garnered from the Memorandum of Understanding (MOU) on Cooperation Regarding Climate Change that Brazil and the United States signed in March 2010. Under this MOU, both countries agreed to cooperate in reducing emissions from deforestation and forest degradation pursuant to the UN's REDD-plus program. It should be pointed out that the goals sought through REDD-plus are compatible with ECPA's sixth pillar of reducing emissions from deforestation and forest degradation, and enhancing carbon sequestration in the land use sector, including through the conservation and sustainable management of forests.

For the Caribbean island states, a hemispheric CDM could have helped to liberate them from their heavy dependence on imported crude oil and refined petroleum for transport and electricity generation, which has made them among the most heavily indebted nations in the world on a debt-to-GDP basis.[19]

Although a wide mix of renewable energy resources is available on different islands, such as hydro (including exploiting strong ocean currents), solar, wind, and geothermal, utilizing them to generate energy is complicated by minuscule markets that make it difficult for private-sector investors to recoup a return on their initial investment within a reasonable time frame (if ever). Accordingly, without the existence of some type of external incentive, the money to develop such projects is unlikely to appear. That scenario changes in the context of a hemispheric cap-and-trade program where a Canadian or U.S. utility company, for example, seeking a carbon offset might be willing to invest in an electricity generation facility in Dominica (which has only 70,000 inhabitants) that makes use of the country's extensive geothermal potential.

The Caribbean Energy Security Initiative

In the face of mounting concerns over the continued sustainability of Venezuela's PetroCaribe initiative, then-U.S. Vice-President Joe Biden launched a Caribbean Energy Security Initiative in June 2014. A Caribbean Energy Security Summit followed in Washington, DC in January 2015, where the U.S. underscored the need for Caribbean nations to create a regulatory environment that would attract private-sector investment. Another reason for U.S. promotion of this particular initiative was that it served as a way to encourage exports of its liquefied natural gas (LNG). The United States government approved export licenses for the first LNG exports to the Caribbean at the beginning of 2016. Whatever the precise motivations of the U.S. government may have been, the Caribbean nations made clear at the January 2015 Summit that what they were most interested in was finding ways to fund ambitious renewable energy projects. At that same Summit, the World Bank presented a proposal to establish a Caribbean Energy Investment Network to improve coordination and communication among development partners to enhance the effectiveness of donor-supported energy programs. In the months after the Summit, the U.S. Overseas Private Investment Corporation (OPIC) announced that that it would disburse the first tranche of approximately US$43 million to finance the Blue Mountains 34-megawatt wind power project in Jamaica. OPIC subsequently financed a 20-megawatt solar photovoltaic installation in Jamaica as well.

Unfortunately, the rhetoric associated with the Caribbean Energy Security Initiative was loftier than the concrete results actually realized. Projects under the initiative tended to be small, such as the technical assistance provided by the U.S. Department of State to Saint Kitts and Nevis to develop its geothermal energy potential. In other cases, the initiative took credit for programs already being implemented and funded by other U.S. government agencies, such as existing USAID projects in Haiti and the Dominican Republic supporting power-sector reform. Another example was the US$2 million in technical support and assistance provided to CARICOM's Caribbean Sustainable Energy Roadmap and Strategy platform to manage regional coordination and action on energy security: the money actually came from USAID and the World Bank, as well as the U.S.

State Department. During a visit to Jamaica in April 2015 to meet with CARICOM leaders, President Obama announced the establishment of a Clean Energy Finance Facility (jointly run by OPIC, the U.S. Trade and Development Agency, and USAID) to serve as a catalyst for greater public- and private-sector investment. Shortly thereafter, the U.S. government provided a US$10 million grant for clean energy projects in Belize and Jamaica, through the Clean Energy Finance Facility. During Obama's last full year in office, the U.S. Congress approved a mere US$2 million for the Caribbean Energy Security Initiative.

Conclusion

ECPA represents the epitome of a liberal international relations policy, beginning with its use of the word "partnership" in a purposeful effort to downplay any predominant leadership role for the United States. In fact, the new Obama administration was intent on not exerting its hegemony, in recognition of the complex and oftentimes abusive exercise of U.S. power in Latin America and the Caribbean in the past. At the Summit of the Americas in Port of Spain, where ECPA was launched in 2009, Obama used key words closely associated with international liberalism, emphasizing that the United States wanted to engage its southern neighbors "based on mutual respect and common interests and shared values." Overall, ECPA is an example of a project premised on very liberal principles of restraint, reciprocity, and sovereign equality.[20]

Despite its potential for success, given the wide range and abundance of energy resources available in the Western Hemisphere, the concrete results actually achieved by ECPA were negligible. The biggest impediment was the fact that the Obama administration was never able to secure climate change legislation at the federal level in the U.S. Congress. Hence, the possibility of a hemispheric cap-and-trade program, whereby U.S. utility companies could obtain carbon offsets from investing in renewable energy projects in the Caribbean, for example, never materialized. When private-sector investment or funding from other governments in the Hemisphere was not forthcoming, the U.S. government was either unable or unwilling to provide its own monies to support ECPA initiatives in any significant way. By the time of the Sixth Summit of the Americas in Cartagena, Colombia in April 2012, neither President Obama, in his remarks to the other gathered leaders, nor any other senior member of the U.S. delegation even mentioned ECPA. This was a glaring omission given that ECPA had been the U.S. government's official submission for fulfilling the energy and climate change-related mandates arising from the Trinidad Summit in 2009.[21]

The United States' failure to support ECPA initiatives with adequate funding displayed an absence of leadership. In that sense, the United States was unable to provide the requisite public goods that would have enticed other countries in the Western Hemisphere to enthusiastically endorse and join it in achieving ECPA's objectives. The refusal of the Republican majority—and certain Democrats from coal-producing states—in the U.S. Congress to pass any type of federal legislation to address climate change, rejecting the overwhelming scientific evidence pointing to the reality of the phenomenon and the preponderant human contribution, provides an example of a hegemon turning in on itself and becoming not only systemically destructive, but self-destructive as well.

Although the absence of political and financial leadership on the part of the United States was a major factor contributing to ECPA's meager results, the concomitant resurgence of resource nationalism in a number of Latin American countries also contributed to undermining efforts to promote the integration of energy markets. Added to this were new technological advances such as hydraulic fracking and horizontal drilling which dramatically expanded U.S. production of natural gas and tight oil from shale rock. Crude oil output in the United States almost doubled, from about five million barrels per day when ECPA was first proposed, to 9.7 million barrels per day by April 2015.[22] The glut in crude production finally spurred the U.S. Congress to lift a 40-year-old ban on U.S. crude oil exports at the end of 2015, and the last restrictions on global exports of U.S. natural gas were lifted in 2016. All of this meant that the urgent U.S. need for energy security at the start of the Obama administration was superseded by a more confident sense of energy self-sufficiency by the time of Obama's second term in office. Hence, expending large amounts of political capital to integrate energy markets in the Western Hemisphere no longer seemed as imperative as it had in early 2009, when ECPA was formally proposed.

Notes

1 Feinberg believes the reasons why the Partnership for Sustainable Energy Use never advanced is that the United States failed to build strong allies elsewhere in the hemisphere and was unable to gain the full support of the two countries with the clearest interest in the subject: Venezuela and Mexico. It also failed to use a preparatory meeting on sustainable development in Quito in October 1994 to flesh out differences and build a durable consensus among key players. Richard E. Feinberg, *Summitry in the Americas: A Progress Report* (Washington, DC: Institute for International Economics, 1997), 123.

2 See Plan of Action of the III Summit of the Americas adopted on April 22, 2001. Available at: www.summit-americas.org/iii_summit/iii_summit_poa_en.pdf.

3 See Declaration of Commitment of Port of Spain signed on April 19, 2009. Available at: www.summit-americas.org/V_Summit/decl_comm_pos_en.pdf.

4 Bolivian concerns were premised on "the view that the development of cooperative policies and arrangements intended to expand biofuels in the Western Hemisphere can adversely affect and impact on the availability of food and raise food prices, increase deforestation, displace populations due to the demand of land, and ultimately aggravate the food crisis." In addition, biofuel expansion "would directly affect low-income persons, especially the poorest economies of the developing countries." Declaration of Commitment of Port of Spain signed on April 19, 2009.

5 See Declaration of Commitment of Port of Spain signed on April 19, 2009. In terms of developing and implementing a voluntary code of corporate responsibility, particular emphasis is to be given to "initiatives that enhance dialogue among government, industry, local communities, indigenous groups, and non-governmental organizations, to enable all stakeholders to better understand, participate in and benefit from energy sector activities."

6 Press Release, *The United States and the 2009 Summit of the Americas: Securing Our Citizens' Future* (Washington, DC: The White House, April 19, 2009). Available at: www.whitehouse.gov/the-press-office/united-states-and-2009-summit-americas-securing-our-citizens-future.

7 See Official Remarks of United States President Barack H. Obama on April 17, 2009 at the Opening Ceremony of the Fifth Summit of the Americas. Text available at: www.summit-americas.org/V_Summit/remarks_usa_en.pdf.

8 See British Petroleum, *BP Statistical Review of World Energy* (London: British Petroleum PLC, June 2017), 12.

9 See British Petroleum, *BP Statistical Review of World Energy* (London: British Petroleum PLC, June 2017), 14–5.

10 See British Petroleum, *BP Statistical Review of World Energy* (London: British Petroleum PLC, June 2017), 28 and 30.

11 Centre for International Governance Innovation (CIGI), *Blueprint for a Sustainable Energy Partnership for the Americas* (Waterloo, ON: CIGI, 2009), 9.

12 The IADB originally hoped to increase this credit line to US$3 billion by 2012. That never happened. Ironically, the bulk of the money that was supplied for this credit line actually originated in countries from outside the Western Hemisphere, including Japan, South Korea, and Spain.

13 The U.S. Department of State finances this program, called the "ECPA Senior Fellows Program," but it is administered by a non-governmental organization called Partners of the Americas. Since it was started in 2010, the program has grown to include up to 23 experts that come from academic institutions, not-for-profit entities, and the private sector. The program also financed two small innovation projects focused on sustainable development.

14 Under the original OAS-administered project that arose out of the 2007 Brazilian–U.S. Memorandum of Understanding, the objective was to work with partner governments and other collaborators to facilitate energy, transport, and agricultural-sector reform; improve energy and agricultural-sector governance; and develop institutional, technical, and legal capacity among the public and private sectors for sustainable bioenergy development and use. The four countries selected by the United States and Brazil for the first phase of this initiative included the Dominican Republic, El Salvador, Haiti, and Saint Kitts and Nevis.

15 For example, USAID supported initiatives to reduce greenhouse gas (GHG) emissions from the energy sector, industry, and urban areas in Central America through a US$10 million Development Credit Authority (DCA) loan guarantee providing credit to small and medium-sized entities to invest in cleaner production technology, industrial and municipal waste reduction and recycling efforts, and pilot municipal-waste methane gas recovery. Through the Initiative for Conservation in the Andean Amazon, USAID and its partners sought to leverage US$65 million from the U.S. government and other public and private sources for conservation in the Amazonian portions of Colombia, Ecuador, Peru, and Bolivia that helped mitigate carbon dioxide emissions. USAID also funded small country-specific projects in Bolivia, Brazil, Ecuador, Guatemala, Honduras, Mexico, Nicaragua, Panama, Paraguay, and Peru that primarily focused on reducing greenhouse gas emissions through changes in current land use practices (namely the destruction of rainforests).

16 Interestingly, because Brazil's emissions primarily come from the burning of tropical rainforests, this practice does not contribute to new global greenhouse emissions *per se*, as live trees naturally remove carbon from the air and, when burned, are simply releasing back into the atmosphere what they initially took out. Accordingly, there is no net gain or loss. See Burton Richter, *Beyond Smoke and Mirrors: Climate Change and Energy in the 21st Century* (New York: Cambridge University Press, 2010), 68–9. "Since plants get the carbon for their growth from the carbon dioxide in the atmosphere and release it on burning, they do not give any net increase in greenhouse

gas as long as they are grown without fertilizers and other modern agriculture technology." The real problem, of course, is the soot released by the mass burning of trees, which creates havoc in the atmosphere in terms of trapping or keeping out solar rays as well as the previously mentioned loss of a natural means for sequestering new carbon dioxide emissions from the heavy global use of fossil fuels.

17 At the UN Conference on Climate Change (COP 17) in Durban, South Africa in December 2011, some 35 industrialized countries agreed to extend their Kyoto Protocol mandates (and, as a consequence, their participation in the CDM) until 2015 or such time as a new climate change agreement to replace the Kyoto Protocol was concluded by all UN member states. Canada, anxious about meeting its obligations to reduce carbon emissions because of the expansion of its oil sands production centered in Alberta, refused to extend its participation in the Kyoto Protocol beyond the original expiration date at the end of 2012. The CDM was extended to 2020 at the UN Conference on Climate Change (COP 18) celebrated in Doha, Qatar in November 2012.

18 Research conducted by two Stanford University professors in 2008 found that a large fraction of the credits generated under the CDM did not represent genuine reductions in greenhouse gas emissions, as many projects that "reduce" emissions would have been built anyway and at a far lower cost as well. Even worse, the CDM creates perverse incentives for developing countries to increase carbon emissions as a way of generating CDM credits that can then be offered to developed nations desperate to find offsets for their own pollution inducing activities. See, Michael Wara and David G. Victor, "A Realistic Policy on International Carbon Offsets" (Program on Energy and Sustainable Development Working Paper # 74. Palo Alto, CA: Freeman Spogli Institute for International Studies, Stanford University, April 2008). Available at: http://fsi.stanford.edu/sites/default/files/WP74_final_final.pdf.

19 Anthony Bryan, "Trinidad and Tobago," in *Energy Cooperation in the Western Hemisphere: Benefits and Impediments*, ed. Sidney Weintraub (Washington, DC: The CSIS Press, 2007), 381. At the time ECPA was first proposed, approximately 93 percent of the Caribbean's energy consumption was fossil fuel based, while only 4 percent came from renewable energy.

20 See, e.g., G. John Ikenberry, "Liberal Internationalism 3.0: America and Dilemmas of Liberal World Order," in *Liberal World Orders*, ed. Tim Dunne et al. (New York: Oxford University Press, 2013), 25. "Liberals assume that people and their governments have deep common interests in the establishment of a cooperative world order organized around principles of restraint, reciprocity, and sovereign equality."

21 See, OAS Summit Implementation Review Group, *Report of the United States Government on Implementation of Mandates from the Fifth Summit of the Americas*, May 27, 2010. Available at: www.summit-americas.org/nat_rep/2010/USA_en.pdf.

22 David Shepard, "Five Crucial Factors Will Decide Oil's Next Move," *Financial Times*, April 6, 2016: 20.

Bibliography

British Petroleum. *BP Statistical Review of World Energy*. London: British Petroleum PLC, June 2017.

Centre for International Governance Innovation (CIGI). *Blueprint for a Sustainable Energy Partnership for the Americas*. Waterloo, ON: CIGI, 2009.

Dunne, Tim and Trine Flockhart, eds. *Liberal World Orders*. New York: Oxford University Press, 2013.

Feinberg, Richard E. *Summitry in the Americas: A Progress Report*. Washington, DC: Institute for International Economics, 1997.

Organization of American States. *Declaration of Commitment of Port of Spain.* Washington, DC: OAS (Summit of the Americas Secretariat). Signed in Port of Spain, Trinidad and Tobago on April 19, 2009. Accessed July 27, 2017: www.summit-americas.org/V_Summit/decl_comm_pos_en.pdf

Organization of American States. *Official Remarks of United States President Barack Obama at the Opening Ceremony of the Fifth Summit of the Americas.* Washington, DC: OAS (Summit of the Americas Secretariat). Delivered in Port of Spain Trinidad and Tobago on April 17, 2009. Accessed July 27, 2017: www.summit-americas. org/V_Summit/remarks_usa_en.pdf

Organization of American States. *Plan of Action.* Washington, DC: OAS (Summit of the Americas Secretariat). Adopted in Quebec City, Canada during the III Summit of the Americas on April 22, 2001. Accessed July 27, 2017: www.summit-americas.org/iii_summit/iii_summit_poa_en.pdf

Organization of American States. *Report of the United States Government on Implementation of Mandates from the Fifth Summit of the Americas.* Washington, DC: OAS (Summit Implementation Review Group). Issued on May 27, 2010. Accessed July 27, 2017: www.summit-americas.org/nat_rep/2010/USA_en.pdf

Press Release. *The United States and the 2009 Summit of the Americas: Securing Our Citizens' Future.* Washington, DC: The White House, April 19, 2009. Accessed July 27, 2017: www.whitehouse.gov/the-press-office/united-states-and-2009-summit-americas-securing-our-citizens-future

Richter, Burton. *Beyond Smoke and Mirrors: Climate Change and Energy in the 21st Century.* New York: Cambridge University Press, 2010.

Shepard, David. "Five Crucial Factors Will Decide Oil's Next Move." *Financial Times,* April 6, 2016: 20.

Wara, Michael and David G. Victor. "A Realistic Policy on International Carbon Offsets." Program on Energy and Sustainable Development Working Paper # 74. Palo Alto, CA: Freeman Spogli Institute for International Studies (Stanford University), April 2008. Accessed July 27, 2017: http://fsi.stanford.edu/sites/default/files/WP74_final_final.pdf

Weintraub, Sidney, ed. *Energy Cooperation in the Western Hemisphere: Benefits Impediments.* Washington, DC: The CSIS Press, 2007.

6   China in Latin America and the Caribbean

Introduction

For much of the post-World War II era, the relationship between the People's Republic of China and the countries of Latin America was colored by Cold War politics and reflected the priorities of the hemispheric hegemon, the United States of America. In January 1950, for example, the Soviet Union proposed that the recently established People's Republic of China replace Chiang Kai-shek's Republic of China, based in Taiwan, as the legitimate representative of the Chinese government in the United Nations (UN), and thereby become one of the five permanent members of the Security Council wielding veto power. The United States vehemently opposed this proposal and successfully lobbied the Latin American governments to vote against the Russian initiative.[1] The first country to break the diplomatic isolation of the People's Republic of China in the Americas was, not surprisingly, Castro's Cuba, in 1961. Despite that, Cuba's relations with Beijing were never as close as those with Moscow, particularly following the post-1960 cooling in relations between the two Communist superpowers. It was not until after the dissolution of the Soviet Union in 1991 that bilateral Chinese–Cuban diplomatic and commercial relations improved significantly.

Not long after Salvador Allende's election to the Chilean presidency in 1970, Chile became the first South American nation to recognize Beijing. Despite the ferociously anti-Communist military government that came to power following Allende's overthrow on September 11, 1973, Chile maintained diplomatic relations with the People's Republic of China. In fact, the Pinochet era was marked by even closer commercial and political ties between Santiago and Beijing than had existed under Allende. Part of the explanation was the Sino–U.S. rapprochement that included President Richard Nixon's visit to China in 1972 and U.S. acquiescence to Beijing replacing the Taipei government at the UN. By the mid-1980s some scholars in China even viewed Pinochet's Chile as a model worth emulating, given the perception that the country, following significant strides in economic growth, was making an orderly transition from repressive authoritarianism to enhanced political liberalization.[2]

One of the lasting legacies of the Cold War is the fact that, of the 20 or so nations in the world that still recognize Taiwan as the legitimate government of

China, 11 are found in Central America and the Caribbean.[3] The only South American country that still maintains diplomatic relations with Taiwan is Paraguay, which makes it the odd man out, given that its MERCOSUR partners all maintain diplomatic relations with Beijing and designated China a market economy before the World Trade Organization (WTO) deadline of 2016 for doing so. Unlike in the past, when recognition of Taiwan was often the result of pressure exerted from Washington, DC, today the explanation is often rooted in economic opportunism.

Beginning in the 1980s and throughout the earlier part of the twenty-first century, Beijing and Taipei engaged in "checkbook diplomacy" in Latin America and the Caribbean to curry favor and diplomatic recognition. Taiwan, for example, has long provided funds for the Central American Bank for Economic Integration and is a major investor in the region's textile and consumer electronics industry. It also has free trade agreements with El Salvador, Guatemala, Honduras, and Sandinista Nicaragua.[4] When Costa Rica switched recognition to Beijing in 2007, Chinese contractors began constructing a major soccer stadium in San José, which finally opened in 2011; this also led to China opening up its market to Costa Rican coffee.[5] President Hu Jintao became the first Chinese leader to ever visit Costa Rica in November 2008. Beijing eventually signed a free trade agreement with Costa Rica in 2010, which came into force a year later.

Following the 2008 election of a Kuomintang government in Taipei that was more amenable to improving commercial and political relations with the mainland, an informal truce was declared in the battle between the People's Republic of China and Taiwan to secure diplomatic recognition. However, the election of Tsai Ing-wen, from the more nationalist Democratic Progressive Party, as president of Taiwan in 2016 revived the former diplomatic tug of war between Beijing and Taipei for diplomatic recognition. In January 2017 the Taiwanese president embarked on an official visit to meet with the presidents of the four Central American nations that, at that point, still recognized Taipei, in an effort to persuade them not to switch recognition to Beijing, as Sao Tomé and Principe in Africa had done the previous month.[6] In an indication that the president's trip to Central America may have been in vain, Panama announced it was switching recognition to Beijing in June 2017.

China's Growing Commercial Presence in Latin America and the Caribbean

Until it became a member of the WTO in 2001 as part of a new national development strategy focused on engagement with the global economy, China was not a major trading partner for most countries in Latin America and the Caribbean. In the twenty-first century, however, trade between China and countries in Latin America and the Caribbean exploded, increasing by some 2,500 percent between 2000 and 2013.[7] One reason for China's newfound interest in Latin America was an effort to diversify its export markets so as to reduce any economic leverage the Americans might be able to exert on Beijing, given how much China exports to the United States.[8] Interestingly, this desire to escape U.S. economic and political domination has long been a goal of many countries in Latin America as well. In addition, China's aim to reform the international political order to better reflect its growing global economic and financial weight is shared by others in the global south, especially Brazil.[9]

The money generated from the explosive growth in commodity exports from Latin America to China that commenced at the start of the twenty-first century allowed countries to pay off debt owed to multilateral organizations such as the International Monetary Fund (IMF) and significantly build up their foreign reserve holdings. By 2011, China had become the most important export destination for Brazil, Chile, and Peru, and the second largest for Argentina, Cuba, Uruguay, and Venezuela. There are important regional differences in the impact and the nature of Chinese trade flows with Latin America and the Caribbean, however.

The Chinese impact in Central America and the Caribbean has trended in favor of major increases in imports from China, which often threaten local industry and displace *maquila*, or mass assembly production (especially of textiles and clothing), to third markets such as the United States. Costa Rica was, for a time, a notable exception in Central America, as trade in manufactured goods went in both directions thanks to Intel's microchip plant outside San José. That plant closed in 2014, however. In general, there is little demand in China for Central America's traditional commodity exports, which include bananas, coffee, and sugar.

The situation with Mexico is more complex as its huge trade deficit with China is often the result of sophisticated manufactured inputs that are incorporated into final products, including automobiles assembled in Mexico, that are then exported duty-free to the United States under the North American Free Trade Agreement, or NAFTA. Nonetheless, the situation at the start of the twenty-first century was rather bleak for Mexico, with China displacing it as the major source of computers, cell phones, and apparel imported into the United States.[10] During the 2000–2005 period, Mexico only managed to increase its share in goods imported into the United States by 25 percent, while China's share in U.S. imports grew by 143 percent.[11] This same time period also saw hundreds of factories close in Mexico and the country lose new manufacturing investment to China. Mexico did positively benefit from China's growing economic prowess at the start of the twenty-first century in terms of the impact this had on raising global petroleum prices. In recent years, Mexico has begun to increase manufactured exports to the U.S. market by specializing in very heavy goods such as airplane engines that are expensive to transport from Asia, and diversifying into product lines requiring higher levels of customization, for which close proximity to the U.S. market offers a distinct advantage. Mexico has also benefited from a trebling of average hourly wages in China's manufacturing sector between 2005 and 2016 to US$3.60, while at the same time manufacturing wages in Mexico fell from US$2.20 to US$2.10 per hour.[12]

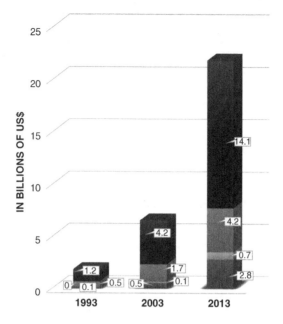

Figure 6.1 Central America* exports to rest of Latin America, China, Europe, and USA.

Source: Inter-American Development Bank/INTAL (INTradebid).
*Costa Rica, El Salvador, Guatemala, Honduras, Nicaragua.

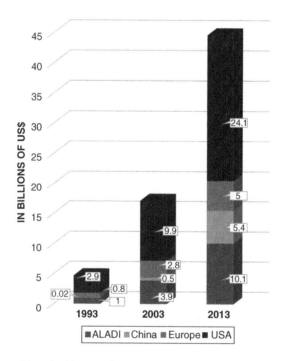

Figure 6.2 Central America* imports from rest of Latin America, China, Europe, and USA.

Source: Inter-American Development Bank/INTAL (INTradebid).
*Costa Rica, El Salvador, Guatemala, Honduras, Nicaragua.

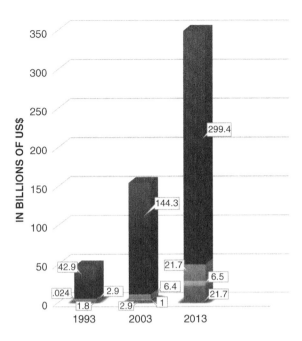

Figure 6.3 Mexico exports to rest of Latin America, China, Europe, and USA.
Source: Inter-American Development Bank/INTAL (INTradebid).

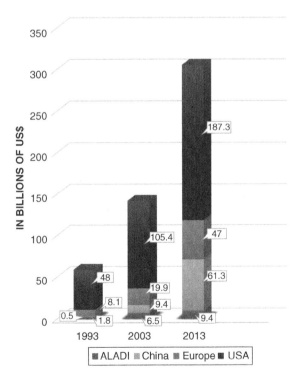

Figure 6.4 Mexico imports from rest of Latin America, China, Europe, and USA.
Source: Inter-American Development Bank/INTAL (INTradebid).

While local industry in South America has also been threatened by cheaper Chinese imports, at least until 2013 this was often compensated by an explosion in high-priced primary commodity exports to China, such as copper, fishmeal, iron ore, oil, and soy. In the particular case of Argentina and Brazil, for example, while both benefited from huge increases in soy exports, at higher prices, to China, and Brazil saw gains from oil, soy, and mineral exports (particularly iron ore), both South American countries also saw important domestic industries, such as shoes, textiles, and toys, threatened by cheaper Chinese imports.[13] In addition, Argentine and Brazilian exports of these products to other South American markets were also negatively impacted by Chinese competition. On the other hand, imports of intermediate and capital goods from China appear to have contributed to an increase in Brazil's share of high-technology exports.[14] For major commodity exporters that have small industrial sectors such as Chile, Ecuador, Paraguay, Peru, and Uruguay, enhanced trade with China has proven to be considerably more beneficial than threatening. This helps explain why Chile had no qualms about signing a free trade agreement with China in 2005, and Peru did so in 2009 (after both obtained exemptions from the Chinese for certain "sensitive" manufactured products).[15] Overall, export earnings from the commodities boom allowed many South American countries to pay down their debts and expand hard currency reserves, and helped to cushion the impact of the global financial meltdown of 2008–9.[16]

If the People's Republic of China was not a major trading partner for Latin America and the Caribbean before the twenty-first century, its role as a direct investor was even less significant. Tallying the full extent of Chinese investment in Latin America and the Caribbean is complicated by the fact that it is often funneled through tax havens such as Grand Cayman and the British Virgin Islands. It would appear, however, that Latin America and the Caribbean is now the destination for 15 percent of Chinese foreign direct investment by both state owned enterprises as well as private investors (versus 65 percent, for example, of Chinese investment that is directed to Asia).[17] The cumulative stock of Chinese direct investment in Latin American and Caribbean nations in the period between 2010 and 2014 is estimated to have been in the neighborhood of US$106 billion.[18]

Chinese investment in Latin America during a first phase that lasted from around 2001 to 2007 was dominated by Chinese state-owned enterprises motivated by a desire to ensure long-term access to strategic resources to preserve, if not enhance, China's place as the world's leading manufacturing country.[19] This explains how Peru became the top destination for Chinese mineral investment in Latin America.[20] It also explains heavy Chinese investment in Ecuador and Venezuela, given the oil reserves of both countries. A second stage after 2007 has seen more private-sector investors from China, as well as a diversification of activities to which investment is directed, particularly services (including electricity generation and transmission, telecommunications, and finance). Examples of this new wave of investment include a Chinese presence in the Brazilian automotive and computer sectors in an attempt to take advantage of

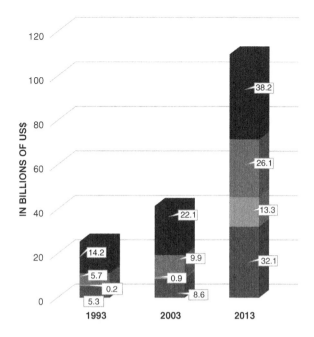

Figure 6.5 Andean Community* exports to rest of Latin America, China, Europe, and USA.

Source: Inter-American Development Bank/INTAL (INTradebid).
*Bolivia, Colombia, Ecuador, Peru, Venezuela.

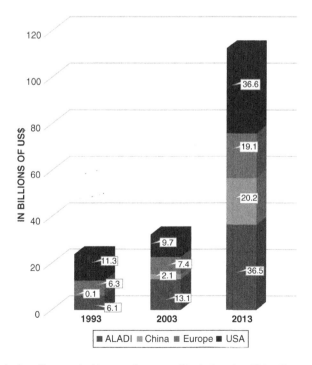

Figure 6.6 Andean Community* imports from rest of Latin America, China, Europe, and USA.

Source: Inter-American Development Bank/INTAL (INTradebid).
*Bolivia, Colombia, Ecuador, Peru, Venezuela.

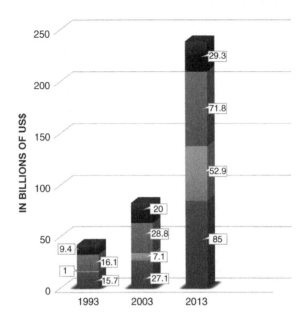

Figure 6.7 Mercosur* exports to rest of Latin America, China, Europe, and USA.

Source: Inter-American Development Bank/INTAL (INTradebid).
*Argentina, Brazil, Paraguay, Uruguay.

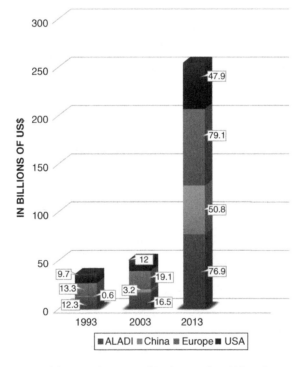

Figure 6.8 Mercosur* imports from rest of Latin America, China, Europe, and USA.

Source: Inter-American Development Bank/INTAL (INTradebid).
*Argentina, Brazil, Paraguay, Uruguay.

that country's huge internal market, protected by high tariff and non-tariff barriers. In 2012 the Commercial Bank of China (ICBC) purchased a majority of the shares of South African-based Standard Bank's Argentine operations (which had in 2006 acquired the venerable Bank of Boston, whose presence in Argentina dated back to the start of the twentieth century). Another example is China State Grid Corporation, which has poured some US$7 billion into Brazil for projects that include the construction of long-distance transmission lines emanating from the controversial Belo Monte hydroelectric dam in the Amazon. Brazil is currently the largest destination for Chinese foreign direct investment in Latin America.[21] Cumulative flows of Chinese foreign direct investment in Brazil are estimated to amount to about US$60 billion.[22]

Chinese construction companies have made major inroads in Latin America and the Caribbean by winning bids to build new highways and ports. "A key part of the Chinese approach has been to bring to the table in a coordinated fashion the company that will do the work and the associated Chinese institution that will finance the project, with a loan relatively free of conditions not directly tied to the project itself."[23] On other occasions a Chinese investor may self-finance an investment and secure repayment by securitizing the revenue earned from the export of a commodity such as petroleum.[24] This is a way to reduce risk, and explains how China is able to provide funding to countries that other lenders avoid. China has "loans-for-oil" agreements with Brazil, Ecuador, and Venezuela, representing two thirds of China's total lending commitments in Latin America.[25]

Although Chinese investment in Latin America has exploded since the beginning of the twenty-first century, China's total investment stock in the region is still low in comparison to more traditional commercial partners. For example, in 2012 the primary foreign investors in Peru were Spain (24.3 percent), the United States (13.3 percent), and South Africa (7.7 percent), while China came in tenth at 3.5 percent.[26] By the end of 2012, total U.S. foreign direct investment in Latin America and the Caribbean was approximately US$870 billion, versus about US$80 billion in total direct investment from China.[27] The European Union as a bloc currently has the largest investment stock in Latin America, ahead of the United States (which is number two). But China is already number three in Latin America, a truly amazing feat given that as recently as the year 2000 there was hardly any Chinese investment in the region.[28]

Since 2005, China has provided approximately US$141 billion in loans and lines of credit to Latin American governments through the China Export-Import Bank and the China Development Bank.[29] On an annualized basis, Chinese finance in Latin America is now larger than that coming from either the World Bank, the Inter-American Development Bank (IADB), or the United States Export-Import Bank, with the bulk of it going to natural resources and natural resource-linked infrastructure projects.[30] What makes Chinese loans especially attractive is that they rarely come with the type of conditionality requirements linked to internal policy changes often imposed by lenders such as the World Bank and the IADB. In the particular case of Argentina under the Kirchners,

Bolivarian Venezuela, and Ecuador under Rafael Correa, Chinese lending also compensated for the fact that these countries were largely shut out from borrowing on the international capital markets because of recent defaults. Interestingly, Chinese financing does not appear to be motivated by political alignments. This is in keeping with China's official policy stance that its relations with Latin America and the Caribbean are in the context of "South–South" solidarity and that it does not intervene in the internal affairs of other sovereign states.[31] Also noteworthy is the fact that loans, at least the biggest ones, are generally offered at market rates.[32]

The Caribbean has also been a beneficiary of heightened Chinese investment and lending, despite the tiny size of many of the island nations' economies and a lack of raw materials of interest to China. During his June 2012 tour of Latin America, then Chinese Prime Minister Wen Jiabao announced the establishment of a new US$5 billion development fund for regional infrastructure projects, to be housed at the Caribbean Development Bank for regional infrastructure projects.[33] This was followed by a March 2013 agreement between the Inter-American Development Bank and the Bank of China whereby Beijing agreed to contribute up to US$2 billion for development projects in the Caribbean, with the underlying presumption that the work would be carried out by Chinese construction companies.[34] Caribbean nations have also been the recipients of concessional loans from the China Export-Import Bank, including for sports stadiums in the Bahamas and Jamaica, schools in Barbados, and the prime minister's residence in

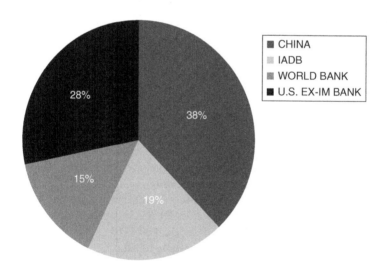

Figure 6.9 Lending to Latin America and the Caribbean in 2016 from China, IADB, World Bank, and U.S. Ex-Im Bank.

Source: Myers and Gallagher, 2017.

Trinidad and Tobago, as well as the foreign ministry building in Suriname.[35] The driving force for Chinese interest in the Caribbean seems to be a desire to project soft power and win over those governments that still diplomatically recognize Taiwan. Interestingly, while the United States of America has no embassies in the mini-states of the Eastern Caribbean, the People's Republic of China does in those with which it has established diplomatic relations.

The Chinese Challenge to U.S. Hegemony in Latin America and the Caribbean

Signs of the growing importance China placed on building its relationship with Latin America became apparent when then President Hu Jintao participated in the 2008 Asia Pacific Economic Council (APEC) summit in Lima, Peru. In conjunction with that visit, the Chinese government issued its first major policy paper on Latin America, making it official that Beijing intended to expand its engagement with the region on a broad variety of fronts, including trade, political and cultural ties, technology contracts, and military relations.[36] The release of the policy paper coincided with the severe economic contraction beginning in both North America and Europe. China was mostly spared this, allowing it to continue buying up huge amounts of South American commodities and thereby helping much of South America escape the deep recessions that engulfed developed economies in North America and Europe. In addition, many Chinese companies found themselves with large amounts of excess capital from export sales. Accordingly, they embarked on a global asset-buying spree in sectors deemed strategically important for the continued expansion of the Chinese economy, as well as greenfield investments and services.[37] Again, South America was a beneficiary of much of this new Chinese investment, while investors from North America and Europe were forced to retrench.

In 2009, China and Argentina reached a US$10.2 billion currency swap agreement to avoid the use of hard currency reserves in bilateral trade, and thereby lower transaction costs. This was followed by a US$11 billion swap in 2014, although this was more about making up for the shrinking foreign currency reserves of the Argentine Central Bank. Brazil signed a US$30 billion currency swap agreement with China's Central Bank in 2013. The Chinese view the swap agreements as a way to maintain steady trade with countries facing shrinking foreign reserves and as a method of internationalizing China's currency.[38] Of more concern to Washington, DC than currency swaps, however, was the announcement in July 2014 from the leaders of Brazil, Russia, India, China, and South Africa (i.e., the so-called BRICS countries) that they planned to set up a US$100 billion reserve fund that could serve as an alternative to the International Monetary Fund (IMF). The BRICS countries also established a US$50 billion development bank that could, in the future, serve as an alternative to the IMF's sister institution, the World Bank. For the time being, at least, Chinese finance appears to be complementing World Bank loans rather than supplanting them completely.[39]

The People's Republic of China hosted a summit in Beijing with all the member states of the Community of Latin American and Caribbean States (CELAC) in January 2015. At the summit, President Xi Jinping pledged to boost bilateral trade to US$500 billion and Chinese investment in Latin America to US$250 billion over the next decade, with another US$35 billion earmarked specifically for infrastructure investment in the region.[40] A China–CELAC Cooperation Plan was also issued that called for, *inter alia*, promoting industrialization, supporting the incorporation of small and medium-sized enterprises into global value chains, and jointly constructing industrial and science and technology parks to promote research and development in new technologies.

In 2015, China announced the creation of the Asian Infrastructure Investment Bank (AIIB). Although the AIIB will directly compete with multilateral institutions long dominated by the United States, such as the World Bank, its main objective appears to be reducing bottlenecks in infrastructure financing that arise from rigorous environmental and social requirements imposed by multilateral lenders. In practical terms, the time-consuming and expensive procedures that must be followed have meant that multilateral development banks now fund less than 1 percent of total infrastructure spending in developing countries.[41] Despite opposition from Washington, DC to its creation, many U.S. allies such as France, Germany, and the United Kingdom, as well as several Latin American countries, have joined the AIIB as capital contributing members.

Until the Chinese economic slowdown in China in 2013, the Chinese provided an attractive alternative of economic development, particularly in those countries that had grown weary of the market-oriented policies preached (although not always practiced) by Washington, DC. Several years into the twenty-first century, a "Beijing consensus" of economic priorities appeared as a rebuke to the market-oriented "Washington Consensus" policies pursued during the 1990s that had failed to address—and, in the eyes of some, may even have deepened—Latin America's deep-rooted problems of inequality, corruption, and stagnant growth.[42] More than a few policy-makers and opinion leaders in Latin America were emboldened by China's success to promote new development strategies in their own countries that included a more activist industrial policy and more generous social transfers.[43] In some cases, generous lending by China, combined with its voracious demand for commodities, allowed certain South American governments to avoid adopting unpopular but much needed policy reforms.

Evan Ellis believes the growing presence of China in Latin America and the Caribbean at the start of the twenty-first century contributed to the viability of regimes opposed to U.S. interests in the region in at least three ways: (1) as a major purchaser of commodities, such as petroleum, that generated important revenue streams; (2) as an important investment partner for populist governments, helping to compensate for policies that have pushed out Western investment; (3) as a purveyor of new technologies.[44] Leaders such as Hugo Chavez of

Venezuela, Evo Morales of Bolivia, and Rafael Correa of Ecuador were particularly aggressive in using China's interest in the region as a way to reinforce their embrace of an anti-U.S. alternative to economic development under the banner of the Bolivarian Alliance for Our America, or ALBA.[45] In addition, the existence of China as an alternative source of military assistance explains how 11 Latin American governments successfully resisted U.S. threats to cut off all military assistance unless they signed agreements not to turn over U.S. military personnel to the new International Criminal Court in The Hague.[46] There is nothing to indicate, however, that China was purposefully using its investment or lending to influence countries to take on a more hostile posture toward the United States. In any event, China is increasingly moving in the direction of targeting its lending and investment at Latin American nations with a track record of good governance. Given the worsening of Venezuela's economic crisis, for example, by the end of 2016 the Chinese had stopped making new loans to Caracas and direct investment had fallen to zero.[47]

The rising importance of China as a commercial power in Latin America and the Caribbean over the past decade and a half has raised alarm bells in Washington, DC. During a 2005 hearing of the Western Hemisphere Subcommittee of the House International Relations Committee, then Congressman Dan Burton of Indiana opined:

> I believe China's rising economic, political, and military influence in the Western Hemisphere poses serious challenges to the United States in the years ahead. And if we are not careful, Beijing's influence could easily unravel the region's hard won, U.S.-backed reforms to fight against corruption and human rights abuses, increase government transparency, and combat intellectual property violations, and the democracies that we see as fledgling democracies could be in real jeopardy.[48]

Statements such as these by U.S. politicians put China in an uncomfortable situation, as it feels compelled to respond by emphasizing that its interests in Latin America and the Caribbean are strictly commercial and that it has no intention to challenge traditional United States hegemony in the region. In addition, China is very cognizant of the fact that—at least for the foreseeable future—the reciprocal significance of Washington–Beijing relations is, for each, greater than their respective relationships with Latin America.[49] On the other hand, China does see its overseas finance and foreign direct investment as a way of reducing that tight bond, by diversifying away from its massive holdings of U.S. treasury bills.[50] In any event, China's ability to utilize its economic leverage over Latin American and Caribbean countries is tempered by the fact that almost all of them have alternative sources for investment, loans, imported inputs, and export markets.

Whatever misgivings may exist among some members of the U.S. Congress, the official line at the U.S. State Department that persisted under both the administrations of George W. Bush and Barack H. Obama was that China's growing presence in Latin America and the Caribbean should not be a matter of inordinate concern and was manageable. In fact, most U.S. officials felt China's economic engagement with Latin America could make positive contributions to the development of the region.[51] That helps explain why the United States dropped its previous opposition to China becoming a shareholder of the Inter-American Development Bank (IADB), as part of a broader agreement with China to support Beijing's expanded integration into the liberal international order long championed by the United States.[52]

In early April 2006, then U.S. Assistant Secretary of State for Hemispheric Affairs Thomas Shannon visited Beijing to meet with Chinese officials, in order to engage in a bilateral dialogue about Latin America, weeks before Hu Jintao's first visit to the United States as Chinese president. Subsequent meetings between Shannon and his Chinese counterparts took place in Washington, DC in 2007 and again in Beijing in 2008, and the bilateral meetings continued into the Obama administration. The main objective of these meetings, institutionalized under the aegis of the U.S.–China Strategic and Economic Dialogue, was for each side to make clear its interests and policies as a way of increasing transparency and avoiding miscalculations.[53] When the bilateral dialogue began in 2006, one of the main U.S. concerns was China's growing relationship with Hugo Chavez's Venezuela, while the Chinese were most concerned with potential U.S. interference in Cuba's political transition process.[54] The United States used the dialogue to convey a message of concern and of limits to China's increasing engagement in the region. It was viewed by the Americans as a mechanism to shape and to influence China's role in the region.[55]

Despite the efforts of the U.S. State Department under the administrations of both George W. Bush and Barack H. Obama to downplay the more alarmist viewpoints emanating from Capitol Hill and some Inside-the-Beltway think tanks, there are aspects of China's growing commercial presence in the Americas that do raise potential concerns. For example, governments that are heavily indebted to Chinese state banks may be pressured into, for example, voting in the UN in ways that support Beijing's position on issues such as sovereignty disputes over the Spratly islands in the South China Sea or the human rights situation in Tibet and Xinjiang. This pressure to toe the Chinese line could even extend to issues such as reform of the UN Security Council, where governments economically dependent on China might vote against giving a fellow Latin American nation, for example, a permanent seat on the Security Council. It is also not unrealistic to expect that China might someday feel compelled to engage in economic retaliation against countries where its investment interests are jeopardized, despite oft-expressed assurances from China that it only seeks peaceful coexistence in the context of South–South cooperation. Such a scenario is heightened by the fact that much of the Chinese investment in South America is centered on extractive industries such as mining or petroleum, which are often tempting targets for populist governments to nationalize or tax exorbitantly.

Of more direct concern to the national security of the United States is the increasingly important role played by Chinese companies in constructing and operating the telecommunication networks of many Latin American and Caribbean countries, which carry sensitive and valuable information that can be exploited for commercial espionage, financial crimes, or attacks against a nation's economy and critical infrastructures.[56] There have also been major Chinese acquisitions of electricity generation plants and transmission lines, cargo handling operations at air and sea ports, and banks. In the event of a future conflict between China and the United States,

> Chinese commercial facilities in all of these areas would represent potential assets for representatives of the Chinese state seeking to use those assets to gather intelligence, conduct blackmail, introduce agents or military goods into the region, disrupt informational, financial and physical flows, resupply forces, or a range of other activities.[57]

For Evan Ellis, China's growing commercial presence in Latin America implies that the Western Hemisphere can no longer be considered an automatic U.S. sanctuary in any potential future conflict with China, and the United States could be forced to devote significant resources to protecting its operations there, as well as in an Asian theater of operations.[58]

The important commercial role that China has assumed in Latin America and the Caribbean over the past decade raises questions as to its long-term geo-political ramifications. This is particularly relevant if one considers that the rise of the United States as a hegemonic power in the Western Hemisphere was preceded by an explosion in U.S. commercial activity. In fact, by the end of the nineteenth century, the United States had displaced Great Britain as the dominant economic power throughout Latin America, with the exception of the Southern Cone of South America. Over the past decade, China has also increased sales of sophisticated military equipment to certain South American nations and expanded its training missions for South American military personnel as well as its participation in joint military exercises.[59] A potentially more ominous phase was inaugurated in February 2015 when Argentina and China signed a series of agreements to co-produce boats for the Argentine Navy and amphibious armored personal carriers for the Argentine Army, offer strategic space cooperation to facilitate China's communication with its satellites and spacecraft in the Southern Hemisphere, and integrate Chinese-made fighter aircraft into the Argentine Air Force.[60]

Conclusion

For an adherent of the realist school of international relations such as John Mearsheimer, China's growing presence in Latin America and the Caribbean poses a serious threat to continued U.S. hegemony in the Western Hemisphere and will inevitably lead to military tensions. That is because, for realists, an established hegemon such as the United States will inevitably attempt to check a country such as China, which ostensibly only aspires to be a regional hegemon in Asia, because of fears that the latter country may eventually cause trouble in the fearful great power's own "backyard."[61] At the same time, China has no other option but to challenge U.S. hegemony, even in the Western Hemisphere. That will remain true whether China becomes a democratic country deeply enmeshed in the global economy or remains autocratic, because amassing ever more hegemonic power is the best way for any state to guarantee its own survival.[62] The great irony with this viewpoint is that much of the defense preparation and modernization for which the United States will need to pay in order to counter the realist threat of inevitable conflict with China will require continued willingness from the Beijing government to purchase U.S. debt.[63]

The neo-realist perspective is less pessimistic, as the United States and China are both motivated by the need to achieve security through a balance of power. Hence, if the United States is willing to live with China becoming a regional hegemon in East Asia, then there is no reason for China to challenge U.S. hegemony—however diminished from historical levels—within the Western Hemisphere. Facilitating such a benign outcome is the fact that a newly energy self-sufficient United States is unlikely to clash with China over competition for energy resources. The U.S. economy is also nowhere near as dependent as the Chinese on imported minerals from South America. More importantly, the Chinese do not claim any territory in the Americas. Any competition that may exist between China and the United States for influence in Latin America and the Caribbean is centered on different visions of the international liberal order and competing models of political governance, and this competition has not involved—and is unlikely to involve—core strategic interests that would lead to outright conflict.[64]

Regardless of whether the realist or neo-realist perspective is correct, China would not be the first country in history to pose a challenge to U.S. hegemony in the Western Hemisphere. According to Mearsheimer, the real danger that the United States faced in the nineteenth century—and continued to face in the twentieth—was the possibility of an anti-American pact between a European great power and a state in the Western Hemisphere that might ultimately be powerful enough to challenge U.S. hegemony in the Americas and adversely affect American security.[65] Those threats—whether actual or perceived—included Germany in both World Wars I and II and the Soviet Union during the Cold War. The Argentine political scientist Gonzalo Paz would add Japan of the 1980s to this list, although the Japanese example also provides a cautionary tale against overreaction to the current Chinese "incursions" in Latin America and the Caribbean.

One important development that could delay what seems like an inevitable realist showdown between the United States and China on the question of hegemony in the Western Hemisphere is the post-2013 economic contraction in China, which has caused global commodity prices to collapse and led to a sharp drop in South American exports to China. At the same time, as commercially viable opportunities for infrastructure, housing, and other construction projects become more scarce in China, and as Chinese banks come under pressure to offset non-performing loans at home with commercially viable ones abroad, these banks, as well as Chinese construction firms and even manufacturers, could become more aggressive in seeking overseas markets such as in Latin America and the Caribbean.[66] Latin American countries will likely react defensively as threats to local manufacturing and construction firms are no longer outweighed by increased commodity exports to China at ever higher prices. There are already examples of Latin American and Caribbean countries standing up to China, including a plethora of unfair trade practice measures created by Argentina and Brazil with regard to Chinese imports.[67] Brazil enacted prohibitions against foreign acquisition of rural land in 2010, while Argentina adopted a similar measure the following year. In both cases, the prohibitions are directed primarily against Chinese overseas agriculture investments. Many Latin American governments have also limited Chinese firms' ability to utilize their compatriots instead of local labor in major infrastructure projects financed by China. Another important check on the future rise of China's power and influence in Latin America is its current repressive internal political model, which is not attractive in a region of the world that spent many years struggling to overcome authoritarianism and brutal military dictatorships. For China to dethrone the United States as regional hegemon in the Western Hemisphere, it would have to be able to offer something superior to the current liberal political and economic order long propagated by the United States.

As noted earlier, it is useful to recall the fears that were raised in the United States after Japan became the world's second largest economy in the early 1970s (a position China took over in 2010, relegating the Japanese to third place). Academics and pundits in the United States during the late 1970s and 1980s made dire predictions that Japan and its superior state-centered model would soon overtake the United States and bury much of its manufacturing industries. Japan was often portrayed in the media as a potential economic rival or adversary rather than a close ally of the United States. By the early 1990s, Japan had even become a significant economic actor in Latin America and, by some measures, was already the largest source of capital for the region.[68] Accordingly, some commentators argued that the United States and Japan would inevitably clash because of the significant threat posed by Japanese trading companies and multinational enterprises to American investment throughout Latin America. "[T]he pursuit of aggressive policies indirectly linking economic aid, recycling, and private investment to Japanese economic influence could in effect represent a challenge to U.S. interests and policy, especially in Latin America."[69] In hindsight, all of this now seems laughable— Japan soon entered a long period of economic stagnation in the late 1990s, from which it has yet to recover, with a concomitant retrenchment of Japanese lending and major investment in Latin America.

There are, of course, major differences between China today and Japan in the 1990s. One of the most important is that Japan was already a mature and highly developed economy at the end of the twentieth century, while China still has tens of millions of potential new consumers to incorporate into its middle class. Therefore, over the long run, Chinese appetite for Latin American commodities is far from being satiated. The importance of China for most Latin American countries also reflects a paradigm shift that will only increase in the decade ahead should predictions that China will replace the United States as the world's largest economy be proved correct. On the other hand, the Communist Party's ability to retain power and ensure a stable transition to a less authoritarian model that will not result in huge economic and political upheaval in China remains an open question. China's impressive economic expansion of the past two decades, for example, has generated a large income divide between the countryside and urban centers, not to mention intolerable levels of environmental degradation and air pollution. All of this is breeding widespread resentment and protest movements throughout China that the Communist Party may not be able to contain.

A more optimistic scenario of what could result from China's increasing presence in Latin America and the Caribbean is, of course, supplied by international liberalism. If the United States continues to reach out to China in an attempt to make it a key partner in the existing international economic order, China's activities in the Western Hemisphere could actually complement and support major U.S. policy objectives. One thing that would help tremendously in facilitating such a partnership would be a peaceful transition away from authoritarian rule to more representative democracy in China. For the moment, this appears to be a pipe dream. Even so, both China and the United States currently have a mutual interest in promoting political stability and respect for the rule of law throughout Latin America and the Caribbean in order to safeguard major investments. Both can also cooperate in efforts to facilitate economic development and combat transnational criminal networks. The Chinese also have a strong incentive to support the global liberal economic order, as this facilitated the country's rapid export-led growth over the past two decades. For China to become an important piece in supporting that order would also be a vindication of international regime theory, as it would demonstrate a shift from past Chinese behavior and a redefinition of their national interests, thereby preserving a global international economic order long supported by the United States. An ascendant and more democratic China that embraces this liberal economic order would also resolve the dilemma posed by hegemonic stability theory as China would eventually step into the shoes of the hegemon offering public goods once filled by the United States.

Another optimistic outlook on what China's increased presence in Latin America and the Caribbean portends is offered by David Lake, who rejects a characterization of the traditional U.S. role in the Western Hemisphere as ever having been hegemonic, preferring his theory of variegated hierarchy. For Lake, the more deeply China is integrated into the current world order, the less likely it is to challenge U.S. authority in the future, even if its coercive capabilities grow. "The hope is that China can be like France in the Western system: a difficult but ultimately loyal ally."[70]

Notes

1 Jiang Shixue, "The Chinese Foreign Policy Perspective," in *China's Expansion into the Western Hemisphere: Implications for Latin America and the United States*, ed. Riordan Roett et al. (Washington, DC: Brookings Institute, 2008), 28. Among other things, the Truman administration "issued a letter to the Latin American embassies in Washington urging them to follow a common policy under the aegis of the United States." Ibid at 29.

2 According to one Chinese scholar, "[t]his intellectual insight established, for the first time in China's history, a link between the internal politics of a Latin American country and the political future of the Communist Party of China (CPC), breaking away from the days when the region was merely viewed as a potential partner in anti-American campaigns." Xiang Lanxin, "An Alternative Chinese View," in *China's Expansion into the Western Hemisphere: Implications for Latin America and the United States*, ed. Riordan Roett et al. (Washington, DC: Brookings Institute, 2008), 49.

3 But for Costa Rica and Panama, all the other Central American countries (i.e., Belize, El Salvador, Guatemala, Honduras, and Nicaragua) currently maintain diplomatic relations with Taiwan. In the Caribbean, Taiwan is still recognized by the Dominican Republic, Haiti, Saint Kitts and Nevis, Saint Lucia, and Saint Vincent and the Grenadines.

4 The Sandinista government actually established diplomatic relations with the People's Republic of China in the 1980s, but they were broken in favor of Taipei when Violeta Barrios de Chamorro became president in 1991 and have yet to be restored despite the return of Daniel Ortega and the Sandinistas to power in 2007. That has not prevented Nicaragua from enjoying good economic relations with Beijing, however, including a controversial plan by a Chinese businessman to build a new canal across Nicaragua.

5 R. Evan Ellis, *China in Latin America: The Whats and Wherefores* (Boulder, CO: Lynne Rienner Publishers, 2009), 271. China also purchased US$300 million in Costa Rican bonds in 2008 and in 2009 and launched a US$1.5 billion mixed capital venture between the Chinese National Petroleum Corporation (CNPC) and Costa Rica's national oil refinery company for the construction of new refineries. Carol Wise, "Playing Both Sides of the Pacific: Latin America's Free Trade Agreements (FTAs) with China," *Pacific Affairs*, Vol. 89, No. 1 (2016): 89. In 2013, President Xi Jinping visited Costa Rica and pledged US$400 million in loans to extend a road from central Costa Rica to its main seaport and US$100 million to replace public transportation vehicles. Barbara Stallings, "Chinese Foreign Aid to Latin America: Trying to Win Friends and Influence People," in *The Political Economy of China–Latin America Relations in the New Millennium: Brave New World*, ed. Margaret Myers et al. (New York: Routledge, 2017), 86.

6 Ironically, Donald Trump's decision to accept a congratulatory telephone call from Taiwanese President Tsai Ing-wen shortly after his election victory appears to have incentivized Beijing's efforts to persuade the Central American countries to switch diplomatic recognition, thereby embarrassing the United States in a part of the world long synonymous with U.S. hegemony. As former Mexican Ambassador to China Jorge Guajardo noted, "China sees an opportunity to establish a beachfront next to the U.S. at an important time when the U.S. is threatening them in the South China Sea." Ben Bland and James Fredrick, "Trip to Central America Underscores Taipei Tension," *Financial Times*, January 7/8, 2017: 4.

7 Cynthia J. Arnson, Introduction to *Reaching Across the Pacific: Latin America and Asia in the New Century*, ed. Cynthia J. Arnson et al. (Washington, DC: Wilson Center, 2014), 10.

8 Jiang Shixue, "The Chinese Foreign Policy Perspective," in *China's Expansion into the Western Hemisphere: Implications for Latin America and the United States*, ed. Riordan Roett et al. (Washington, DC: Brookings Institute, 2008), 34.

9 Ted Piccone, "The Geopolitics of China's Rise in Latin America," *Geo-economics and Global Issues Paper 2* (Washington, DC: Brookings Institute, November 2016), 2. See also Juan Gabriel Tokatlian, "A View from Latin America," in *China's Expansion into the Western Hemisphere: Implications for Latin America and the United States*, ed. Riordan Roett et al. (Washington, DC: Brookings Institute, 2008), 62: "The main goal of the countries in Latin America is to foster development and increase international autonomy, consistent with the view that domestic prosperity and national security are more likely to prevail in an international system with a wider distribution and diffusion of power."

10 Cecilia Posadas Perez, "China and Mexico in the US Market," in *Sino-Latin American Economic Relations*, ed. K.C. Fung et al. (New York: Routledge, 2012), 262 and 265. The loss in Mexican competitiveness in apparel exports in the United States is particularly ironic given that it was Chinese textile products that lost what had been a dominant position in the U.S. market until NAFTA.

11 Carol Wise, "China and Latin America's Emerging Economies: New Realities amid Old Challenges," *Latin America Policy*, Vol. 7, No. 1 (2016): 33. During the period 2000–2006, 72 percent of Mexican exports were directly threatened by China in world markets, a figure that fell to 24 percent from 2008 to 2013. Kevin P. Gallagher, *The China Triangle: Latin America's China Boom and the Fate of the Washington Consensus* (New York: Oxford University Press, 2016), 170.

12 Steve Johnson, "Chinese Wages Play Catch-Up with the West after Salaries Triple in a Decade," *Financial Times*, February 27, 2017: 1. At the start of the twenty-first century, hourly wages in Mexico were about three times more than those in China. Luis Alberto Moreno, Preface to *Reaching Across the Pacific: Latin America and Asia in the New Century*, ed. Cynthia J. Arnson et al. (Washington, DC: Wilson Center, 2014), 3.

13 An interesting aspect of Argentina's soy exports to China is that this commodity was not produced in significant quantities in Argentina prior to the 1990s. In addition, unlike minerals or oil, soy is a renewable bio-commodity resilient to drought and whose derivatives include oil, pellets for animal feed, flour, and biodiesel. Gonzalo S. Paz, "Argentina and Asia: China's Reemergence, Argentina's Recovery," in *Reaching Across the Pacific: Latin America and Asia in the New Century*, ed. Cynthia J. Arnson et al. (Washington, DC: Wilson Center, 2014), 162. Furthermore, the Argentine soy industry utilizes a sophisticated "direct planting" method of production which minimizes soil erosion, reduces expensive labor costs and the heavy use of fossil fuels, and reduces the use of herbicides. Ibid at 164. Soy production has also fostered backward linkages within Argentina to a sophisticated support industry that has created new job opportunities in rural Argentina. Ibid at 165. For example, computerized "big data" from on-the-ground sensors and GPS feeds are used to alert and activate soil and plant treatments as needed.

14 Ernesto Dos Santos and Soledad Zignago, "The Impact of the Emergence of China on Brazilian International Trade," in *Sino-Latin American Economic Relations*, ed. K.C. Fung et al. (New York: Routledge, 2012), 245 and 247. It should be noted, however, that Brazil's contribution to the share of global high technology remains small.

15 "The overriding narrative in the literature on China's motives for pursuing FTAs in Latin America rests largely on cross-Pacific diplomacy." Carol Wise, "Playing Both Sides of the Pacific: Latin America's Free Trade Agreements (FTAs) with China," *Pacific Affairs*, Vol. 89, No. 1 (2016): 88. According to Wise, however, another important objective was China's concern over resource security and its need for Latin America's abundant raw materials to fuel its growth. Ibid. For Chile and Peru, the specific motivation for a free trade agreement with China is linked to efforts to diversify exports away from unprocessed minerals to non-traditional, higher value-added products as well as to attract non-mineral resource related investment. Ibid at 89.

16 Cynthia J. Arnson, Introduction to *Reaching Across the Pacific: Latin America and Asia in the New Century*, ed. Cynthia J. Arnson et al. (Washington, DC: Wilson Center, 2014), 12.

17 Carol Wise, "China and Latin America's Emerging Economies: New Realities amid Old Challenges," *Latin America Policy*, Vol. 7, No. 1 (2016): 27. It is important to underscore that most of China's foreign direct investment is in developed economies, and no Latin American country is among the top ten destinations. David Dollar, "China's Investment in Latin America," *Geo-economics and Global Issues Paper 4* (Washington, DC: Brookings Institute, January 2017), 3.

18 David Dollar, "China's Investment in Latin America," *Geo-economics and Global Issues Paper 4* (Washington, DC: Brookings Institute, January 2017), 1.

19 Gaston Fornés and Alan Butt Philip, *The China–Latin America Axis* (Houndmills: Palgrave Macmillan, 2012), 75–6 and 96.

20 Cynthia A. Sanborn and Alexis Yong, "Peru's Economic Boom and the Asian Connection," in *Reaching Across the Pacific: Latin America and Asia in the New Century*, ed. Cynthia J. Arnson et al. (Washington, DC: Wilson Center, 2014), 65. Interestingly, it is precisely the mining sector that has sparked the greatest conflicts—oftentimes violent—with environmentalists, local communities, and indigenous groups.

21 David Dollar, "China's Investment in Latin America," *Geo-economics and Global Issues Paper 4* (Washington, DC: Brookings Institute, January 2017), 4 and 5.

22 Rolando Avendano, Angel Melguizo, and Sean Miner, *Chinese FDI in Latin America: New Trends with Global Implications* (Washington, DC: Atlantic Council & Paris: OECD Development Center, June 2017), 6.

23 R. Evan Ellis, *China on the Ground in Latin America: Challenges for the Chinese and Impacts on the Region* (New York: Palgrave Macmillan, 2014), 47.

24 R. Evan Ellis, *China on the Ground in Latin America: Challenges for the Chinese and Impacts on the Region* (New York: Palgrave Macmillan, 2014), 57. These loans are structured in such a way that payment is based on the proceeds obtained from the oil at spot market prices on the actual day of sale. Kevin P. Gallagher, *The China Triangle: Latin America's China Boom and the Fate of the Washington Consensus* (New York: Oxford University Press, 2016), 78.

25 Kevin P. Gallagher and Amos Irwin, "China's Economic Statecraft in Latin America: Evidence from China's Policy Banks," in *The Political Economy of China–Latin America Relations in the New Millennium: Brave New World*, ed. Margaret Myers et al. (New York: Routledge, 2017), 59. Gallagher and Amos point out that Venezuela has negotiated five such loans since 2007, totaling US$36 billion, while Brazil signed one for US$10 billion in 2009 and Ecuador initially signed a US$1 billion deal in 2009, followed by a second in 2010, with two more in 2011 totaling US$3 billion.

26 Cynthia A. Sanborn and Alexis Yong, "Peru's Economic Boom and the Asian Connection," in *Reaching Across the Pacific: Latin America and Asia in the New Century*, ed. Cynthia J. Arnson et al. (Washington, DC: Wilson Center, 2014), 76 and 82. By 2012 China had become the largest single investor in Peru's mining sector, representing about 20 percent of total foreign direct investment in that specific sector.

27 Margaret Myers and Carol Wise, eds., *The Political Economy of China–Latin America Relations in the New Millennium: Brave New World* (New York: Routledge, 2017), 9.

28 Kevin P. Gallagher, *The China Triangle: Latin America's China Boom and the Fate of the Washington Consensus* (New York: Oxford University Press, 2016), 50. The pattern of Chinese foreign investment in Latin America, at least initially, largely tracked the patterns of trade, with more than 94 percent of all Chinese FDI into Latin America going into the energy, mining, and food sectors. Ibid at 51.

29 Kevin P. Gallagher, *The China Triangle: Latin America's China Boom and the Fate of the Washington Consensus* (New York: Oxford University Press, 2016), 7.

30 Kevin P. Gallagher and Amos Irwin, "China's Economic Statecraft in Latin America: Evidence from China's Policy Banks," in *The Political Economy of China–Latin America Relations in the New Millennium: Brave New World*, ed. Margaret Myers et al. (New York: Routledge, 2017), 51 and 54. Given the pattern of activities for which Chinese lending has been earmarked to date, it should not be a surprise that some 95 percent of lending has been concentrated on four countries: Venezuela, Ecuador, Argentina, and Brazil. Harold Trinkunas, "Renminbi Diplomacy? The Limits of China's Influence on Latin America's Domestic Politics," *Geo-economics and Global Issues Paper 3* (Washington, DC: Brookings Institute, November 2016), 7.

31 Harold Trinkunas, "Renminbi Diplomacy?: The Limits of China's Influence on Latin America's Domestic Politics," *Geo-economics and Global Issues Paper 3* (Washington, DC: Brookings Institute, November 2016), 8. Chinese loans have, however, had an impact on Latin American politics by further enabling the region's chief executives to act independently of other branches of government, as China's loans tend to focus on government-to-government agreements or on state-owned enterprises, and such negotiations are generally handled by the executive branch. Ibid at 20.

32 Kevin P. Gallagher and Amos Irwin, "China's Economic Statecraft in Latin America: Evidence from China's Policy Banks," in *The Political Economy of China–Latin America Relations in the New Millennium: Brave New World*, ed. Margaret Myers et al. (New York: Routledge, 2017), 51. According to Gallagher and Irwin, when Chinese rates are measurably more favorable than those offered by international financial institutions or private-sector banks, it is due to China's commodity-based risk instruments and the way the Chinese structure financing between sovereign governments and Chinese state-owned enterprises. Ibid. In addition, some small loans, most of which are categorized as foreign aid, do carry concessional or subsidized interest rates. Ibid at 54.

33 R. Evan Ellis, *China on the Ground in Latin America: Challenges for the Chinese and Impacts on the Region* (New York: Palgrave Macmillan, 2014), 59. As part of a strategy to increase its influence in the region, China joined the Caribbean Development Bank in 1998 as a non-regional member. Initially taking a 5.77 percent capital stake, China contributed US$1 million in 2002 to establish a technical cooperation fund. Jiang Shixue, "The Chinese Foreign Policy Perspective," in *China's Expansion into the Western Hemisphere: Implications for Latin America and the United States*, ed. Riordan Roett et al. (Washington, DC: Brookings Institute, 2008), 36.

34 R. Evan Ellis, *China on the Ground in Latin America: Challenges for the Chinese and Impacts on the Region* (New York: Palgrave Macmillan, 2014), 59.

35 Barbara Stallings, "Chinese Foreign Aid to Latin America: Trying to Win Friends and Influence People," in *The Political Economy of China–Latin America Relations in the New Millennium: Brave New World*, ed. Margaret Myers et al. (New York: Routledge, 2017), 80. Stallings notes that these types of loans typically have an amortization period of 20 years, with ten years of grace.

36 R. Evan Ellis, *China on the Ground in Latin America: Challenges for the Chinese and Impacts on the Region* (New York: Palgrave Macmillan, 2014), 7. Hu Jintao had already attended an APEC Summit in Chile and visited a number of other Latin American countries in November 2004, during which he promised substantial increases in trade and investment. Two months later, Vice-President Zeng Qinghong made a follow up tour of Latin America. After Hu Jintao's visit to Latin America in November 2008, then Vice-President Xi Jinping visited the region in early 2009.

37 R. Evan Ellis, *China on the Ground in Latin America: Challenges for the Chinese and Impacts on the Region* (New York: Palgrave Macmillan, 2014), 7.

38 Yang Zhimin, "Policy Choice in China–Latin America Trade Cooperation in Response to the Financial Crisis," in *China–Latin America Relations: Review and Analysis*, ed. He Shuangrong (Beijing: Social Sciences Academic Press, 2012), 108.

39 See Kevin P. Gallagher, *The China Triangle: Latin America's China Boom and the Fate of the Washington Consensus* (New York: Oxford University Press, 2016), 72. "The vast majority of Chinese finance in [Latin America] goes into large infrastructure, energy, and mining projects. Finance from banks like the World Bank and IADB span a wider range of governmental, social, and environmental purposes. The Chinese banks channel 87 percent of their loans into energy, mining, and infrastructure sectors. Only 29 percent of IADB loans and 34 percent of World Bank loans go to those sectors. Instead, the IADB and World Bank direct over a third of their loans toward the health, social, and environmental sectors, which do not receive Chinese investment."

40 Kevin P. Gallagher, *The China Triangle: Latin America's China Boom and the Fate of the Washington Consensus* (New York: Oxford University Press, 2016), 11. In terms of infrastructure, China committed US$20 billion in special loans for Latin American infrastructure cooperation, US$10 billion in preferential loans, and US$5 billion earmarked for the China–CELAC Cooperation Fund. Ibid at 87 and 171.

41 David Dollar, "China's Investment in Latin America," *Geo-economics and Global Issues Paper 4* (Washington, DC: Brookings Institute, January 2017), 12. Dollar points out that the AIIB approach differs from that of the more risk-averse World Bank, for example, by avoiding detailed regulations that make implementation of projects slow and bureaucratic.

42 R. Evan Ellis, *China in Latin America: The Whats and Wherefores* (Boulder, CO: Lynne Rienner Publishers, 2009), 28. See, e.g., Alfredo Toro Hardy, *The World Turned Upside Down: The Complex Partnership between China and Latin America* (Singapore: World Scientific Publishing Company, 2013), 14. Among the negative impacts of the Washington Consensus "were the high unemployment and dramatic social costs resulting from the reduction or disappearance of the social safety nets provided by the State, there was also the loss of important parcels of the national wealth, through the privatization of state industries and public utilities, and the abandonment of endogenous research and development efforts." In contrast to the inflexible mandates of the Washington Consensus, Toro Hardy claims the Beijing Consensus allows for trial and error. "While clearly defining a goal to aim at through strategic planning, [China] allowed itself an ample tactical room of maneuvering, leaving space to react to undesirable effects or changing circumstances." Ibid at 21.

43 Rolando Avedaño and Jeff Dayton-Johnson, "Central America, China, and the US: What Prospects for Development," in *The Political Economy of China–Latin America Relations in the New Millennium: Brave New World*, ed. Margaret Myers et al. (New York: Routledge, 2017), 214.

44 R. Evan Ellis, *China in Latin America: The Whats and Wherefores* (Boulder, CO: Lynne Rienner Publishers, 2009), 29.

45 Ted Piccone, "The Geopolitics of China's Rise in Latin America," *Geo-economics and Global Issues Paper 2* (Washington, DC: Brookings Institute, November 2016), 6. The actions of the governments of Bolivia, Ecuador, Nicaragua, and Venezuela over the past decade suggest that having China as an alternative market and source of credit and investment emboldened these states not to pursue policies advanced by the United States on issues such as democratic governance, human rights, and free trade. R. Evan Ellis, *China on the Ground in Latin America: Challenges for the Chinese and Impacts on the Region* (New York: Palgrave Macmillan, 2014), 207.

46 R. Evan Ellis, *China in Latin America: The Whats and Wherefores* (Boulder, CO: Lynne Rienner Publishers, 2009), 284. Those 11 countries had refused to comply with provisions of the American Servicemen's Protection Act of 2002 that required recipients of U.S. military assistance to exempt U.S. soldiers from being handed over for prosecution before the International Criminal Court of Justice or be cut off from participating in the International Military and Education Training (IMET) program. The U.S. government did impose the sanction, but in an admission of defeat exempted these countries in November 2004 and restored their eligibility to participate.

47 David Dollar, "China's Investment in Latin America," *Geo-economics and Global Issues Paper 4* (Washington, DC: Brookings Institute, January 2017), 8 and 9. Another reason why China is increasingly moving away from investing and lending to countries with poor governance is the fact that new oil and natural gas resources are being developed in countries with less risky political and economic environments. Ibid at 17–18.

48 Jiang Shixue, "The Chinese Foreign Policy Perspective," in *China's Expansion into the Western Hemisphere: Implications for Latin America and the United States*, ed. Riordan Roett et al. (Washington, DC: Brookings Institute, 2008), 39–40. Disquiet over China's expanding presence in the Western Hemisphere has also been accompanied by growing concern about China's resurgence as a global power. For example, in the Pentagon's Quadrennial Defense Review for 2006, China was already judged to be the country with the greatest potential to compete militarily with the United States. Riordan Roett and Guadalupe Paz, eds., *China's Expansion into the Western Hemisphere: Implications for Latin America and the United States* (Washington, DC: Brookings Institute, 2008), 5.

49 Juan Gabriel Tokatlian, "A View from Latin America," in *China's Expansion into the Western Hemisphere: Implications for Latin America and the United States*, ed. Riordan Roett et al. (Washington, DC: Brookings Institute, 2008), 61. Throughout the Bush and Obama administrations, China's goal and main challenge was to deepen its relations with the countries of Latin America without irritating Washington, DC. Ibid at 60. One example of how this sensitivity has played itself out was the decision by the Saudi Arabian company SABIC in 2012 to withdraw from a joint venture with the Chinese company Sinopec to build a US$5.3 billion methanol refinery in Trinidad and Tobago because of U.S. opposition. R. Evan Ellis, *China on the Ground in Latin America: Challenges for the Chinese and Impacts on the Region* (New York: Palgrave Macmillan, 2014), 141. China also never followed up on President Nestor Kirchner's "Grand Strategy" in 2004 to liberate Argentina from IMF dependency by obtaining Chinese loans to pay off its IMF debt. "Hu Jintao decided not to risk China's truly strategic relationship—that with the United States—with a distracting move on the periphery of the global game." Gonzalo S. Paz, "Argentina and Asia: China's Reemergence, Argentina's Recovery," in *Reaching Across the Pacific: Latin America and Asia in the New Century*, ed. Cynthia J. Arnson et al. (Washington, DC: Wilson Center, 2014), 160 and 181.

50 Kevin P. Gallagher, *The China Triangle: Latin America's China Boom and the Fate of the Washington Consensus* (New York: Oxford University Press, 2016), 171.

51 R. Evan Ellis, "Cooperation and Mistrust Between China and the U.S. in Latin America," in *The Political Economy of China–Latin America Relations in the New Millennium: Brave New World*, ed. Margaret Myers et al. (New York: Routledge, 2017), 32. For example, Ellis explains that increased revenues from exports to China in the past helped to contribute to economic growth in Latin America and provided new resources of funding for much needed improvements to infrastructure, health care, education, and security.

52 Beijing made an unsuccessful bid in 1993 to become a shareholder of the IADB. The decision to accept the People's Republic of China as an IADB shareholder in 2009 was the result of intense lobbying by the IADB's president, Luis Alberto Moreno, who felt the country's inclusion would attract more capital and enhance the institution's visibility. Although China's membership was long resisted by Japan, which had been the only Asian member of the IADB until South Korea joined in 2005, the Obama administration eventually convinced Tokyo to drop its objections. R. Evan Ellis, *China in Latin America: The Whats and Wherefores* (Boulder, CO: Lynne Rienner Publishers, 2009), 8, fn. 16.

53 Gonzalo Sebastian Paz, "China, United States and Hegemonic Challenge in Latin America: An Overview and Some Lessons from Previous Instances of Hegemonic

Challenge in the Region," *The China Quarterly*, Vol. 209 (March 2012): 23. See, also, R. Evan Ellis, "Cooperation and Mistrust Between China and the U.S. in Latin America," in *The Political Economy of China–Latin America Relations in the New Millennium: Brave New World*, ed. Margaret Myers et al. (New York: Routledge, 2017), 35. "The dialogue seeks to avoid misunderstanding and build political trust between the U.S. and China as the latter expands its engagement with the Western Hemisphere" and allows "the U.S. and China to explore possible areas of cooperation in the region."

54 Gonzalo Sebastian Paz, "China, United States and Hegemonic Challenge in Latin America: An Overview and Some Lessons from Previous Instances of Hegemonic Challenge in the Region," *The China Quarterly*, Vol. 209 (March 2012): 23. Many commentators have suggested that U.S. concerns over Chinese involvement in Venezuela were always overblown. See, e.g., Juan Gabriel Tokatlian, "A View from Latin America," in *China's Expansion into the Western Hemisphere: Implications for Latin America and the United States*, ed. Riordan Roett et al. (Washington, DC: Brookings Institute, 2008), 73. "China does not seem interested in a high-profile relationship with Venezuela should it have a detrimental impact on Sino–U.S. ties."

55 Gonzalo Sebastian Paz, "China, United States and Hegemonic Challenge in Latin America: An Overview and Some Lessons from Previous Instances of Hegemonic Challenge in the Region," *The China Quarterly*, Vol. 209 (March 2012): 24. For the Chinese, the dialogue "offers an opportunity to reassure the United States over the stress in economic relations and to dispel any mistrust of potential political effects." Ibid.

56 R. Evan Ellis, *China on the Ground in Latin America: Challenges for the Chinese and Impacts on the Region* (New York: Palgrave Macmillan, 2014), 125. Expanding Chinese engagement with Latin America and the Caribbean is also generating unintended consequences such as the expansion of criminal activities facilitated by the growth of black market commerce in contraband goods, human trafficking, drugs and related chemicals, arms trafficking, and money laundering. R. Evan Ellis, "Cooperation and Mistrust Between China and the U.S. in Latin America," in *The Political Economy of China–Latin America Relations in the New Millennium: Brave New World*, ed. Margaret Myers et al. (New York: Routledge, 2017), 34.

57 R. Evan Ellis, *China on the Ground in Latin America: Challenges for the Chinese and Impacts on the Region* (New York: Palgrave Macmillan, 2014), 126. While particular concerns were raised by some U.S. military intelligence analysts in Washington, DC with respect to China's joint venture with Venezuela to develop and eventually launch the Simon Bolivar communications satellite in 2008, this type of technology-assistance agreement was certainly not a new phenomenon. In 1999, for example, Brazil and China jointly launched the first of what would eventually expand to encompass three satellites that are used, *inter alia*, to monitor the burning of tropical rain forests.

58 R. Evan Ellis, *China in Latin America: The Whats and Wherefores* (Boulder, CO: Lynne Rienner Publishers, 2009), 286.

59 "Ties between Chinese and Latin American militaries have expanded beyond the PLA [*i.e.*, People's Liberation Army] National Defense University to exchange programs, official visits, and increasingly, the sale of Chinese arms in the region." Cynthia A. Watson, "The Obama Administration, Latin America, and the Middle Kingdom," in *China Engages Latin America: Tracing the Trajectory,* ed. Adrian H. Hearn et al. (Boulder, CO: Lynne Rienner Publishers, 2011), 110.

60 Ted Piccone, "The Geopolitics of China's Rise in Latin America," *Geo-economics and Global Issues Paper 2* (Washington, DC: Brookings Institute, November 2016), 9.

61 John J. Mearsheimer, *The Tragedy of Great Power Politics* (New York: W.W. Norton & Co., 2001), 41–2. "States that achieve regional hegemony seek to prevent great

powers in other regions from duplicating their feat. Regional hegemons, in other words, do not want peers." Ibid at 41. This type of realist rationale may be what motivated the U.S. Navy in July 2008 to resurrect the mothballed World War II-era Fourth Fleet in Mayport, Florida, in response to China's growing presence in the Caribbean.

62 John J. Mearsheimer, *The Tragedy of Great Power Politics* (New York: W.W. Norton & Co., 2001), 4.

63 Cynthia A Watson, "The Obama Administration, Latin America, and the Middle Kingdom," in *China Engages Latin America: Tracing the Trajectory*, ed. Adrian H. Hearn et al. (Boulder, CO: Lynne Rienner Publishers, 2011), 115.

64 Ted Piccone, "The Geopolitics of China's Rise in Latin America," *Geo-economics and Global Issues Paper 2* (Washington, DC: Brookings Institute, November 2016), 12.

65 John J. Mearsheimer, *The Tragedy of Great Power Politics* (New York: W.W. Norton & Co., 2001), 249. Interestingly, long before World War II actually broke out, U.S. concerns over the threat Germany posed to U.S. hegemony in Latin America were premised on the explosion in trade. Gonzalo Sebastian Paz, "China, United States and Hegemonic Challenge in Latin America: An Overview and Some Lessons from Previous Instances of Hegemonic Challenge in the Region," *The China Quarterly*, Vol. 209 (March 2012): 27.

66 R. Evan Ellis, "O Novo Ambiente Estratégico do Transpacífico: Uma Perspectiva dos EUA," *Política Externa*, Vol. 23, No. 4 (2015): 44.

67 See, e.g., Welber Barral, "Brazil and China: Trade in the Twenty-First Century," in *Settlements of Trade Disputes between China and Latin American Countries*, ed. Dan Wei (Heidelberg: Springer, 2015), 9. "An analysis of WTO data regarding the number of antidumping investigations and measures applied shows that Brazil, notably in recent years, is one of the more frequent users of antidumping measures, especially against Chinese products."

68 Barbara Stallings and Gabriel Székely, eds., *Japan, the United States, and Latin America* (Baltimore: The Johns Hopkins University Press, 1993), 3. In an ironic parallel to China's activities in Latin America today, Brazil's iron ore exports to Tokyo and Japan's interest in building a second canal in Panama (recalling the Chinese entrepreneur who now wants to build a canal across Nicaragua) were cited as evidence of Japan's rising economic importance in Latin America.

69 A. Blake Firiscia, "Japanese Economic Relations with Latin America: An Overview," in *Japan and Latin America in the New Global Order*, ed. Susan Kaufman Purcell et al. (Boulder, CO: Lynne Rienner Publishers, 1992), 64.

70 David A. Lake, *Hierarchy in International Relations* (Ithaca, NY: Cornell University Press, 2009), 183. Lake also acknowledges, however, that as China continues to expand it may build a network of subordinates that can counter hierarchies headed by the United States, and China may also try to outbid the United States by offering a better deal to some subordinates currently safely lodged in an American hierarchy. Ibid at 184.

Bibliography

Arnson, Cynthia J. and Jorge Heine, eds. *Reaching Across the Pacific: Latin America and Asia in the New Century*. Washington, DC: The Wilson Center, 2014.

Avendano, Rolando, Angel Melguizo, and Sean Miner. *Chinese FDI in Latin America: New Trends with Global Implications*. Washington, DC: Atlantic Council & Paris: OECD Development Center, June 2017.

Bland, Ben and James Fredrick. "Trip to Central America Underscores Taipei Tension." *Financial Times*, January 7/8, 2017: 4.

Dollar, David. "China's Investment in Latin America." *Geo-economics and Global Issues Paper 4*. Washington, DC: Brookings Institute, January 2017.

Ellis, R. Evan. *China in Latin America: The Whats and Wherefores*. Boulder, CO: Lynne Rienner Publishers, 2009.

Ellis, R. Evan. *China on the Ground in Latin America: Challenges for the Chinese and Impacts on the Region*. New York: Palgrave Macmillan, 2014.

Ellis, R. Evan. "O Novo Ambiente Estratégico do Transpacífico: Uma Perspectiva dos EUA." *Política Externa* Vol. 23, No. 4 (2015): 37–48.

Fornés, Gaston and Alan Butt Philip. *The China–Latin America Axis*. Houndmills: Palgrave Macmillan, 2012.

Fung, K.C. and Alicia García-Herrero, eds. *Sino-Latin American Economic Relations*. New York: Routledge, 2012.

Gallagher, Kevin P. *The China Triangle: Latin America's China Boom and the Fate of the Washington Consensus*. New York: Oxford University Press, 2016.

Hearn, Adrian H. and José Luis León-Manriuez, eds. *China Engages Latin America: Tracing the Trajectory*. Boulder, CO: Lynne Rienner Publishers, 2011.

Johnson, Steve. "Chinese Wages Play Catch-Up with the West after Salaries Triple in a Decade." *Financial Times*, February 27, 2017: 1.

Kaufman Purcell, Susan and Robert M. Immerman, eds. *Japan and Latin America in the New Global Order*. Boulder, CO: Lynne Rienner Publishers, 1992.

Lake, David A. *Hierarchy in International Relations*. Ithaca, NY: Cornell University Press, 2009.

Mearsheimer, John J. *The Tragedy of Great Power Politics*. New York: W.W. Norton & Co., 2001.

Myers, Margaret and Carol Wise, eds. *The Political Economy of China–Latin America Relations in the New Millennium: Brave New World*. New York: Routledge, 2017.

Myers, Margaret and Kevin Gallagher. *China–Latin America Report: Chinese Finance to LAC in 2016*. Washington, DC: Inter-American Dialogue & Boston: Global Governance Initiative (Boston University), February 2017.

Paz, Gonzalo Sebastian. "China, United States and Hegemonic Challenge in Latin America: An Overview and Some Lessons from Previous Instances of Hegemonic Challenge in the Region." *The China Quarterly* Vol. 209 (March 2012):18–34.

Piccone, Ted. "The Geopolitics of China's Rise in Latin America." *Geo-economics and Global Issues Paper 2*. Washington, DC: Brookings Institute, November 2016.

Roett, Riordan and Guadalupe Paz, eds. *China's Expansion into the Western Hemisphere: Implications for Latin America and the United States*. Washington, DC: Brookings Institute, 2008.

Shuangrong, He, ed. *China–Latin America Relations: Review and Analysis*. Beijing: Social Sciences Academic Press, 2012.

Stallings, Barbara and Gabriel Székely, eds. *Japan, the United States, and Latin America*. Baltimore: The Johns Hopkins University Press, 1993.

Toro Hardy, Alfredo. *The World Turned Upside Down: The Complex Partnership between China and Latin America*. Singapore: World Scientific Publishing Company, 2013.

Trinkunas, Harold. "Renminbi Diplomacy? The Limits of China's Influence on Latin America's Domestic Politics." *Geo-economics and Global Issues Paper 3*. Washington, DC: Brookings Institute, November 2016.

Wei, Dan, ed. *Settlements of Trade Disputes between China and Latin American Countries*. Heidelberg: Springer, 2015.

Wise, Carol. "China and Latin America's Emerging Economies: New Realities amid Old Challenges." *Latin America Policy* Vol. 7, No. 1 (2016): 26–51.

Wise, Carol. "Playing Both Sides of the Pacific: Latin America's Free Trade Agreements (FTAs) with China." *Pacific Affairs* Vol. 89, No. 1 (2016): 75–100.

7 The Record on Other Major United States Foreign Policy Initiatives in the Western Hemisphere under George W. Bush and Barack H. Obama

Introduction

Many in Latin America greeted George W. Bush's inauguration as president of the United States with guarded optimism. Bush had previously been the governor of Texas and had encouraged cross-border cooperation between his state and Mexico. The fact that Bush's first foreign visit was to Mexico City and not Ottawa, thereby breaking a long-standing tradition set by past U.S. presidents, also raised hopes that Washington, DC would pay greater attention to Latin America. During his first year in office, Bush expressed an interest in reforming U.S. immigration policies by acknowledging the need to facilitate the legalization of millions of undocumented workers, most of them from Latin America and the Caribbean.[1] The terrorist attacks in the northeastern United States on September 11, 2001, however, quickly brought a halt to any heightened attention the Bush White House may have shown countries south of the border. The administration instead became preoccupied with fighting real or imagined terrorist threats in Central Asia and the Near East. Although Latin American governments rallied behind the United States in the immediate weeks after the attacks on the World Trade Center and the Pentagon, with the OAS even invoking the mutual assistance provisions of the Rio Treaty of 1947, that support eroded as the civilian death toll from U.S. planes' high-altitude bombing of Afghanistan steadily mounted. Latin American sympathy for the United States plunged after the Bush administration decided to invade Iraq in March 2003 without the authorization of the UN Security Council.

In the latter part of 2002, the United States had begun a concerted effort to get UN Security Council approval for armed intervention in Iraq, based on the premise that Saddam Hussein had acquired weapons of mass destruction that threatened the security not only of the United States but of the entire world community. At the time, both Mexico and Chile were temporary members of the Security Council and the United States was unable to obtain their vote. The Chilean government would not budge, even after U.S. Secretary of State Colin Powell indirectly apologized for the Nixon administration's covert activities in Chile that had contributed to the overthrow of Chilean President Salvador Allende on September 11, 1973. The Chilean government also remained impervious to veiled threats that the ratification of its recently concluded free trade agreement with the United States might be at risk if Chile did not vote in favor of military action in Iraq. Both Chile and Mexico felt the Bush administration had failed to present credible evidence of Saddam Hussein stockpiling weapons of mass destruction. Mexican President Vicente Fox went as far as to publicly state that because Iraq had not aggressed against the United States or any other country, a U.S. attack on Iraq was immoral.[2] Unable to secure a simple majority in the UN Security Council, the United States unilaterally invaded and subsequently occupied Iraq. These actions revived memories of the worst excesses of historical U.S. violations of national sovereignty in Latin America and the Caribbean, particularly when the alleged weapons of mass destruction failed to materialize.[3] Even among the handful of Latin American nations that contributed small numbers of military or security personnel for the U.S. occupation of Iraq, namely the Dominican Republic, El Salvador, Honduras, and Nicaragua, a majority of citizens remained opposed to the original U.S. military action.

The sadistic abuse of prisoners by U.S. military personnel and civilian contractors at detention centers in Iraq and in Afghanistan further soured Latin Americans on the Bush administration's vision of a United States acting unilaterally and unrestrained by international legal obligations. The stories of systemic torture that emerged from Guantanamo reminded many Latin Americans of the widespread human rights abuses carried out in the 1970s and 1980s by their own military rulers, a significant number of whom had received training in "enhanced interrogation methods" at the U.S.-administered School of the Americas in the Panama Canal Zone. The Bush administration's counter-terrorism policies and its unilateralist military actions in Afghanistan and Iraq undermined U.S. credibility in the Western Hemisphere and made it difficult to achieve progress on issues where a consensus might otherwise have existed. The most notable exception was Colombia, although even the Uribe government never contributed troops to Bush's coalition for the invasion or subsequent occupation of Iraq.

The election of Barack H. Obama to the White House in November 2008 was welcomed in most of Latin America and the Caribbean—as in much of the rest of the world—with a profound sense of relief. The new U.S. president, the first with visible sub-Saharan African ancestry, came across as charismatic, articulate, and intelligent, and promised to put an end to the divisive unilateralism that had characterized the foreign policy of his predecessor. Nothing during the campaign indicated, however, that an Obama presidency would heighten U.S. attention toward the region. During the entire campaign, candidate Obama gave only one speech outlining what would be his policies for Latin America and the Caribbean if elected. That was in May 2008, before the Cuban American National Foundation in Miami. The prime objectives of Obama's address were to attract votes from Cuban-Americans and increase support for three Cuban-Americans running for the U.S. House of Representatives as Democrats, against three entrenched Cuban-American Republicans from south Florida.[4] Accordingly, policy proposals for Cuba dominated Obama's talk in Miami, including a pledge to retain the U.S. trade embargo on Cuba. Obama also pledged to fight drug trafficking in Colombia. He subsequently undermined that promise, however, by expressing opposition to ratification of the Colombia–U.S. free trade agreement that would enhance opportunities for Colombians to engage in alternative export activities not centered on the drug trade.

Upon his inauguration, Obama inherited an economy that was in free fall, with many of the country's largest financial institutions teetering on bankruptcy. Obama's foreign policy agenda focused on fulfilling his campaign promises to withdraw U.S. troops from Iraq and stabilize Afghanistan while at the same time combatting the growing terrorist threat from Islamist extremism. Accordingly, Obama had little time or resources to devote attention to other parts of the world that did not pose an imminent national security threat. For the most part, Latin America and the Caribbean did not pose such a threat. When the Obama administration evinced any interest in the region, it was usually in the form of partnerships that required little expenditure of U.S. political or financial capital. The region, long accustomed to a domineering United States trying to impose its will on its weaker neighbors, enthusiastically welcomed the new emphasis on partnership. This enthusiasm was soon to be tempered, however, upon the realization that these partnerships implied "shared responsibility," and did not include any significant increase in U.S. economic support. In retrospect, the Obama years offered Latin America a unique opportunity to experiment with a variety of economic and even political models that could run their course and prove their worth (or lack thereof) without the type of suffocating paternalism and outright intervention that had, in the past, frequently interrupted the learning of invaluable lessons.

Plan Colombia

U.S. President Bill Clinton and his Colombian counterpart, Andrés Pastrana, launched Plan Colombia in 1999 in an attempt to reverse the dire circumstances facing the country. Plan Colombia was also part of an effort to repair U.S.–Colombian relations, which had reached a nadir under Pastrana's predecessor, Ernesto Samper (1994–1998). Samper's relationship with the United States was frayed even before his inauguration, as a result of allegations that his presidential campaign had accepted contributions from the Cali drug cartel. During Samper's presidency, the U.S. government twice decertified Colombia for not sufficiently cooperating in the fight against illicit narcotics production and trafficking, and it lost crucial U.S. aid funding as a result. At one point, Samper himself had his visa to visit the United States revoked. As Samper prepared to hand over the Colombian presidency to his successor, Colombia's military was poorly equipped and thoroughly demoralized, the nation's economy was in a deep recession, and its foreign currency reserves were depleted. Moreover, guerillas from the *Fuerzas Armadas Revolucionarias de Colombia* (FARC) or the smaller *Ejercito de Liberación Nacional* (ELN) controlled significant parts of the Colombian countryside. Ominously, the FARC had become deeply enmeshed in the illegal drug trade as a way to fund its insurgency.[5] Profits from the drug trade also contributed to the expansion of right-wing paramilitary groups who would soon be responsible for more than three quarters of the extrajudicial killings and massacres in the country.[6]

Upon assuming the Colombia presidency, Pastrana and his advisers elaborated a series of initiatives to stop the flow of illegal narcotics production and finally end a half-century of internal conflict by, in part, resolving the social inequities in rural Colombia that contributed to both problems. At the same time, Pastrana would attempt to negotiate a peace agreement with the guerillas. In subsequent months, Pastrana's initiative took on a decidedly more militarized hue, as more emphasis was placed on security and anti-drug trafficking issues, and less on social reforms such as land redistribution. Although this change is often attributed to Pastrana's need to obtain U.S. financial support for his initiative, the reality is that the security issue was as much a priority for the Colombians as it was for the Americans.[7]

What finally emerged as Plan Colombia reflected a close collaboration between the Colombian and U.S. governments, adjusted to the changing conditions in Colombia.[8] Previous U.S. anti-narcotics assistance to Colombia had focused almost exclusively on fumigation and interdiction. In addition, during Samper's time in office, U.S. funding was directed to the Colombian National Police, viewed as less corrupt and not as subservient to the Colombian president (and not as tainted by the human rights abuses that plagued the Colombian army). Because Pastrana was able to reframe the Colombian conflict with the guerillas as a fight against "narco-guerillas," he succeeded in obtaining adequate U.S. funding to rebuild the Colombian Army into an effective fighting force, supplemented with aid for alternative crop development programs as well as for human rights training and judicial reform.[9]

After a delay of almost a year because of partisan wrangling in the U.S. Congress, President Bill Clinton signed Plan Colombia into law on July 13, 2000.[10] As a result, Colombia quickly become the third leading recipient of U.S. foreign assistance in the world, behind Israel and Egypt.[11] Between 2000 and 2016, the U.S. Congress appropriated some US$10 billion in assistance to carry out Plan Colombia and its follow-on strategies.[12] Bogota's contribution to Plan Colombia, however, was significantly more, as special taxes were imposed on the country's wealthiest citizens and corporations to fund security initiatives, with the Colombians eventually financing nearly 95 percent of the total investment in Plan Colombia.[13] The bulk of U.S. aid under the Clinton administration went to both the Colombian armed forces and the country's national police, for counternarcotics and military operations. The percentage of U.S. aid earmarked for military operations actually decreased under the subsequent administration of George W. Bush, although the Colombian government was able to make up for this by substantially increasing its military spending as a result of revenue obtained from the special taxes levied on the wealthy. At the same time, the United States' military role in Colombia moved away from counter-narcotics operations and toward direct assistance to the Colombian military for counter-insurgency efforts.[14] This broadly reshaped the United States' military role in Colombia's internal armed struggle.[15] For Tom Long, this is an example of derivative power at work, whereby Colombian leaders were able to exploit a perceived commonality of interests to obtain, commit, and manipulate U.S. power and concerns for their own domestic political ends.[16]

Colombian President Álvaro Uribe (2002–2010) came to office following the dismantling of the demilitarized zones that Pastrana had created in an attempt to entice the guerillas to negotiate a peace agreement. In response, the FARC had unleashed a brutal offensive in which the guerillas increased urban attacks, set off car bombs, and began destroying Colombia's energy and transport infrastructure. Uribe was convinced that a weak state had created permissive conditions for the growth of armed actors and the drug trade, and that a necessary precondition for guaranteeing the rule of law was to strengthen state control over the national territory.[18] He therefore favored using the military to extend the national government's presence where it had previously been absent for many years, if not decades. Uribe also embarked on a concerted effort to rid the political system of corrupt politicians beholden to organized criminal groups, in an attempt to restore citizen confidence in the legitimacy of the state and its institutions.[19] Among Uribe's most controversial moves was his decision in 2002 to brand the FARC and ELN as "terrorist" organizations. In doing so, Uribe hoped to garner U.S. moral and material support for Colombian military offensives by encompassing the FARC and ELN within Bush's fight against global terrorism. The U.S. Congress responded favorably by lifting the prohibition against using U.S. assistance for counter-insurgency or counter-terrorism activities found in the original implementing legislation for Plan Colombia. Introducing the concept of terrorism, however, obfuscated the deep social, economic, political, and historical roots of Colombia's protracted armed conflict and led to an escalation of hostilities and combat operations.[20]

At the conclusion of the Uribe administration, the United States was hailing Plan Colombia as a major success story.[21] The FARC had suffered major military defeats and lost effective control over large swaths of territory (including land under coca production) in which it had once acted as the *de facto* government. Homicides and kidnappings dramatically decreased, as well, and it once again became safe to travel overland between Colombia's main cities. The succeeding government of Juan Manuel Santos argued that had it not been for Plan Colombia, the FARC would never have entered into peace talks in 2012. In 2016, the ELN also began negotiating for peace with the central government in Bogotá.

Critics contend that any successes that may be attributable to Plan Colombia are outweighed by the huge social costs the country paid in terms of lost lives and a further undermining of its already fragile institutions. For example, in an attempt to boost statistical evidence of the success of military campaigns against the FARC, the Colombian military under Uribe rounded up and killed thousands of poor youth and claimed they were guerilla casualties. Uribe's administration was also associated with massive wiretapping abuses involving journalists, opposition politicians, judges, and human rights organizations. If that were not bad enough, in 2006 the Colombian military seized the laptop of a paramilitary commander in an act that led to evidence of significant collusion between the paramilitaries and government officials. Critics also point out that a controversial aerial fumigation program linked to Plan Colombia, while reducing the amount of land devoted to coca production, fell well below the original reduction targets and was compensated by an increase in coca production in Peru and Bolivia.[23] In addition, aerial fumigation decimated food crops and poisoned pastures, forests, and waterways, while alternative agricultural programs funded by USAID eroded public confidence in the Colombian government in rural areas due to consistently failing to deliver on what was promised.[24] In place of the 30,000-member-strong United Self-Defense Forces of Colombia (AUC) paramilitary group that Uribe succeeded in demobilizing, there soon appeared the *bandas criminales*, or BACRIM.[25] Most damning of all, given Plan Colombia's original objective as a counter-narcotics strategy, is the fact that Colombia is the largest producer of cocaine in the world today.[26]

Uribe's two terms in office are also associated with Colombia's isolation from its South American neighbors. Ecuador broke off diplomatic relations with Bogotá in 2008 following Colombian soldiers' raid on a FARC camp in Ecuadorian territory, which killed an important FARC commander. Venezuelan President Hugo Chavez responded by mobilizing his country's army and ordering troops to the border with Colombia. The raid also led to the creation of UNASUR's South American Defense Council, at the insistence of Brazil, which viewed the Colombian incursion as inspired by the United States, "a geopolitical interloper in a region where Brazil felt it should be the primary power and lead the resolution of political and security crises."[27] Uribe's 2009 invitation for the United States to utilize several Colombian bases for counternarcotics operations, after Ecuadorian President Rafael Correa did not renew a base agreement in Manta for a similar objective, also brought a sharp rebuke from UNASUR. Venezuela broke off diplomatic relations with Bogotá in July 2010 after Colombia threatened to file a complaint at the OAS charging that Chavez was harboring FARC guerillas.

Soon after assuming the Colombian presidency in August 2010, President Juan Manuel Santos launched peace negotiations with the FARC. The decision to pursue a peace agreement with the FARC marked an abrupt reversal from policies pursued by Uribe and by Santos himself when he served as Minister of Defense under Uribe between 2006 and 2009.[28] Santos also sought to mend fences with his South American neighbors by, *inter alia*, downplaying the extremely close relationship that had marked bilateral relations with the United States under Uribe. An example of this was the Santos government's decision to extradite to Venezuela a drug trafficker wanted by both Washington, DC and Caracas (even though the drug trafficker's high-level connections in Venezuela ensured he would never be jailed). In addition, within days of taking office, Santos and Venezuelan President Chavez met and agreed upon a blueprint for reinstating diplomatic relations while the Colombian also extracted a pledge from Chavez that the presence of illegal armed groups such as the FARC would not be permitted in Venezuelan territory.[29] Thereafter, Venezuela was invited to facilitate the Colombian government's peace negotiations with the FARC in Havana (along with the official guarantors of the negotiations: Chile, Cuba, and Norway). Santos also restored relations with Quito soon after his inauguration (which the Ecuadorian President Rafael Correa had attended). Colombia took on a more active role in UNASUR as well, with two Colombians serving as secretary general of the organization (including the hapless former president, Ernesto Samper).

The Mérida Initiative

Implemented in the last year of George W. Bush's second term in office, the Mérida Initiative grew out of an understanding reached by the Mexican and United States governments of their shared responsibility to combat drug trafficking by, among other things, disrupting organized criminal groups and institutionalizing reforms to the Mexican criminal justice system.[30] It originally included the Central American countries, but a new program called the Central American Regional Security Initiative, or CARSI, established early during the Obama administration led to the Mérida program focusing only on Mexico. One explanation why drugs became such an important bilateral U.S.–Mexican issue was an unintended consequence of the successful campaign waged by the United States in the 1980s and 1990s to disrupt cocaine-smuggling from South to North America through the Caribbean. The new route to the United States now went through Central America and Mexico. By the mid-1990s Mexican criminal organizations and traffickers had become major international players, often replacing Colombian organizations as the main buyers, transporters, and distributors of cocaine into the United States.[31] At around the same time, Mexico became an important source of synthetic drugs such as methamphetamine, as well as homegrown heroin and marijuana sold illegally in the U.S. market. A contributing factor, albeit wholly unintentional in terms of its impact on illicit narcotics, was the dramatic increase in cross-border trade that followed the implementation of the North American Free Trade Agreement, or NAFTA, after 1994.

The main goal of the Mérida Initiative was to provide assistance to the embattled administration of Mexican President Felipe Calderón (2006–2012), who, shortly after taking office, enlisted the country's armed forces to crush the drug cartels. In particular, Calderón's decision to metaphorically decapitate the cartel leadership set off turf battles among the newer and smaller gangs that appeared in place of the larger syndicates, as they fought among each other to control different aspects of the lucrative narcotics trade.[32] In addition, Calderón's political party, the PAN (National Action Party), never exercised the type of control over all the country's major societal actors that had been enjoyed by the notoriously corrupt PRI (Institutional Revolutionary Party) before it lost its seven-decade stranglehold over Mexican politics in 2000 with the victory of the PAN's Vicente Fox. During the PRI's heyday, from the 1940s through the 1990s, a "live and let live" relationship existed between some Mexican authorities and drug lords that allowed the former to get rich but also to maintain relative public peace and a semblance of law and order through the containment of drug syndicates.[33] Calderón's fateful decision unleashed a wave of violence in Mexico as the number of homicides escalated from 8,900 in 2007, the first full year of Calderón's presidency, to a peak of 27,200 in 2011.[34] Although the PRI's return to the Mexican presidency with Enrique Peña Nieto in 2012 was accompanied by a drop in homicides (albeit not kidnappings or extortions), in 2016 the homicide rate began to increase once more.[35] Perhaps not coincidentally, in 2014 Peña Nieto resumed his predecessor's policy of capturing or assassinating cartel leaders (this included the February 2014 re-arrest of Joaquin "El Chapo" Guzman, head of the Sinaloa cartel, who escaped from a maximum-security prison in Jalisco in 2001, and then from another maximum-security facility outside of Mexico City in July 2015).

Between 2008 and 2016, the U.S. Congress appropriated some US$2.6 billion for the purchase of equipment such as helicopters to confront criminal organizations, as well as machinery and trained dogs to detect illicit goods at internal checkpoints and border posts. The money has also gone toward training to enhance the intelligence-gathering capabilities of law enforcement personnel. An original goal of the Mérida Initiative was to put a halt to the widespread illegal importation of firearms from the United States into Mexico, often purchased legally in U.S. border states such as Arizona and Texas. Throughout its existence, the Mérida Initiative has often had to confront challenges arising from the increasingly dysfunctional federal government in the United States, hamstrung by partisan infighting. At one point during Obama's first term in the White House, President Calderón had to plead with then U.S. Secretary of State Hillary Clinton to intervene to accelerate the disbursement of US$500 million in equipment and training for security forces.[36] The Mexican government also bristled at the U.S. Congress's insistence that funding be linked to compliance with human rights obligations, as Mexico was anxious to avoid repeating its humiliating experience of drug certification with the U.S. government in the 1980s and 1990s.[37]

During the Obama administration, the Mérida Initiative retained an emphasis on security but shifted away from the Bush administration's militarized counternarcotics and counter-terrorism focus in favor of establishing a new professional police force at the federal level in Mexico, improving intelligence collaboration, and enhancing the institutional effectiveness of the judicial system. On the latter, the Mérida Initiative provided technical and financial support for Mexico to adopt a new, oral accusatory criminal justice system as well as to create drug treatment courts in five Mexican states that offered alternatives to incarceration. The Obama administration also adopted a "risk segregation" border management strategy that included the increased use of pre-clearance programs to determine which individuals or cargo shipments coming into the United States merited lesser or greater scrutiny. At the same time, the U.S. government provided funding to strengthen Mexico's southern border with Guatemala in an attempt to halt the flow of refugees fleeing the violence and chaos in northern Central America.[38] Furthermore, the Obama administration pushed for a violence-reduction and -prevention program that entailed the improvement of public spaces, job creation, and efforts to reduce the demand for illegal drugs.[39]

The Mérida Initiative never addressed key Mexican concerns, such as reducing the demand for drugs in the United States and halting the cross-border traffic in illegal arms, drug precursors, and bulk cash.[40] There is little evidence that judicial reforms under the Mérida Initiative have had any noticeable impact in ending the widespread impunity of the rich and politically connected in Mexico. The September 2014 disappearance of 43 students from a teacher's college in Ayotzinapa provides the most vivid example of many involving government cover-ups in which no one with any real authority is ever made to account for their actions. This incident, as well as the involvement of government personnel in other serious human rights abuses in fiscal year 2014, led the United States to withhold US$5 million in counter-narcotics assistance for Mexico in October 2015. Overall, the amount of money the U.S. Congress has approved for Mérida Initiative programs has been steadily declining in recent years.

The lackluster accomplishments of the Mérida Initiative are not surprising, as it never addressed what Edgardo Buscaglia asserts to be the main issue in the escalating violence in Mexico: the failure to go after the cartels' assets, obtained from a wide range of illicit activities beyond just narcotics, and invested in legal endeavors within the formal economy.[41] Closely tied to this is the failure to adopt strict campaign financing rules to minimize the cartels' influence on the political system and to prosecute government officials with links to organized criminal organizations.[42] With their asset base intact and no meaningful campaign finance reform or major house-cleaning within government, the cartels are able to respond to any aggressive security-oriented campaign directed against them by raising their violence to intolerable levels and further corrupting the political system to buy themselves even more protection.[43] In fact, even if the leaders of the cartels are put behind bars, their business (both illicit and legal) continues as usual.

Pathways to Prosperity in the Americas

Pathways to Prosperity in the Americas was originally a Bush administration effort, launched in response to the collapse of the Free Trade Area of the Americas (FTAA) negotiations as an attempt to try to stitch together all the exiting bilateral and sub-regional free trade agreements among countries in the Western Hemisphere. Although such an effort would never encompass all the countries in the Americas, it was seen as a second-best option to an FTAA. A key focus was to try to harmonize the plethora of different rules of origin that existed in these different bilateral or sub-regional trade arrangements. Pathways to Prosperity initially included only the 11 countries in Latin America that had a free trade agreement with the United States, as well as Belize, Canada, and Uruguay. Brazil had observer status, as did Trinidad and Tobago. The OAS, the Inter-American Development Bank, and the UN Economic Commission for Latin America and the Caribbean were designated "strategic partners." Given that the Bush administration's foreign policy priorities lay elsewhere in the world, however, the initiative soon floundered, and achieved nothing tangible.

The Obama administration revived Pathways to Prosperity in the Americas, but this time as an initiative to promote inclusive growth, prosperity, and social justice throughout the Americas. A Pathways Clearinghouse Mechanism was established at the OAS General Secretariat in Washington, DC to foster and facilitate the regular exchange of ideas and best practices among participating governments. The initiative was open to all OAS member states that wished to participate. Among other things, Pathways to Prosperity in the Americas sought to encourage public policies and public–private partnerships aimed at empowering small farmers, small businesses, women, indigenous communities, Afro-descendants, youth, and vulnerable groups to participate effectively in the global economy through four pillars:

1   empowering small businesses by providing access to financial and technical support mechanisms for micro, small, and medium-sized enterprises;
2   facilitating trade and regional competitiveness by improving the regulatory environment and infrastructure;
3   building a modern workforce through the sharing of best practices and by supporting workers' rights and fair labor standards as well as promoting the education, training, jobs, and entrepreneurship that will prepare citizens to achieve their full potential; and,
4   promoting sustainable business practices and environmental cooperation, particularly among small and medium-sized enterprises.

Like the Energy and Climate Partnership of the Americas (ECPA), Pathways to Prosperity in the Americas was rhetorically ambitious, but its record of tangible and sustainable deliverables was even more constrained and disappointing than that of the ECPA. Although there were some interesting achievements, such as setting up Small Business Development Centers modeled on the U.S. equivalent in a number of Central American countries, Colombia, the Dominican Republic, and Mexico, a lack of adequate funding hampered other potentially valuable programs, such as the technical training programs envisioned by the Women Entrepreneurs Mentoring Network. Most of the other proposed initiatives never made it beyond the planning workshop stage or visits by small delegations to the United States. The Pathways to Prosperity in the Americas initiative eventually withered into irrelevancy after Hillary Clinton stepped down as U.S. Secretary of State in 2013.

The Central American Regional Security Initiative (CARSI)

The Obama administration established the Central American Regional Security Initiative (CARSI) in 2010 as a separate program from the Mérida Initiative (which would thereafter focus only on Mexico), upon the realization of how widespread threats to citizen security had become in Central America. CARSI, which would also serve as the new regional umbrella for previously existing bilateral programs, had two tranches. The first consisted of programs to enhance the capacity of law enforcement and legal institutions in an attempt to reduce the high levels of crime and violence afflicting the so-called Northern Triangle countries of El Salvador, Guatemala, and Honduras. The second would support pre-existing national programs bolstering citizen security and the capabilities of legal institutions in Belize, Costa Rica, Nicaragua, and Panama. By the end of the Obama administration, the U.S. government had funneled about a billion U.S. dollars into various programs falling strictly under the CARSI umbrella.

The severe deterioration of the security situation in at least one of the three Northern Triangle countries stems from the presence of youth gangs with roots in the United States, particularly Los Angeles and the suburbs of Washington, DC. These areas received large numbers of Salvadoran refugees fleeing their country's civil war in the 1980s. Some of these refugees were infants or young children who later, as teenagers, joined urban gangs such as 18th Street (once an exclusively Mexican–American gang, and which takes its name from a thoroughfare in East Los Angeles) and Mara Salvatrucha, or MS 13. Eventually many gang members were deported to their country of birth following criminal convictions in U.S. courts. The problem was that they returned to a society that was now foreign to them and where they enjoyed no close familial ties; many could no longer even speak fluent Spanish. Aggravating the situation was a Salvadoran economy with too few jobs, particularly for people with no marketable skills and a criminal record. Accordingly, the deported gang members soon regrouped and teamed up with organized criminals already present in El Salvador; taking advantage of a weak state with severe institutional constraints, they engaged in widespread extortion of shopkeepers, bus drivers, and business owners, as well as in other criminal activities.

The rapid expansion of gangs in Guatemala and Honduras is less influenced by expatriates being deported from the United States (although it is a factor here too). Like El Salvador, both countries have large pools of poorly educated young people with few marketable skills competing for a limited number of employment opportunities. In addition, the institutional frameworks (particularly the judicial system and the police) in both countries are fragile and plagued by systemic corruption. A major difference with the gangs in El Salvador is that their counterparts in Guatemala and Honduras have closer links to large transnational criminal organizations based in Colombia and Mexico that funnel South American cocaine destined for the United States.[44] This drug trafficking often occurs under the noses of public officials and police forces that have either been co-opted into narcotic trafficking or bought off, or who are in other ways complicit in narcotics trafficking. The lucrative nature of the drug trade in particular has degenerated into intra-gang warfare for control of territory and trafficking routes. This has contributed to giving Honduras the dubious distinction of having the highest number of civilian homicides per capita in the world in certain years. It is important to emphasize, however, that organized criminal activity in Guatemala and Honduras is not restricted to the narcotics trade, but (as is true in El Salvador) also includes kidnappings, robbery, and extortion.

The United States is not the only country working on security-related issues in Central America (even though it is a major contributor to the violence, as the end destination of the drugs funneled through Central America and the source of the criminal deportees and many of the illegal firearms wreaking havoc there). During the Obama administration, the United States enlisted the assistance of Canada, Chile, Colombia, the European Union (spearheaded by the governments of Germany, Italy, and Spain), Mexico, and even Australia. President Obama also added a Central American Citizen Security Partnership under the CARSI umbrella following his March 2011 visit to El Salvador in an attempt to coordinate foreign and regional contributions to improve citizen safety by reducing criminal organizations' ability to destabilize governments and engage in the illicit trafficking of firearms, narcotics, and people. One priority area for this partnership was re-establishing an effective state presence in areas of El Salvador, Guatemala, and Honduras that had fallen under the control of local gangs and transnational criminal organizations.

When Obama proposed the Central American Citizen Security Partnership, U.S. government officials went to great lengths to point out that the use of the word "partnership" implied shared responsibility and accountability. A more cynical interpretation would posit that the emphasis on partnership betrayed Washington, DC's inability to provide the requisite funding due to budget shortfalls and/or Republican resistance in the U.S. Congress against any initiative proposed by the Obama White House. The idea of a partnership also responded to criticisms leveled at Central America's wealthiest individuals and businesses for failing to provide sufficient financial contributions to support previous CARSI programs. With the exception of Costa Rica, Central America has traditionally had among the lowest effective tax collection rates in the world. Guatemala is especially notorious in this regard: historically, the wealthy in this country have simply refused to pay taxes. Again, with the exception of Costa Rica, the results have been poor public services (including security), highly deficient public education and health care systems, and a wholly inadequate energy, telecommunication, and transportation infrastructure. Things did begin to change in 2012, however, when Honduras enacted special security taxes and Guatemala finally implemented a tax reform so that it could begin adequately funding basic government services, including enhanced police protection. El Salvador eventually followed with a 5 percent tax on telecommunication services to fund security-related measures.

One successful CARSI program established model police precincts in certain municipalities and high-crime neighborhoods in the Northern Triangle countries, leading to reduced crime rates in the beneficiary communities. The program uses community-based policing techniques, with the usually newly hired police officers (as many veterans are considered to be irredeemably corrupt) receiving classroom and on-the-job training to increase their investigative and patrolling capabilities. Another CARSI program established more than 100 youth outreach centers throughout Central America providing vocational training and recreational and cultural activities for at-risk youth in the most vulnerable communities.[45] One of the more controversial aspects of CARSI was the decision to use retired or active Colombian military personnel and law enforcement officials as advisers and trainers. In the recent past, members of the Colombian Armed Forces have been implicated in cases of serious human rights violations. In response to these concerns, U.S. government officials countered that the U.S. State Department vets all the Colombians, many of whom are veterans of Plan Colombia counter-narcotics and counter-insurgency activities, to ensure they have no record of involvement in past human rights abuses.

By 2014, tens of thousands of Central American mothers and their children, as well as unaccompanied minors, were fleeing to the United States from the Northern Triangle to escape the gang violence. Even the most ardent *spinmeister* at the U.S. State Department would be hard pressed to deny that CARSI was falling short and that something more ambitious was required to address the root causes of this growing humanitarian catastrophe in Central America. Vocational training and gang prevention programs targeting at-risk youth, for example, are meaningless in societies without opportunities for gainful employment. Similarly, incarcerating massive numbers of alleged gang members in severely overcrowded jails that they brazenly control resolves nothing, as they continue to oversee illicit behavior beyond prison walls. One common criticism leveled at most CARSI-funded programs was the absence of rigorous impact evaluations, particularly in the areas of institutional strengthening and drug interdiction.[46] U.S.-supported specialized law enforcement units under CARSI, although often successful in carrying out sensitive operations against high-impact criminals, raised questions in terms of these units' contributions to broader law enforcement reform and professionalization.[47]

In November 2014, the presidents of El Salvador, Guatemala, and Honduras announced a Plan for an Alliance for Prosperity in the Northern Triangle that included getting rid of the excessive government red tape that undermined entrepreneurship and hindered the free trade of goods and services among the three countries and the outside world. Other initiatives included major improvements to the public health care and education systems, targeting rural development, energy integration, and reforming tax systems with assistance from the U.S. Treasury Department. While the Alliance retains a security angle, most of its programs target structural reforms to the police, courts, and prisons that are aimed at improving citizen security. Then U.S. Vice-President

Joseph Biden was a frequent guest at meetings of the three Northern Triangle presidents as they put together elements of the Plan with technical assistance from the Inter-American Development Bank, given the initial expectation that the United States would contribute a billion U.S. dollars.

In late 2015, the U.S. Congress finally approved a US$750 million aid package to support the Alliance for Prosperity in the Northern Triangle, conditioned on the three governments taking effective steps to reduce crime, impunity, and corruption as well as to protect human rights. Although the Alliance represents a welcome shift in focus from earlier programs under CARSI that overemphasized security issues narrowly focused on counter-narcotics, it has been subject to the same type of institutional and political inertia in Washington, DC that eventually undermined CARSI.[48] Accordingly, some 80 percent of the money for Alliance for Prosperity programs has, to date, come from the three Central American governments.[49] So far, funding provided by the Alliance has been used to replace thousands of corrupt police officers in Honduras and increase the salaries of the police in both El Salvador and Honduras. It remains to be seen, however, if there will be a concerted effort to seriously diminish the impact of dirty money on local political systems and remove corrupt government officials from office and prosecute them. Regardless of questions about when and if this will ever happen, at least Honduras has had an asset forfeiture law since 2010, El Salvador adopted one at the end of 2013, and Guatemala has legislation allowing the government to seize assets of organized crime. Another welcome sign of progress was the resignation and arrest of the then President and Vice-President of Guatemala in 2015, following an investigation by the Attorney General into corruption in the country's customs service.

The Caribbean Basin Security Initiative (CBSI)

The Caribbean Basin Security Initiative (CBSI) was an outgrowth of a pledge made by U.S. President Obama at the Fifth Summit of the Americas, held in Trinidad in April 2009, to deepen regional security cooperation and complement similar programs the United States had with Mexico and Central America. Formally launched in May 2010, CBSI grouped together the 15 member states of CARICOM plus the Dominican Republic in an ongoing dialogue to reduce the illicit trafficking of drugs and firearms throughout the Caribbean, increase public safety and security, and promote social justice.[50] CBSI was a response to very high levels of homicides in the Caribbean nations fomented by the rising use of the region as a major transit route for funneling illicit drugs from South America to Europe as well as the United States.[51] This increased use of the Caribbean as a transit route for illegal narcotics was a direct result of disruptions to routes through Mexico following Calderón's war against the drug cartels after 2007. This resurgence suggests a potential return to the role the Caribbean played in the 1970s and 1980s as the main transit route for funneling Andean cocaine to the United States. By the mid-1990s that transit route was significantly disrupted by a Clinton-administration program that, among other things, permitted U.S. Coast Guard boats to patrol the territorial waters of many understaffed and economically challenged island nation states (so long as there was a local law enforcement representative on board). It was also during the Clinton administration that Cuba began cooperating with U.S. counter-narcotics operations by passing information about suspicious vessels or aircraft to the U.S. Coast Guard.

As Obama's time in the White House drew to a close, the United States had spent an estimated US$450 million or so on CBSI programs. In particular, these monies were used to pay for equipment and training to improve aerial and maritime surveillance, enhance the ability of Caribbean nations to share ballistics and fingerprint information, and intercept smuggled narcotics, weapons, bulk cash, and contraband at air and seaports. In an attempt to contain the growth of criminal gangs, funding was also directed at reforming and strengthening both the criminal justice and juvenile justice systems in Caribbean countries by incorporating sentencing alternatives to imprisonment such as rehabilitation services, and the wider adoption of plea bargaining to capture drug kingpins. Among the tangible equipment and hardware provided to Caribbean nations under CBSI were patrol boats and coastal radars.

To counter the growth and spread of drug-trafficking organizations, CBSI allowed the U.S. Drug Enforcement Agency to offer training equipment and operational support to police units in the Bahamas, the Dominican Republic, and Jamaica. CBSI also partially paid the salary of a British prosecutor based in the region to offer technical assistance and training to judges and prosecutors in the tiny Eastern Caribbean island nations. Another CBSI program collaborated with the Royal Canadian Mounted Police to establish a regional certification center for polygraph examiners, while three hubs were set up in Barbados, Jamaica, and Trinidad and Tobago to share digital ballistics data with law enforcement agencies throughout the Caribbean. In December 2012, the U.S. government launched a US$3.43 million assistance program through CBSI to combat illicit trafficking in firearms spearheaded by the U.S. Department of Justice's Bureau of Alcohol, Tobacco, Firearms and Explosives (ATF). Among other things, the program provided two firearms advisors to render on-site assistance, established a forensic training program, and developed an exchange program allowing law enforcement officials from various Caribbean island nations to work alongside their ATF counterparts in the United States. The United States is the source for most of the firearms circulating in the Caribbean, and guns are responsible for the bulk of the region's high homicide rates.

CBSI was the inspiration for a 911 system for reporting crime in the Dominican Republic that was intended to reduce emergency response times. CBSI provided resources to Trinidad and Tobago's police academy to train police officers from nine other Caribbean nations, and paid lawyers to draft asset-forfeiture legislation in four Eastern Caribbean countries. One important goal of asset forfeiture is to direct part of the seized funds to help finance more law enforcement and crime prevention initiatives. Working under CBSI's umbrella, USAID has funded juvenile justice and community-based policing projects to strengthen alternative sentencing options and provide skills training to wayward youth. Undermining these efforts is the fact that unemployment rates, in general and among youth in particular, are very high throughout the Caribbean. Interestingly, CBSI does not address other security threats that CARICOM leaders have identified as "significant," including cyber and financial crimes as well as government corruption.[52]

Less successful programs associated with CBSI included one that provided training and resources for the Jamaican Constabulary Forces to carry out internal investigations to weed out corrupt personnel. Although it did succeed in identifying a significant number of wayward police officers, leading to their dismissal, CBSI involvement was suspended when credible accusations surfaced of extrajudicial killings committed by members of the Constabulary. A similar suspension based on torture accusations occurred in Saint Lucia. Under the Leahy Law, the U.S. government cannot provide financial or technical assistance to any unit of a foreign government's military or security forces credibly implicated in serious human rights abuses.

Independent of CBSI, CARICOM has attempted to develop regional organizations to tackle security issues, in light of the severe human capacity and financial restraints of many member states. Accordingly, a Regional Intelligence Fusion Centre serves as a centralized coordinator of intelligence gathering, analysis, training, strategic risk, and threat assessment. A CARICOM Integrated Border Security System (CARIBSEC) has developed a watch list of persons who are known security threats, and facilitates the sharing and analysis of intelligence information, including on lost or stolen passports, criminal convictions, and potential terrorist affiliations. An Advance Passenger Information System exists for persons arriving, transiting through, or departing from CARICOM nations, and member governments are working on implementing a similar system for cargo shipments. All of these regional efforts are only as good as the intelligence provided by national governments, however, and this is an area where there is still much work to do in strengthening domestic capacity.

100,000 Strong in the Americas

The Obama administration launched the *100,000 Strong in the Americas* initiative in 2011, with a goal of annual exchanges of up to 100,000 university students in each direction between the United States and other countries in the Western Hemisphere by 2020. The U.S. government's financial contribution to the program was minimal, however. The expectation was that it would be a public–private partnership and the bulk of the money would come from other governments, the private sector, foundations, and universities themselves. A number of multinationals stepped up to the plate, including Coca-Cola, ExxonMobil, Freeport-McMoRan Copper & Gold, and Banco Santander. Together, these multinationals pledged a total of US$3.65 million to create a *100,000 Strong in the Americas* Innovation Fund in late 2013 that would provide challenge grants to universities to strengthen their capacity to both send and host student exchange programs. The Ford Foundation also contributed money to this fund. Eventually other companies and foundations stepped up to the plate, such as the Andean Development Bank (CAF), Chevron, MetLife, Sempra Energy, and Televisa, as well as Colombia and the Commonwealth of Puerto Rico. During Obama's visit to Cuba in March 2016, groups from the Cuban-American community pledged another million dollars to the Innovation Fund in order to increase bidirectional student mobility between Cuba and the United States. The *100,000 Strong in the Americas* Innovation Fund is administered by Partners for the Americas (a not-for-profit organization that grew out of the Alliance for Progress) and the Association of International Educators, or NAFSA.

The *100,000 Strong in the Americas* program benefited from the fact that it complemented the "Science without Borders" initiative launched by Brazilian President Dilma Rousseff in 2012, which sought to send 101,000 Brazilian students abroad to study in the science and technology fields by 2016. One interesting aspect about the *100,000 Strong* initiative is that it attempted to steer students to universities other than elite institutions in the northeast of the United States or California, such as historically African-American majority schools or colleges in the interior or more rural areas of the United States. The goal was also to reach out to students from historically disadvantaged backgrounds throughout Latin America and the Caribbean to come study in the United States. By the time Obama's presidency ended in January 2017, the Innovation Fund had grown to US$10 million in pledges. Some 93 grants averaging about US$25,000.00 had been awarded, benefiting just over 200 institutions of higher learning in 20 countries. Universities awarded grants are required to commit matching funds. By the end of the Obama administration, the average match was close to double the initial grant awarded. The grants are used to facilitate the establishment of credit-earning study-abroad programs between institutions of higher learning in the United States and those in other nations throughout the Western Hemisphere. They are not individual student scholarships. Institutions are required to demonstrate the sustainability of the student exchange program beyond the grant period of one year.

Restoring Normal Diplomatic Relations with Cuba

Shortly after his inauguration, U.S. President Obama took steps to facilitate more travel by U.S. citizens to Cuba and increased the amount of money U.S. residents could send back to family members on the island in the form of remittances. In 2013, the United States and Cuba began secret negotiations in Canada, facilitated by the Vatican, following the election of a new Pope from Argentina. On December 17, 2014, President Obama announced that, following the successful conclusion of those secret talks, the United States would renew normal diplomatic relations with Havana, thereby ending more than half a century of hostile relations. This was premised on Cuba's decision to free an American who had been working as an independent contractor on a USAID-funded project to supply and help install telecommunication equipment that would benefit the island's tiny Jewish community. The American contractor had been under arrest since December 2009, charged with espionage. He was exchanged for three Cubans convicted by the U.S. of spying. Havana also agreed to free 53 political prisoners and to permit on-site inspections of detention centers by the International Red Cross.

In January 2015, the U.S. government announced that American citizens could henceforth travel to Cuba on general licenses under a wide range of categories that did not require prior authorization from the Treasury Department. Prior to this time, U.S. nationals and permanent residents, while not prohibited outright from traveling to the island, had to obtain special waivers from the Treasury Department in order to utilize U.S. currency to purchase goods and services on the island. In addition, more flexible arrangements for selling U.S. agricultural products in Cuba were adopted that waived the previous strict "cash payment upon sale" requirement. By May 2015, the U.S. had finally complied with a long-standing demand of the Castro government: Cuba was removed from the U.S. government's "state sponsor of terrorism" list. In July 2015, both Cuba and the United States reopened their embassies in each other's respective capital cities. President Obama himself visited Havana with his family in March 2016, the first sitting U.S. president to do so since Calvin Coolidge attended a summit of Inter-American states in Havana in 1928. When Obama stepped down from the presidency in January 2017, however, the U.S. trade embargo remained in place, as the White House was unable to certify to the U.S. Congress that Cuba had taken steps to become a representative democracy. In 1996 the Cuban Liberty and Democratic Solidarity Act, aka the Helms–Burton Bill, removed what had previously been the exclusive prerogative of the executive branch to decide whether to lift the trade embargo or not.

Obama's re-establishment of normal diplomatic relations with Havana was the culmination of a long process of previous attempts begun decades earlier that had always ended in failure. In June 1974, the Ford administration had initiated a "discreet dialogue" with Cuba, with both countries dropping preconditions: Washington set aside demands that Cuba sever all military ties to the Soviet Union; Havana held back its claim that the United States lift the embargo unilaterally.[53] These negotiations collapsed, however, after Cuba sent thousands of troops to Angola at the end of 1975 in support of the embattled government of the leftist Movement for the Liberation of Angola, under attack by guerillas from the National Union for the Total Independence of Angola (UNITA), which was supported by the CIA and apartheid South Africa.

Within months of his January 1977 inauguration, U.S. President Jimmy Carter authorized the opening of a U.S. Interests Section in Havana headed by Wayne Smith and lifted the ban on Americans spending U.S. money in Cuba (thereby easing travel restrictions). These efforts at rapprochement soon came to naught, however, when Cuba sent a large contingent of its soldiers to help the Ethiopian government repel a Somali invasion over the disputed territory in the Ogaden. Havana's intervention in the Ogaden War was followed by the Mariel boatlift between April and October 1980, when Castro temporarily permitted

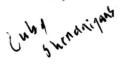

any Cuban who could secure transport to leave the island. Taking advantage of this opening, some 125,000 Cubans fled to Florida. Included were many patients of mental hospitals and inmates from Cuban jails, thoroughly embarrassing Carter, who faced a tough re-election battle that November that he ultimately lost to Ronald Reagan.

The Clinton administration was equally unsuccessful in its overtures to Castro, after Cuba shot down two planes in February 1996 that killed four Cuban-American pilots affiliated with Brothers to the Rescue. This group ostensibly flew over the Straits of Florida looking for Cubans fleeing their homeland by boat, in order to alert the U.S. Coast Guard to conduct rescue operations. Cuba had long accused Brothers to the Rescue of violating its air space and dropping propaganda leaflets over the island. Since the incident came at the start of the same year in which Clinton was seeking re-election based on a strategy of winning Florida's votes in the Electoral College, the president felt compelled to sign the Helms–Burton Bill in March 1996, thereby ceding to Congress his prerogative (and that of all his successors) to lift the U.S. trade embargo on Cuba.

One important explanation for why Obama succeeded in his overtures to Havana, in contrast to his predecessors, is that Raul Castro, and not his more intransigent brother Fidel, was the president of Cuba. In addition, the steady economic deterioration of Venezuela following the collapse in global oil prices that began in 2014 meant that Havana could no longer count on continued Venezuelan petroleum shipments under generous repayment terms. As a result, Cuba faced the prospect of another "special period" such as that which it experienced in the 1990s following the collapse of the Soviet Union, when guaranteed high levels of sugar exports to that country, as well as subsidized oil imports, came to an abrupt halt. The loss of revenue from sugar exports and increased energy prices at that time wreaked havoc on Cuba's finances and caused living standards on the island to plummet.

Conclusion

Plan Colombia, the Mérida Initiative, CARSI, and CBSI are difficult to explain from a realist perspective of hegemony. While the illegal narcotics trade certainly has a negative societal impact in the United States, it is hard to argue it poses an existential threat to U.S. national security. There are no balance of power concerns, either, as the drug cartels have nowhere near the military force or hardware to challenge the United States, nor is there any expressed desire on their part to overthrow the U.S. government and take over the country. If the United States really wants to protect its citizens from the pernicious effects of imported illicit narcotics, it has many other options at its disposal, including tightening border controls and imposing draconian punishments on drug offenders up and down the value chain. It could also adopt stringent anti-corruption protocols to prevent foreigners laundering their ill-gotten gains through the U.S. real estate market or U.S. financial institutions. Accordingly, alternatives exist to spending billions of dollars on counter-narcotics operations that do nothing to enhance U.S. security.

Hegemonic stability and international regime theories offer more satisfying explanations for U.S. behavior through Plan Colombia, the Mérida Initiative, CARSI, and CBSI. All four are examples of the U.S. hegemon offering a public good—in this case money, technical assistance, and trainers for counter-narcotics (and, in the case of Colombia, eventually counter-insurgency) operations—in an attempt to restore citizen security in the targeted subaltern states. Plan Colombia, in particular, provides an interesting application of international regime theory at work in the real world, as the United States offered the crucial initial seed money but it was the Colombians who eventually supplied the bulk of the total investment. There are indications that the same thing may be happening with CARSI and CBSI, as some of the Central American governments have overcome strong elite resistance to impose new taxes to support specific CARSI programs, while CARICOM has complemented or provided deeper financial and logistical support for programs initiated under CBSI. The leaders of El Salvador, Guatemala, and Honduras have also realized that they must move beyond drug interdiction and cosmetic institutional reforms to a deeper reorganization of their societies by providing meaningful economic opportunities for their citizens. Hence the reason for the appearance of the Alliance for Prosperity in the Northern Triangle.

Without doubt, the best explanations for U.S. actions under Plan Colombia, the Mérida Initiative, CARSI, and CBSI are offered by the liberal school of international relations, Lake's theory of variegated hierarchy, and Gramscian notions of hegemony. In the specific case of Gramsci, the four initiatives reflect a consensus of interests among the dominant elites in the United States, Colombia, Mexico, and the Central American and Caribbean nations to implement their hegemonic economic and political agendas free of the threats posed by rising actors with an alternative economic or political outlook. The agenda of these new actors has the potential to become counter-hegemonic if they cannot be co-opted into the dominant consensus, hence the need to confront them. For liberals, the four initiatives represent cross-border cooperation based on a harmony of interests. In particular, the United States has a strong desire to keep illegal narcotics out and stem the flow into its territory of economic and political migrants fleeing the violence and turmoil in Colombia, Mexico, Central America, and the Caribbean. The United States is also by far the wealthiest country in the Western Hemisphere, and therefore in the strongest position to bankroll efforts to achieve the common goals shared with its smaller and poorer southern neighbors. That all four initiatives have changed and been modified over time is in keeping with the liberal notion that the interests of states are multiple and changing, as well as both self-interested and other-regarding.

What the United States has tried to accomplish through Plan Colombia, the Mérida Initiative, CARSI, and CBSI is consistent with those liberals who acknowledge and accept a more limited and constrained form of hegemony than the one realists have in mind. As the leader of the Western Hemisphere, the

United States undertook the initial decision to confront a threat to itself and its southern neighbors, and proposed a way to redress it that culminated in a consensus on what set of actions to pursue. On the other hand, even this limited liberal conception of hegemony underscores how all four initiatives reflect its decline, in terms of the United States, in Latin America and the Caribbean. None of the four initiatives has been adequately funded by the "hegemon." Instead, they have necessitated significant financial contributions from other countries (including the beneficiaries). Although it can be argued that this too is very much in keeping with liberal notions of shared responsibility or partnerships, the funding Bogotá itself provided for Plan Colombia far exceeded whatever came from the United States. In fact, the Colombians were also responsible for shifting the focus of Plan Colombia from the initial narrow U.S. counternarcotics objective to one that also encompassed efforts to combat the FARC and restore the presence of the national government in areas from which it had long been absent. The narrow security focus, centered on drug interdiction, of all four initiatives also betrays a lack of intellectual rigor and a long-term strategic vision—both qualities normally associated with leadership.

Pathways to Prosperity and *100,000 Strong in the Americas* are textbook examples of classic liberal international relations theory. Both evince the liberal ethos of human progress through education and the expansion of economic opportunities to traditionally marginalized individuals under a liberal, market-oriented ethos. Both initiatives evince a decline of U.S. leadership in Latin America and the Caribbean, however, as both were woefully underfunded and there was little follow-through so that Pathways to Prosperity eventually fell into obscurity. *100,000 Strong in the Americas* would have succumbed to a similar fate if not for a complementary Brazilian government program that provided academic scholarships for its youth to study at universities abroad.

Cuba underscores the limitations that even a hegemon can face in imposing its will on a smaller and weaker country. In fact, Cuba is the only successful example of Gramscian counter-hegemony in the Western Hemisphere (albeit that all indications are that even this half-century experiment is approaching its end). The United States was never able to achieve its stated goal of ousting either Fidel Castro or his brother Raul from power after the successful Cuban revolution of 1959, despite covert operations to spark a counter-revolution or assassinate Fidel Castro in the early 1960s. For its part, the hawkish Reagan administration was compelled to include Cuba in the peace negotiations that finally brought the fighting in Angola and Namibia to an end. The United States even betrayed its own long-term interests when it employed Luis Posada Carriles as a CIA operative in Central America and granted residency to Orlando Bosch, despite both being implicated in the 1976 bombing of a *Cubana de Aviación* flight en route from Barbados to Havana that killed all 73 passengers on board.[54] Cuban exile groups also played a role in what was, until September 11, 2001, the worst act of foreign terrorism committed on U.S. soil in modern history. In September 1976 Orlando Letelier, the former Chilean ambassador to the U.S. and minister of various portfolios under President Salvador Allende, was killed along with an American co-worker when a remote-controlled bomb was detonated in the car in which they were traveling, near Sheridan Square in Washington, DC. Although the assassination was carried out by Chile's secret police, the DINA, Cuban exile groups based in Miami provided important logistical support and even operatives.[55]

In the end, therefore, Obama's efforts to normalize diplomatic relations with Cuba were successful because Havana finally wanted them to be.

Notes

1 See, e.g., Ginger Thompson, "U.S. and Mexico to Open Talks on Freer Migration of Workers," *New York Times*, February 16, 2001: 1 and Tim Weiner and Ginger Thompson, "Bush Gives Mexico Backing on Drive Against Narcotics," *New York Times*, February 17, 2001: 1.

2 Mark Eric Williams, *Understanding U.S.–Latin American Relations* (New York: Routledge, 2012), 332.

3 The Latinobarómetro Report 2008 notes that positive views of the United States among Latin Americans fell from 73 percent in 2001 to 58 percent by 2008. The Southern Cone of South America was the most critical, with only 32 percent of Argentines, for example, having a positive image of the United States. The 40 to 61-year-old group throughout Latin America had the least positive image of the United States (31 percent)—the report points out that this was the generation that experienced the brunt of U.S. support for brutal military dictatorships, between the 1960s and the 1980s (with a respite during the Carter administration). The full report can be accessed at: www.latinobarometro.org/docs/INFORME_LATINO-BAROMETRO_2008.pdf. The impact of the Iraq War on generating negative opinions of the United States can also be surmised from a survey by the Pew Global Attitudes Project which showed that favorable images of the U.S. held by Brazilians, for example, fell from 52 percent in 2002 to 34 percent one year later. See June 3, 2003 *Views of a Changing World 2003* report, available at: www.pewglobal.org/2003/06/03/views-of-a-changing-world-2003/.

4 Edward Luce, "Obama Woos Cuban-Americans with Promises," *Financial Times*, May 24, 2008: 4. One of those Democrats was himself the then president of the Cuban American National Foundation. Notwithstanding Obama's endorsement, all three Democratic candidates lost to the Republican incumbents.

5 By 1998, "Colombia was estimated to be the source of 90 percent of the cocaine entering the United States, and as much as half of this came from coca leaf cultivated in areas under FARC control." Tom Long, *Latin America Confronts the United States: Asymmetry and Influence* (New York: Cambridge University Press, 2015), 182.

6 Marc W. Chernick, "Colombia: Does Injustice Cause Violence?" in *What Justice? Whose Justice? Fighting for Fairness in Latin America*, ed. Susan Eckstein et al. (Berkeley: University of California Press, 2003), 192–3. Drug traffickers invested a considerable portion of their illicit earnings in rural landholdings and these new narco-elites in turn invested in private armies to protect themselves and their investments from the guerillas. Ibid at 192. By mid-1989, approximately 11,000 paramilitary commandos were operating in Colombia, most under the control of the Medellin cartel. Russell Crandall, *Driven by Drugs: U.S. Policy Toward Colombia* (Boulder, CO: Lynne Rienner Publishers, 2008), 65.

7 Tom Long, *Latin America Confronts the United States: Asymmetry and Influence* (New York: Cambridge University Press, 2015), 174–216. During its first week in office, the Pastrana administration sought 14 Blackhawk helicopters as a first step toward addressing the army's inability to pursue guerillas and traffickers. Ibid at 186.

Pastrana also sought to convince the Clinton administration of "the importance of drug trafficking in financing armed groups, in part because he wanted to involve the Colombian military in attacking both traffickers and guerillas." Ibid at 187. While still a candidate, Pastrana had promised to professionalize the Colombian military should he become president. Ibid at 197.

8 Tom Long, *Latin America Confronts the United States: Asymmetry and Influence* (New York: Cambridge University Press, 2015), 200. The most dramatic of these changed conditions was the collapse of the peace process Pastrana had secretly launched shortly after he won the elections and before his inauguration, which eventually led to the creation of a demilitarized zone the size of Switzerland with a heavy FARC presence. In February 2002, Pastrana ordered a now much strengthened Colombian military to retake the demilitarized zones from the FARC when it refused to agree to a timetable for reducing the intensity of the conflict, and after FARC guerillas had hijacked a Colombian airliner and kidnapped one of its passengers, a Colombian senator. Ibid at 212.

9 Tom Long, *Latin America Confronts the United States: Asymmetry and Influence* (New York: Cambridge University Press, 2015), 221. Pastrana also initially convinced the Clinton administration to continue supporting his peace process, including the controversial demilitarized zones that were deeply unpopular among conservatives in the U.S. Congress and high-ranking members of the Colombian Armed Forces, who felt peace negotiations with the FARC might undermine anti-drug efforts. Russell Crandall, *Driven by Drugs: U.S. Policy Toward Colombia* (Boulder, CO: Lynne Rienner Publishers, 2008), 119.

10 Winifred Tate, *Drugs, Thugs, and Diplomats: U.S. Policymaking in Colombia* (Stanford, CA: Stanford University Press, 2015), 161. The bill authorized US$1.3 billion in spending in Colombia, almost 80 percent of it on military aid, at a time when the Colombian security forces were linked to abusive, drug-trafficking paramilitary groups. Ibid at 3. "The [Clinton] administration's attempts to distance itself from Colombia's internal conflict by focusing solely on drugs helped to ensure a relatively quick and controversy-free approval through Congress." Russell Crandall, *Driven by Drugs: U.S. Policy Toward Colombia* (Boulder, CO: Lynne Rienner Publishers, 2008), 124.

11 Russell Crandall, *Driven by Drugs: U.S. Policy Toward Colombia* (Boulder, CO: Lynne Rienner Publishers, 2008), 1.

12 Mark P. Sullivan, *Latin America and the Caribbean: Key Issues and Actions in the 114th Congress* (Washington, DC: Congressional Research Service, January 4, 2017), 34. With the increasing nationalization of Plan Colombia-related programs since 2008, U.S. foreign assistance to Colombia declined. The Colombia Strategic Development Initiative was begun in 2011 to align U.S. assistance with the follow-up strategy to Plan Colombia, designed to develop a functioning state presence in remote, but strategically important, areas. Ibid at 10. This reflects the ultimate triumph of the Colombian government's effort to steer Plan Colombia away from the original U.S. focus strictly on counter-narcotics.

13 Atlantic Council, *Building a Better Future: A Blueprint for Central America's Northern Triangle* (Washington, DC: Atlantic Council, May 2017), 13. In 2002 Uribe enacted a so-called war tax to pay for military expenditures that required companies and individuals with US$60,000 or more in assets to pay a one-time contribution equal to 1.2 percent of their capital. Juan Forero, "Burdened Colombians Back Tax to Fight Rebels," *New York Times*, September 8, 2002: 16. In subsequent years, new taxes levied on high-income individual and corporate earners in Colombia raised billions of dollars every year to fund further security initiatives. This allowed Colombia's defense budget alone to triple to nearly US$12 billion between 2000 and 2009. Michael Shifter, "Plan Colombia: A Retrospective," *Americas Quarterly*, Vol. 6, No. 2 (2012): 41.

14 Russell Crandall, *Driven by Drugs: U.S. Policy Toward Colombia* (Boulder, CO: Lynne Rienner Publishers, 2008), 36–8. "Collapse of the [Pastrana] peace process helped fuel the Bush administration's efforts to expand its Colombia policy, especially breaking down the 'firewall' between counter-narcotics and counterinsurgency assistance." Ibid at 138.

15 Marc Chernick, "Santos, the FARC, and the Evolution of Peace Negotiations in Colombia," in *Colombia's Political Economy at the Outset of the Twenty-first Century: From Uribe to Santos and Beyond*, ed. Bruce M. Bagley et al. (Lanham, MD: Lexington Books, 2015), 142. The U.S. military presence in Colombia tripled between late 2001 and mid-2003. Russell Crandall, *Driven by Drugs: U.S. Policy Toward Colombia* (Boulder, CO: Lynne Rienner Publishers, 2008), 151.

16 Tom Long, *Latin America Confronts the United States: Asymmetry and Influence* (New York: Cambridge University Press, 2015), 224. Through derivative power, a weaker state compensates for its own limited capabilities by accessing the greater resources of more powerful states. Ibid. at 223.

17 Russell Crandall, *Driven by Drugs: U.S. Policy Toward Colombia* (Boulder, CO: Lynne Rienner Publishers, 2008), 138. The guerillas also attacked Colombia's political institutions, forcing half the country's mayors to abandon their posts. Ibid at 145.

18 Cynthia J. Arnson and Arlene B. Tickner, "Colombia and the United States: The Path to Strategic Partnership," in *Contemporary U.S.–Latin American Relations*, ed. Jorge I. Domínguez et al. (New York: Routledge, 2016), 154–5. The United States had already declared the FARC a terrorist group back in 1999, when FARC guerillas killed three North American indigenous rights activists.

19 Beginning in 2002, Colombia commenced legal proceedings against approximately a third of the country's national legislators of whatever political party or allegiance for ties to organized criminal groups. Edgardo Buscaglia, "La Paradoja Mexicana de la Delincuencia Organizada: Policías, Violencia y Corrupción," *Revista Policía y Seguridad Pública* Año 2, Vol. 1 (2012): 277.

20 Marc Chernick, "Santos, the FARC, and the Evolution of Peace Negotiations in Colombia" in *Colombia's Political Economy at the Outset of the Twenty-first Century: From Uribe to Santos and Beyond*, ed. Bruce M. Bagley et al. (Lanham, MD: Lexington Books, 2015), 142–3. For the United States, Colombia was transformed into the principal non-Islamic site in the war on terrorism. Ibid at 143.

21 The then U.S. Ambassador to Colombia, William Brownfield, asserted in 2009 that Plan Colombia "has been the most successful nation-building exercise the United States has associated itself with perhaps over the last 25–30 years." Cynthia J. Arnson and Arlene B. Tickner, "Colombia and the United States: The Path to Strategic Partnership," in *Contemporary U.S.–Latin American Relations*, ed. Jorge I. Domínguez et al. (New York: Routledge, 2016), 168.

22 Russell Crandall, *Driven by Drugs: U.S. Policy Toward Colombia* (Boulder, CO: Lynne Rienner Publishers, 2008), 167. The unfolding scandal eventually landed many Uribe allies in jail, including the former head of the Department of Administrative Security (DAS), Jorge Noguera Cotes, who was sentenced to 25 years in prison for, among other things, providing information on trade union leaders for paramilitary groups to assassinate.

23 According to Winifred Tate, assessments of Plan Colombia have largely downplayed counter-narcotics objectives because these programs failed according to the metrics contained within the project itself. A 2007 study by the Center for Strategic and International Studies, for example, pointed out that Plan Colombia's target for a 50 percent reduction in coca production was not achieved. Winifred Tate, *Drugs, Thugs, and Diplomats: U.S. Policymaking in Colombia* (Stanford, CA: Stanford University Press, 2015), 222. See also, Megan Alpert, "15 Years and $10 Billion Later, U.S. Efforts to Curb Colombia's Cocaine Trade Have Failed," *Foreign Policy,*

February 8, 2016. Available at: http://foreignpolicy.com/2016/02/08/15-years-and-10-billion-later-u-s-efforts-to-curb-colombias-cocaine-trade-have-failed/.

24 Winifred Tate, *Drugs, Thugs, and Diplomats: U.S. Policymaking in Colombia* (Stanford, CA: Stanford University Press, 2015), 224.

25 Rodrigo Tavares, *Security in South America: The Role of States and Regional Organizations* (Boulder, CO: First Forum Press, 2014), 210–211. Among other enticements, Uribe used the threat of extradition to the United States as a way to get the paramilitary leadership to demobilize.

26 A report by the UN Office on Drugs and Crime (UNODC) noted that land used for growing coca leaf in Colombia had increased 52 percent in 2016 over the year before, reaching levels not seen in two decades, and translating into a potential increase in cocaine output of 34 percent. Joshua Goodman, "Cultivos de Hoja de Coca en Colombia Subieron 52% en 2016, Según la ONU," *El Mercurio* (Santiago), July 15, 2017: A4. Among the reasons offered for this dramatic increase was President Juan Manuel Santos's decision in 2015 to suspend aerial fumigation over public health concerns, and the peace agreement with the FARC that offers subsidies to peasant farmers to produce crops other than coca (hence the rush to expand production in order to obtain greater subsidies in the future).

27 Carlos Espinosa, "The Origins of the Union of South American Nations: A Multicausal Account of South American Regionalism," in *Exploring the New South American Regionalism*, ed. Ernesto Vivares (Farnham, UK: Ashgate Publishing, 2014), 39. Brazilian geo-strategists looked at Plan Colombia with concern as it "not only implied a direct US military presence in a region that Brazil saw as its theater of operations, but also posed a threat to Brazil's strategic objectives of exerting control over the Amazon." Ibid.

28 A crucial difference between the peace efforts of Santos and those of Pastrana a decade earlier was the absence of any ceasefire while the peace negotiations were being conducted. Nor was the FARC granted any safe havens within the country. In fact, government military actions against the FARC continued unabated, so as to put further pressure on the FARC to negotiate on six crucial points: 1) agrarian reform; 2) political participation of the guerilla forces; 3) drug trafficking; 4) victims and reparations; 5) definitively ending the conflict; 6) implementation of the peace deal.

29 Cynthia J. Arnson and Arlene B. Tickner, "Colombia and the United States: The Path to Strategic Partnership," in *Contemporary U.S.–Latin American Relations*, ed. Jorge I. Domínguez (New York: Routledge, 2016), 161. Bilateral working groups were also established "to address the payment of Venezuela's debt to Colombian exporters, trade and economic integration, border development and infrastructure, and, most important of all, security." Ibid.

30 The Anti-Drug Abuse Act of 1986, which mandated tough sentences for drug offenses and helped turn the United States into the country with the world's highest level of incarcerated citizens, also required the White House to transmit biannual reports to Congress certifying whether drug-producing and transit countries were cooperating with U.S. antinarcotics efforts, at the risk of losing financial aid. Major changes to the Act in 2002 eliminated certification and sanctions, and reduced the White House obligation to filing an annual report highlighting countries that failed to take appropriate counter-narcotics measures. "The abandonment of the certification procedure lifted a cloud from U.S.–Mexican relations and would pave the way for the launching of the Mérida Initiative in 2007." Jorge I. Domínguez and Rafael Fernández de Castro, "U.S.–Mexican Relations: Coping with Domestic and International Crisis," in *Contemporary U.S.–Latin American Relations*, ed. Jorge I. Domínguez et al. (New York: Routledge, 2016), 44.

31 Eric L. Olson, *The Evolving Mérida Initiative and the Policy of Shared Responsibility in U.S.–Mexico Security Relations* (Washington, DC: Mexico Institute [Woodrow Wilson International Center for Scholars], February 2017), 3. Following the demise

of the Medellin and Cali drug cartels in Colombia, "[w]hat had once been primarily a Mexican marijuana trafficking business now became a lucrative transnational criminal enterprise with the capacity to move large quantities of cocaine and other illegal drugs into the United States." Ibid.

32 There were plenty of warning signs that going after the leaders of the drug cartels would escalate the level of violence in Mexico, based on the experience of Calderón's predecessor, Vicente Fox. "The capture of Benjamín Arellano Felix, head of the Tijuana cartel, in 2002, and of Osiél Cardenas Guillén, head of the Gulf cartel, in 2003, led to a vicious war within and among the criminal organizations, as upcoming drug leaders battled to assert or reassert control over territory, resources, and manpower." Francisco E. González, "Mexico's Drug Wars Get Brutal," *Current History*, Vol. 108, No. 715 (2009): 74.

33 Francisco E. González, "Mexico's Drug Wars Get Brutal," *Current History*, Vol. 108, No. 715 (2009): 73. This does not mean that all or most government officials were involved in the illicit narcotics trade, but, given Mexico's complex and fragmented territorial politics, the country's governors, mayors, military officers, and police chiefs retained some autonomy to advance their interests and those of their allies, including, in some cases, drug traffickers. Ibid.

34 Jorge I. Domínguez and Rafael Fernández de Castro, "U.S.–Mexican Relations: Coping with Domestic and International Crisis," in *Contemporary U.S.–Latin American Relations*, ed. Jorge I. Domínguez et al. (New York: Routledge, 2016), 45. The most conservative estimates of the total number of drug-related homicides over the course of Calderón's presidency approximated 60,000 persons. As of July 2017, official Mexican government figures admitted that 186,000 persons had lost their lives since Calderón initiated his military offensive against organized crime in 2006.

35 With recorded murders of 2,566 persons, June 2017 registered the highest number of homicides in Mexico in a single month since 1997, when the offices of local prosecutors began furnishing the Federal Secretariat of Public Security with such statistics. "Violencia Se Expande y Homicidios Llegan a Su Mayor Nivel en 20 Años en México," *El Mercurio* (Santiago), July 22, 2017: A6. More alarming still is the fact that these murders are no longer concentrated in a handful of states, but are now dispersed throughout Mexico.

36 Jorge I. Domínguez and Rafael Fernández de Castro, "U.S.–Mexican Relations: Coping with Domestic and International Crisis," in *Contemporary U.S.–Latin American Relations*, ed. Jorge I. Domínguez et al. (New York: Routledge, 2016), 45. An office in Mexico City for U.S. and Mexican government officials working on Mérida-related programs opened, to much fanfare, in 2009, but shrinking U.S. funding ensured it never became fully operational and it was eventually shut down in 2014. Ibid at 48.

37 Eric L. Olson, *The Evolving Mérida Initiative and the Policy of Shared Responsibility in U.S.–Mexico Security Relations* (Washington, DC: Mexico Institute [Woodrow Wilson International Center for Scholars], February 2017), 7. The Mérida Initiative requires that the U.S. State Department keep the Federal Congress appraised of progress by Mexico in fulfilling its obligations under international human rights law, including ensuring civilian-led investigations of police and military forces for alleged human rights abuses as well as prohibiting the use of testimony obtained through torture.

38 Much of this money went toward improving border infrastructure and training to enhance the capacity of security and immigration personnel to enforce migration laws as well as the incorporation of new technology to process migrants. Eric L. Olson, *The Evolving Mérida Initiative and the Policy of Shared Responsibility in U.S.–Mexico Security Relations* (Washington, DC: Mexico Institute [Woodrow Wilson International Center for Scholars], February 2017), 15.

39 Eric L. Olson, *The Evolving Mérida Initiative and the Policy of Shared Responsibility in U.S.–Mexico Security Relations* (Washington, DC: Mexico Institute [Woodrow

Wilson International Center for Scholars], February 2017), 10. The original focus of these efforts sought to address the social determinants and drivers of violence in Tijuana, Ciudad Juarez, and Monterrey, three of the Mexican cities with the highest levels of homicides.

40 Jorge I. Domínguez and Rafael Fernández de Castro, "U.S.–Mexican Relations: Coping with Domestic and International Crisis," in *Contemporary U.S.–Latin American Relations*, ed. Jorge I. Domínguez et al. (New York: Routledge, 2016), 48. One explanation for this is that public commitments made by U.S. officials were not tied to specific targets or funding initiatives that could better ensure their fulfillment. Eric L. Olson, *The Evolving Mérida Initiative and the Policy of Shared Responsibility in U.S.–Mexico Security Relations* (Washington, DC: Mexico Institute [Woodrow Wilson International Center for Scholars], February 2017), 7.

41 Edgardo Buscaglia, "La Paradoja Mexicana de la Delincuencia Organizada: Policías, Violencia y Corrupción," *Revista Policía y Seguridad Pública* Año 2, Vol. 1 (2012): 277. Buscaglia suggests that one explanation for why there is no effective asset forfeiture mechanism or major cleansing of the political system in Mexico is the inability of all law enforcement agencies (including the intelligence agencies, police, judiciary, and prison systems) to work together in a coordinated fashion. Ibid at 278. He highlights the turf battles that exist between the Federal Secretariat of Public Security and the Office of the Prosecutor General of the Republic, for example, and even involving the armed forces.

42 Edgardo Buscaglia, "La Paradoja Mexicana de la Delincuencia Organizada: Policías, Violencia y Corrupción," *Revista Policía y Seguridad Pública* Año 2, Vol. 1 (2012): 277. Buscaglia also recognizes the need for civil society groups to work closely with the government to dissuade young people from joining criminal gangs, whether through enhancing educational opportunities, creating more jobs in the formal sector, or developing public health and social development campaigns. Ibid at 278. This was actually one of the new elements the Obama administration added to the Mérida Initiative.

43 Edgardo Buscaglia, "La Paradoja Mexicana de la Delincuencia Organizada: Policías, Violencia y Corrupción," *Revista Policía y Seguridad Pública* Año 2, Vol. 1 (2012): 279. Buscaglia would argue that only after you have tackled the issues of asset forfeiture, campaign finance reform, getting all the law enforcement agencies to work in unison, and building effective public–private partnerships to provide youth with alternatives to a life of crime, can you then work on a major overhaul of the judicial system that will produce sustainable outcomes. Ibid at 280.

44 "More than 90 percent of the cocaine trafficked to the United States is of Colombian origin . . . and approximately 83 percent of the cocaine that enters the United States transits through the Mexico-Central America corridor." Gema Santamaria, "Breaking the Vicious Cycle: Criminal Violence in U.S.–Latin American Relations," in *Contemporary U.S.–Latin American Relations*, ed. Jorge I. Domínguez et al. (New York: Routledge, 2016), 256. In addition, the U.S. State Department estimates that as much as 87 percent of all cocaine-smuggling flights departing South America first land in Honduras. Eric L. Olson, ed., *Crime and Violence in Central America's Northern Triangle* (Washington, DC: Woodrow Wilson International Center for Scholars, 2015), 24.

45 Interestingly, there are no CARSI programs to support the thousands of youth already ensnared in gang life, who might be enticed to leave if there were acceptable exit programs as well as alternative education and job-training schemes. Eric L. Olson, ed., *Crime and Violence in Central America's Northern Triangle* (Washington, DC: Woodrow Wilson International Center for Scholars, 2015), 39–40. In the Salvadoran case (and to an extent in Guatemala) this is, in part, the result of the U.S. Treasury Department designating the Mara Salvatrucha, or MS-13, and its supporters as a transnational criminal organization, therefore prohibiting U.S. citizens and organizations from engaging in transactions with them. Ibid at 39.

46 Eric L. Olson, ed., *Crime and Violence in Central America's Northern Triangle* (Washington, DC: Woodrow Wilson International Center for Scholars, 2015), 7. "Drug seizures, arrests, and number of people trained [were] . . . used as indicators of success even though these offer little evidence of long term impact on violence or crime rates or institutional capacity." Ibid. "The most common problem is that evaluations tend to measure the wrong things—inputs instead of outcomes." Ibid at 49.

47 Eric L. Olson, ed., *Crime and Violence in Central America's Northern Triangle* (Washington, DC: Woodrow Wilson International Center for Scholars, 2015), 46–7. These specialized units are generally established within an existing law enforcement agency and "tend to become isolated within the broader institutional framework, can create resentment and unnecessary competition within their institution, and, because of their sensitive nature, have been accused of undertaking operations that contradict or undermine other law enforcement priorities." Ibid at 4 and 46–7.

48 Gema Santamaria, "Breaking the Vicious Cycle: Criminal Violence in U.S.–Latin American Relations," in *Contemporary U.S.–Latin American Relations*, ed. Jorge I. Domínguez et al. (New York: Routledge, 2016), 257. By the time Obama left office, the U.S. Congress had appropriated an estimated US$1.5 billion of assistance through CARSI. Mark P. Sullivan, *Latin America and the Caribbean: Key Issues and Actions in the 114th Congress* (Washington, DC: Congressional Research Service, January 4, 2017), 32.

49 By February 2017, of the US$750 million approved by the U.S. Congress at the end of 2015, only US$125 million had reached Honduras, while El Salvador had only received US$98 million. Atlantic Council, *Building a Better Future: A Blueprint for Central America's Northern Triangle* (Washington, DC: Atlantic Council, May 2017), 14. By contrast, Guatemala, El Salvador, and Honduras collectively budgeted US$2.8 billion for the Alliance for Prosperity in 2016 and another US$2.9 billion in 2017, representing some 80 percent of the Alliance's total budgeted resources. Ibid at 15.

50 The member states of the Caribbean Community and Common Market, or CARICOM, are: 1) Antigua and Barbuda; 2) the Bahamas; 3) Barbados; 4) Belize; 5) Dominica; 6) Grenada; 7) Guyana; 8) Haiti; 9) Jamaica; 10) Montserrat; 11) Saint Kitts and Nevis; 12) Saint Lucia; 13) Saint Vincent and the Grenadines; 14) Suriname; 15) Trinidad and Tobago.

51 Then U.S. President Obama identified five Caribbean countries—the Bahamas, Belize, the Dominican Republic, Haiti, and Jamaica—as major drug-producing or drug-transit countries in September 2016, pursuant to requirements imposed by the U.S. Congress on the White House to publicly identify on an annual basis those countries that fail to take appropriate counter-narcotics measures. Mark P. Sullivan, *Latin America and the Caribbean: Key Issues and Actions in the 114th Congress* (Washington, DC: Congressional Research Service, January 4, 2017), 30.

52 See "CARICOM Crime and Security Strategy 2013: Securing the Region," adopted at the 24th Inter-Sessional Meeting of the Conference of Heads of Government of CARICOM, February 18–19, 2013, Port-au-Prince, Haiti. Available at: http://caricom.org/media-center/multimedia/document-library/ or www.state.gov/p/wha/rls/210635.htm.

53 Marifeli Pérez-Stable, "The United States and Cuba: Intimate Neighbors?" in *Contemporary U.S.–Latin American Relations*, ed. Jorge I. Domínguez et al. (New York: Routledge, 2016), 63.

54 See, e.g., Ann Louise Bardach, "Twilight of the Assassins," *The Atlantic*, Vol. 298, No. 4 (2006): 88–101. Cuban exile groups based in the United States also carried out assassinations in Miami, New York, and Puerto Rico, and bombed travel agencies that chartered flights to Cuba and the businesses or homes of some pro-rapprochement exiles. Marifeli Pérez-Stable, "The United States and Cuba: Intimate Neighbors?" in *Contemporary U.S.–Latin American Relations*, ed. Jorge I.

Domínguez et al. (New York: Routledge, 2016), 70. Cuban authorities arrested a Salvadoran man who claimed that individuals tied to the Miami-based Cuban American National Foundation had paid him for each bomb he placed in Havana hotels in 1997 to discourage foreign tourism to the island. Ibid at fn. 25, 79. Luis Posada Carriles boasted of launching that bombing campaign. Ann Louise Bardach, "Twilight of the Assassins," *The Atlantic*, Vol. 298, No. 4 (2006): 92.

55 See, e.g., John Dinges and Saul Landau, *Assassination on Embassy Row* (New York: McGraw Hill, 1981).

Bibliography

Alpert, Megan. "15 Years and $10 Billion Later, U.S. Efforts to Curb Colombia's Cocaine Trade Have Failed." *Foreign Policy*. February 8, 2016. Accessed July 27, 2017: http://foreignpolicy.com/2016/02/08/15-years-and-10-billion-later-u-s-efforts-to-curb-colombias-cocaine-trade-have-failed/.

Atlantic Council. *Building a Better Future: A Blueprint for Central America's Northern Triangle*. Washington, DC: Atlantic Council, May 2017.

Bagley, Bruce M. and Jonathan D. Rosen, eds. *Colombia's Political Economy at the Outset of the Twenty-first Century: From Uribe to Santos and Beyond*. Lanham, MD: Lexington Books, 2015.

Bardach, Ann Louise. "Twilight of the Assassins." *The Atlantic* Vol. 298, No. 4 (2006): 88–101.

Buscaglia, Edgardo. "La Paradoja Mexicana de la Delincuencia Organizada: Policías, Violencia y Corrupción." *Revista Policía y Seguridad Pública* Año 2, Vol. 1 (2012): 275–282.

CARICOM. "CARICOM Crime and Security Strategy 2013: Securing the Region." Georgetown, Guyana: CARICOM Secretariat. Adopted at the 24th Inter-Sessional Meeting of the Conference of Heads of Government of CARICOM in Port-Au-Prince, Haiti on February 18–19, 2013. Accessed July 27, 2017: http://caricom.org/media-center/multimedia/document-library/ or www.state.gov/p/wha/rls/210635.htm

Crandall, Russell. *Driven by Drugs: U.S. Policy Toward Colombia*. Boulder, CO: Lynne Rienner Publishers, 2008.

Dinges, John and Saul Landau. *Assassination on Embassy Row*. New York: McGraw Hill, 1981.

Domínguez, Jorge I. and Rafael Fernández de Castro, eds. *Contemporary U.S.–Latin American Relations*. New York: Routledge, 2016.

Eckstein, Susan and Timothy P. Wickham, eds. *What Justice? Whose Justice? Fighting for Fairness in Latin America*. Berkeley: University of California Press, 2003.

El Mercurio, "Violencia Se Expande y Homicidios Llegan a Su Mayor Nivel en 20 Años en México." *El Mercurio* (Santiago), July 22, 2017: A6.

Forero, Juan. "Burdened Colombians Back Tax to Fight Rebels." *New York Times*, September 8, 2002: 16.

González, Francisco E. "Mexico's Drug Wars Get Brutal." *Current History* Vol. 108, No. 715 (2009): 72–76.

Goodman, Joshua. "Cultivos de Hoja de Coca en Colombia Subieron 52% en 2016, Según la ONU." *El Mercurio* (Santiago), July 15, 2017: A4.

Latinobarómetro. *Informe 2008*. Santiago: Corporación Latinobarómetro, November 2008. Accessed July 27, 2017: www.latinobarometro.org/docs/INFORME_LATINOBAROMETRO_2008.pdf

Long, Tom. *Latin America Confronts the United States: Asymmetry and Influence.* New York: Cambridge University Press, 2015.

Luce, Edward. "Obama Woos Cuban-Americans with Promises." *Financial Times,* May 24, 2008: 4.

Olson, Eric L. ed. *Crime and Violence in Central America's Northern Tringle.* Washington, DC: Woodrow Wilson International Center for Scholars, 2015.

Olson, Eric L. *The Evolving Mérida Initiative and the Policy of Shared Responsibility in U.S.–Mexico Security Relations.* Washington, DC: Mexico Institute [Woodrow Wilson International Center for Scholars], February 2017.

Pew Global Attitudes Project. "Views of a Changing World 2003." Washington, DC: Pew Research Center, June 3, 2003. Accessed July 27, 2017: www.pewglobal.org/ 2003/06/03/views-of-a-changing-world-2003/

Shifter, Michael. "Plan Colombia: A Retrospective." *Americas Quarterly* Vol. 6, No. 2 (2012): 36–42.

Sullivan, Mark P. *Latin America and the Caribbean: Key Issues and Actions in the 114th Congress.* Washington, DC: Congressional Research Service, January 4, 2017.

Tate, Winifred. *Drugs, Thugs, and Diplomats: U.S. Policymaking in Colombia.* Stanford, CA: Stanford University Press, 2015.

Tavares, Rodrigo. *Security in South America: The Role of States and Regional Organizations.* Boulder, CO: First Forum Press, 2014.

Thompson, Ginger. "U.S. and Mexico to Open Talks on Freer Migration of Workers." *New York Times,* February 16, 2001: 1.

Vivares, Ernesto, ed. *Exploring the New South American Regionalism.* Farnham, UK: Ashgate Publishing, 2014.

Weiner, Tim and Ginger Thompson. "Bush Gives Mexico Backing on Drive Against Narcotics." *New York Times,* February 17, 2001: 1.

Williams, Mark Eric. *Understanding U.S.–Latin American Relations.* New York: Routledge, 2012.

8 The Current State of Affairs and Future Ramifications

With the exception of Gramsci's conception of hegemony, it is difficult to argue that the dominance and leadership traditionally exerted over the Western Hemisphere by the United States has not significantly diminished since George W. Bush became President of the United States of America at the start of the twenty-first century. In the case of Bush, much of this is attributable to two disastrous wars of choice, one in Afghanistan and the other in Iraq. A decade and a half later, the United States has still not been able to extricate itself from either quagmire and has little to show for the trillions of dollars squandered, not to mention countless human lives lost or ruined.[1] Both wars also had ripple effects throughout Asia, northern Africa, and Europe that unleashed further bloodshed and saw the appearance of new groups of extremists. During this time period, there was a lack of any visionary leadership or proactive engagement on the part of the United States in the Western Hemisphere, which would have been beneficial in terms of equitable economic growth and addressing a myriad of challenges, including climate change. Instead, a narrow security agenda dominated U.S. concerns in the region, especially where it could be linked to the global war on terrorism. Hence, the only noteworthy accomplishment was the reassertion of the central government's presence throughout Colombia's national territory, and most of that is attributable to the Colombians themselves, who bankrolled the bulk of Plan Colombia and steered it in such a way as to meet their basic objectives.

A lack of visionary leadership when it came to Latin America and the Caribbean also characterized Barack H. Obama's time in the White House, albeit excused in part by the severe economic crisis he faced upon taking office as well as two raging land wars in the Near East. In particular, the United States was engulfed in the worst economic crisis since the Great Depression. Approximately US$40 trillion in equity value in the global economy was destroyed, the U.S. government was forced to nationalize the country's largest mortgage lenders, the Lehman Brothers investment bank disappeared following the largest bankruptcy in history, and the bailouts and stimulus packages issued around the world totaled trillions of dollars.[2] These massive bailouts of banks, insurers, and industry carried out by both the Bush and Obama administrations contradicted the free market sermons that Washington, DC had long preached to Latin American governments. In addition, most of the individuals responsible for the financial corruption that caused the severe economic dislocations managed to escape punishment, with this thereby rivaling the worst impunity scandals that had long bedeviled countries to the south.

Obama's ability to devise a bold new policy for the Western Hemisphere was further stymied by an intransigent Republican majority in both the Senate and House of Representatives after the mid-term legislative elections of November 2010. This led to a threatened shutdown of the Federal government in 2011 and an actual closure in 2013 stemming from the U.S. Congress' inability to agree on a budget. The initial refusal of the Republican majority in Congress to raise the federal debt ceiling in 2011, thereby threatening default, also led Standard & Poor's to take the previously unheard-of step of downgrading the United States of America's credit rating.

The one notable achievement of the Obama administration in terms of U.S. relations with Latin America and the Caribbean was the decision to restore normal diplomatic relations with Cuba in 2015. If this effort bore fruit, however, it was primarily because Havana now felt that it was in its best interests for it to do so.

Of the four case studies examined in this book, all of them exhibit the United States' diminished ability to control the course of events or positively influence outcomes. At least three of the four case studies also underscore the failure of the United States to exert any type of meaningful leadership that might have resulted in success. The fourth case study—China's rising presence in Latin America and the Caribbean—is still a work in progress, although there is no doubt the Chinese commercial presence, particularly in South America, is already challenging U.S. economic domination of the continent. In fact, if the Free Trade Area of the Americas (FTAA) were to be proposed today, it is doubtful there would be as many enthusiastic participants from South America as was the case two decades ago.

The Energy and Climate Partnership of the Americas (ECPA) is perhaps the most glaring example of a U.S. foreign policy initiative that stumbled because of a lack of leadership on the part of Washington, DC (albeit that this may have been by design). The United States never put its money where its mouth was in adequately funding ECPA initiatives, expecting the private sector or other governments in the Western Hemisphere to step up to the plate (something that failed to materialize in any significant manner). The United States' failure to ratify the Kyoto Protocol or to enact any type of meaningful climate change legislation at the federal level undermined its moral authority on the issue. The inability to enact national climate change legislation also removed the possibility of establishing a hemispheric carbon offset program that would have provided an important boost for raising ECPA's profile.

Although the United States did play a predominant role in supplying the parameters for the FTAA and steering the negotiations, it failed to make the necessary sacrifices that would have sealed the deal. While the United States claimed it was in favor of free trade, it refused to give up re-imposing tariffs in response to alleged dumping even if there were alternative means (namely competition policy) to redress the detrimental impacts of unfair trade practices. It also preferred to refer discussions on the highly distortive impacts of its agricultural subsidies to other fora. By kowtowing to vested domestic interest groups, the United States was left unable to offer meaningful concessions to the largest South American governments, particularly Brazil, making it politically untenable for them to table offers on issues that were of most interest to the Americans. Undoubtedly contributing to the intransigent U.S. negotiating position was the triumphalism that arose from the collapse of the USSR and the Marxist alternative to free market economic liberalism. This put ideological blinders on U.S. political leaders, who were deaf to pleas that the FTAA required a well-funded economic development component in order to succeed. Free trade by itself was not going to produce an equitable expansion of opportunities for the citizens and entrepreneurs throughout the Americas, given the huge asymmetries among the countries participating in the FTAA. This failure in U.S. leadership helped consign the FTAA to the dustbin of history.

The Organization of American States (OAS), the centerpiece of an inter-American system championed by the United States to exert its power and influence in the Western Hemisphere, is today a victim of U.S. neglect.[3] The United States often finds itself outvoted and incapable of pushing its foreign policy agenda through the OAS. In frustration, it pulls back from exerting any proactive leadership role and, in the past, has retaliated by failing to make timely payments of its annual dues.[4] The most effective component of the inter-American system relates to the promotion and protection of human rights. The U.S. Senate has never ratified the American Convention on Human Rights, however, even though President Jimmy Carter signed it back in the 1970s. That means, by definition, the United States does not participate in the Inter-American Court of Human Rights in San José, Costa Rica. The United States also rejects the binding character of decisions from the Inter-American Commission on Human Rights interpreting provisions of the American Declaration on Human Rights (which is applicable to all OAS member states, including the United States). As a result, the United States is incapable of exercising effective leadership in ensuring compliance with the most important legal instruments for the protection of human rights within the Western Hemisphere. This scenario has provided an opening for governments with deplorable human rights records to question and, in the case of Bolivarian Venezuela, even refuse to participate in the inter-American human rights system. One of the most notable developments in the twenty-first century has been governments' enthusiasm for forming alternative institutions to the OAS, such as the Community of Latin American and Caribbean States (CELAC), that purposefully exclude the United States. The fact that these countries no longer feel it necessary to focus all their diplomatic efforts on the OAS in order to contain the United States is perhaps the most revealing indication of how widespread the perception of U.S. hegemony's decline in the Western Hemisphere has become.

It is still too early to tell whether the explosion in Chinese investment and trade with Latin America and the Caribbean that coincided with the start of the twenty-first century means that China will become the new hegemon to replace the United States in all or part of the Americas. Regardless, China is now the largest trading partner for many South American nations. It is difficult to visit any retailer in Latin America and the Caribbean today and not find the shelves and racks full of Chinese-made goods. The boom in South American commodity exports to China allowed governments to build up their reserves, pay off debts, and liberate themselves from dependence on multilateral lending agencies centered on Washington, DC. The Chinese have also become major investors throughout Latin America and the Caribbean, particularly in the mining and energy sectors, and are playing an ever more important role in building the region's energy, telecommunication, and transportation infrastructure. In fact, Chinese banks now contribute more money, on an annual basis, to economic development projects in Latin America and the Caribbean than do traditional lenders such as the World Bank and the Inter-American Development Bank. China's banks also stand out for their lending to governments which the private sector and the multilateral institutions based in Washington, DC tend to avoid, and also allow borrowing countries to pay them back with natural resource commodities such as oil. China's role in building ports and telecommunication systems gives Beijing an intelligence advantage that could be used militarily against the United States in the future. Chinese military assistance and arms sales have already played a role in allowing many Latin American governments to resist American pressure that they do not comply with International Criminal Court requests to turn over U.S. military personnel accused of war crimes. Accordingly, China is emerging not only as an economic but also, potentially, a military rival to the United States in the Western Hemisphere.

The other foreign policy initiatives directed at Latin America and the Caribbean under the George W. Bush and Obama administrations that are discussed in this book display a diminishment of influence and an absence of leadership on the part of the United States. While the U.S. took the initial lead in providing the funds for and supplying the original parameters of Plan Colombia, Bogotá was responsible for footing the bulk of the money and eventually determined what strategic objectives would be prioritized. Any accomplishments achieved under Plan Colombia, therefore, are much more attributable to the Colombians than to the political establishment in Washington, DC. The Mérida Initiative, the Central American Regional Security Initiative (CARSI), and the Caribbean Basin Security Initiative (CBSI) are bereft of a comprehensive and long-term strategic vision required to resolve the myriad root causes of the escalating violence in the beneficiary countries. Instead, all three initiatives are myopically fixated on a narrow, short-term security agenda with precarious and uncertain funding streams. While Pathways to Prosperity and *100,000 Strong in the Americas* exemplify American liberal idealism at its best, both were woefully underfunded. In addition, the U.S. government provided no sustained oversight or direction, so that both initiatives eventually floundered. Finally, the resumption of normal diplomatic relations between Washington, DC and Havana while Cuba was still under the Communist rule of a Castro is an indictment of a half-century-long policy that failed to accomplish any of its main objectives. In the end, the United States was forced to bow to reality more than the Cubans were.

As previously noted, the one conception of hegemony that most strongly supports the argument that the political values and economic principles long championed by the United States remain predominant throughout the Western Hemisphere is provided by the neo-Marxist Antonio Gramsci. Representative democracy is the norm throughout the Western Hemisphere, even though there have been a number of recent challenges and temporary setbacks. On the economic front, there has been a return to more market-friendly policies following the end of the so-called Pink Tide in Latin America, when governments assumed a more interventionist role in the economy. This has been particularly noticeable in Argentina and Brazil. In Bolivia, despite the socialist rhetoric of the ruling party, the administration of Evo Morales has generally adhered to orthodox macroeconomic policies that mesh with standard IMF prescriptions. Similarly, Ecuador under Rafael Correa and Nicaragua under Daniel Ortega never fully abandoned all of the economic policy recommendations of the Washington Consensus. The one country that did, Venezuela, is currently an economic basket case. In addition, although Hugo Chavez did manage to find new export markets for Venezuelan petroleum and reduce his country's previous heavy dependency on the American market, the United States continues to be the primary destination for Venezuelan oil exports. Paradoxically, the country is even more dependent on U.S. imports today than it was before Chavez became president in 1999. Only Cuba has provided a sustained counter-hegemonic alternative to the dominant capitalist economic model and ethos of representative democracy that prevails in the Americas. All indications are that this alternative model appears exhausted, however, and the country may find itself moving closer to the norms that prevail in the rest of the Americas after Raul Castro steps down as president of Cuba in 2018.

Even under David Lake's alternative theory of variegated hierarchy, which he uses instead of hegemony to characterize the role of the United States in the Western Hemisphere since the end of the nineteenth century, there is plenty of evidence that the U.S. position at the apex of an economic and security pyramid is contested in the twenty-first century. For one thing, there is the rise of CELAC and UNASUR as alternatives to the OAS. UNASUR, in particular, has marginalized the inter-American defense system and created an alternative forum for South American governments to address their defense priorities and develop their own defense technologies. The OAS has itself evolved from an institution that more often than not rubber-stamped policy dictates emanating from Washington, DC to one that increasingly serves as a brake (explaining U.S. policy-makers' growing frustration with the organization). The appearance of China as a major trade partner, investor, and lender—particularly in South America—has significantly reduced the influence of the multilateral institutions centered on Washington, DC that enforce U.S. policy prescriptions through conditionality requirements on loans. The Bush administration's unilateral military interventions and the Obama administration's failure to adhere to the same economic policy advice that, for decades, Washington, DC dispensed to Latin American governments when they faced grave economic troubles have led to a loss of U.S. legitimacy. This, in turn, has diminished U.S. authority to command and destabilized—perhaps fatally—the hierarchical status quo in force for more than a century. Exacerbating this phenomenon is the fact the United States has been unable or unwilling to provide wise policy advice and adequate funding for a number of proposed policy initiatives, ranging from ECPA to Pathways to Prosperity in the Americas. Hence, there is no longer any strong incentive for many countries in the Americas—particularly the further south one goes—to strategically sacrifice part of their sovereignty in exchange for the meager public goods the United States may now be offering to entice compliance.

From a Latin American perspective, the United States' inability to project its authority and influence throughout the Western Hemisphere since the start of the twenty-first century in the way it historically did is a positive development. For one thing, it has allowed many Latin American governments to experiment with new forms of governance and economic policies free of interruptions from the Colossus of the North. Hence, they have been able to run their full course, as in Venezuela, and have been shown to be abject failures, hopefully never to be repeated again. This marks a dramatic change from the twentieth century, when experiments of this type were often cut short—for example, Salvador Allende's "Chilean road to socialism under democracy" that ended prematurely in a blood-soaked military coup encouraged by the Nixon administration. These interruptions always provided ammunition for arguments that the experiments might have succeeded if not for the intervention of the United States, and, worse, allowed them to be tried again elsewhere, often with negative consequences for the citizens of these countries.

The financial absence of the United States in recent decades has also forced Latin American and Caribbean governments to look to domestic and regional financing to resolve long-standing deficiencies in economic development and inequitable distribution of wealth, and the societal maladies these produce. After a long history of resistance, the elites of the Northern Triangle countries of Central America have finally acquiesced to the imposition of new taxes to pay for enhanced government services (including security) in order to prevent a wave of violence that threatens to undermine their own livelihoods. The Colombians themselves provided the bulk of the money expended to halt and reverse their country's slide into becoming a failed state. While its economy boomed during the Lula administration, Brazil was an important contributor to development aid, both in Latin America and in sub-Saharan Africa.[5] The Brazilian National Development Bank (BNDES) also funded major infrastructure projects throughout South America. After the implosion of the Argentine economy at the end of 2001, which also had a recessionary impact on Paraguay and Uruguay, BNDES allowed the local subsidiaries of Brazilian firms operating in the other MERCOSUR countries to be eligible for its loans.[6] The objective was to provide an economic stimulus to prevent a severe contraction of intra-MERCOSUR trade flows that could have put the entire Southern Cone integration project at risk.

Overall, Latin America has made significant progress in reducing extreme poverty in the twenty-first century. In 2002, almost 44 percent of the region's population were considered to be living in poverty, but by 2012 that figure had dropped to 28 percent, representing 164 million people.[7] This was, in part, the result of the surge in Asian demand for the region's commodities, sparking economic growth and creating many new jobs. Another important factor was the conditional cash-transfer programs pioneered by Brazil and Mexico in the late 1990s but eventually enacted by at least 18 other countries in Latin America and the Caribbean, which provide government subsidies to poor families who keep their children in school and have them properly vaccinated. The fact that Latin American governments were forced to look to themselves for solutions to resolve domestic challenges, including supplying the requisite financing, has enhanced national self-confidence. A case in point is Brazil, which under the Lula administration sought a greater regional and even global role, exerting its diplomatic and economic muscle as an alternative to the United States, such as in the UN drive to sanction Iran for its nuclear ambitions.[8]

Chile provides an interesting example of a Latin American country that has not waited for the United States to lead the Western Hemisphere in efforts to reduce greenhouse gas emissions or fund initiatives to mitigate vulnerabilities exacerbated by climate change. Chile's national energy plan aims to have 70 percent of the country's energy generated from domestic renewable and non-conventional resources by 2050, and 60 percent by 2035. This is, in part, the result of painful lessons from the recent past in which natural gas from neighboring Argentina was interrupted after 2004, and eventually stopped altogether (making the handful of cross-border pipelines built in the 1990s obsolete). Chile's decision to encourage the building of those pipelines and thermal plants to generate electricity from natural gas was, in turn, the result of a severe drought in the mid-1990s which hindered its previous extensive reliance on hydropower. In response to the energy crisis generated by the Argentine cut-off, two expensive receiving terminals were built to import liquefied natural gas (LNG) from East Asia and Trinidad and Tobago. The Chileans were also forced to use more coal, exacerbating the already problematic air quality in many Chilean cities. The move to a matrix in which the vast majority of its electricity is generated from domestically sourced renewable and non-conventional resources aims to drastically reduce Chile's greenhouse gas emissions and enhance energy security. At present, more than half of the investment in non-conventional, renewable energy in Latin America and the Caribbean is directed to Chile.[9] The most interesting aspect of the Chilean experience is that the shift to renewable energy has largely been financed by the private sector, with no expensive subsidies (other than reimbursement payments at the full retail price to photovoltaic contributors to the grid). The investment has come because of a transparent business climate based on respect for the rule of law and an attractive regulatory environment.

The cumulative effect of all these examples of Latin American governments stepping up to the plate to resolve long-standing societal problems, rather than waiting for a hegemon to step in to resolve it for them, means that when a future American administration appears offering "partnership and shared responsibility," as the Obama administration did, more countries will be in a position to respond positively. Such a scenario might also revive the comatose inter-American system and convert it into an effective tool of hemispheric governance premised on a genuine congruence of interests.

Up to now, the premise of this book has revolved around the debate over whether there has been a decline in U.S. hegemony since the start of the new millennium. The extent of that decline, if any, is premised on the particular definition of hegemony utilized. The conclusion is that, using standard definitions supplied by the different schools of international relations theory, U.S. hegemony in the Western Hemisphere has diminished in comparison to the situation that existed throughout the twentieth century. The exception is reliance on the Gramscian notion of hegemony, through which there has been no decline—although in that case we are not talking about an American hegemony *per se*, but rather a hegemony of ideas and precepts propagated by transnational elites. In any event, the use of the word "decline" is purposeful as it rests on an optimistic premise that the phenomenon can still be halted and even reversed.[10] At least, that was the assumption prior to the election of Donald Trump as the 45th President of the United States of America.

The public pronouncements and actions taken by Trump since his inauguration on January 20, 2017 could well spell the demise of U.S. hegemony, not only in terms of the Western Hemisphere, but globally as well. His threats to ignore the rulings of the World Trade Organization and abrogate the North American Free Trade Agreement, if carried out, will undoubtedly undermine the international economic order that American political leaders spent decades constructing after the conclusion of World War II. For the moment, the Trump administration seems determined to undermine an already enfeebled inter-American system, precisely when it is most needed to facilitate a peaceful resolution to the escalating political and economic crisis in Venezuela. In March 2017, the Trump administration boycotted hearings of the Inter-American Commission on Human Rights examining the human rights situation within the United States. This was followed by a failure at the June 2017 meeting of the OAS General Assembly in Cancun to secure the necessary two-thirds majority to approve a resolution on Venezuela. The resolution called on President Nicolás Maduro to, among other things, admit a delegation of representatives from OAS member states to try to mediate a solution to the Venezuelan crisis. Some commentators have attributed the inability to pass this resolution to U.S. Secretary of State Rex Tillerson's last-minute decision not to attend the meeting and personally lobby for votes in favor of the resolution.[11]

If the draconian budget cuts for U.S. foreign assistance proposed by the Trump White House go through, this will reduce Washington, DC's ability to provide public goods in return for acquiescence to American leadership.

Trump's decision to withdraw from the Trans-Pacific Partnership (TPP)—which included Chile, Mexico, and Peru—and adoption of more protectionist trade policies have already led to a revival of dormant trade arrangements such as the Latin American Integration Association (ALADI) and MERCOSUR. A protectionist United States may well end up providing the catalyst for the European Union and MERCOSUR to conclude a free trade agreement, after two decades of previous failed attempts. Even if much of what Trump is threatening turns out to be empty bluster, there is a price to pay in international diplomacy when one fails to follow through on promises or threats, in terms of credibility and respect. The Obama administration learned that lesson in Syria when it failed to respond forcefully after Bashar al-Assad crossed the U.S.-imposed "red line" and used chemical weapons against civilians.

Despite a further decline in the authority and influence of the United States, the rest of the Western Hemisphere, and particularly the countries in the Caribbean Basin, is not yet in a position to ignore the latest antics in Washington, DC and carry on without the Americans. The United States is still the richest country in the Western Hemisphere and as such remains a magnet for immigrants, both legal and undocumented. El Salvador, Haiti, Honduras, and Nicaragua are currently beneficiaries of deferred deportation programs that have allowed hundreds of thousands of their citizens to remain in the United States, decades after the initial crises that allowed them to obtain Temporary Protected Status (TPS). Any decision by the White House to terminate this discretionary mechanism would have a severely destabilizing impact on the politics and economies of the beneficiary countries. The United States' mass deportations of Central Americans from the Northern Triangle countries who had criminal records, beginning in the late 1990s, are in part responsible for the high levels of violence and homicides afflicting those countries today.

Latin American and Caribbean countries also benefit from the United States' overwhelming military predominance in the Western Hemisphere. For one thing, the U.S.-supplied security blanket that insulates the Americas from external threats allows Latin American and Caribbean governments to spend their limited resources on human capital development, rather than on building up and maintaining a huge military apparatus that could encourage wars over border disputes or be abused domestically in ways that violate basic human rights. Tellingly, UNASUR's defense arrangements do not include any references to collective security. The Trump administration's questioning of the value of NATO, coupled with demands that European countries "pay their fair share" and increase national defense budgets, ought to raise questions in capitals throughout the Americas as to the future sustainability of the U.S. security blanket.

Given its position as the largest contributor to greenhouse gas emissions in the Western Hemisphere (and the second in the world after China), it is imperative to engage the United States in efforts to reduce such emissions on a global level. Latin America and the Caribbean face numerous risks from climate change, including rising sea levels that threaten major population centers and the entire territory of island nations, as well as melting glaciers in the Andes that would eliminate the most important source of fresh-water supply and energy from hydropower in South America. Latin American and Caribbean governments should also be concerned about massive U.S. budget cuts proposed by the Trump administration with regard to the National Institutes of Health, the Centers for Disease Control and Prevention, and the Pan-American Health Organization. The United States, after all, has traditionally taken the lead on providing funding for the research and development of medications to treat pandemics and other maladies that have historically broken out in the Americas, including the introduction of the first effective vaccine for yellow fever.

Notes

1 A comprehensive academic study in 2012 put the actual costs of both the Iraq and Afghan wars through the end of 2011 at US$4.4 trillion, counting expenses such as veterans' medical benefits. By contrast, the Congressional Budget Office's estimation was a more modest US$1.5 trillion through the end of 2011. Joel Brinkley, "Iraq Outlook Looks Dim After U.S. Troop Pullout: Some Predict Another Brutal Dictatorship," *Politico,* February 27, 2012: 1. In June 2015, Obama deployed up to 450 more troops to join the 3,000 or so already in Iraq to train local forces to fight Islamic State militants. At least 300 U.S. paratroopers were sent to Iraq by the Trump administration in March 2017 to help the Iraqi military retake Mosul. W.J. Hennigan, "U.S. Military Escalation, Off the Radar: The Trump Administration has Stopped Disclosing the Number of Troops in Iraq and Syria," *Los Angeles Times,* March 30, 2017: 1. Some 9,000 U.S. soldiers were still present in Afghanistan by the time Obama left office. In June 2017 the Trump administration announced the deployment of an additional 4,000 troops to Afghanistan to help the Afghan army against a resurgent Taliban insurgency.
2 Alfredo Toro Hardy, *The World Turned Upside Down: The Complex Partnership between China and Latin America* (Singapore: World Scientific Publishing Company, 2013), 81. The Great Recession of 2008 was the result of excessive deregulation and *laissez faire* policies in the U.S. financial services sector that contributed to a global wave of mistrust of private institutions, subsequently transferred onto governments. Ibid at xxi. This phenomenon explains the eventual rise of populist political parties in Europe, Brexit, and the election of Donald Trump to the U.S. presidency.
3 Signs of cracks in the inter-American system were already evident in the 1970s and 1980s, most notably with respect to major Latin American countries' interest in quickly ending the civil wars in Central America despite initial U.S. resistance. With the end of the Cold War and the hemispheric consensus that followed regarding adherence to free-market economic policies and representative democracy, those fissures were papered over until they could no longer be hidden in the twenty-first century, as new governments appeared in Latin America with different ideological frameworks than those of Washington, DC.
4 Paradoxically, while complaining about the emergence of new regional bodies in Latin America and the Caribbean that exclude the United States, the U.S. government has proceeded to weaken the most established and ancient pan-American body, the OAS. Jorge Heine and Brigitte Weiffen, *21st Century Democracy Promotion in the Americas: Standing Up for the Polity* (New York: Routledge, 2015), 140.
5 The value of all Brazilian development aid, broadly defined, reached US$4 billion a year during Lula's second term in office—less than China but similar to generous

donors such as Sweden and Canada. "Brazil's Foreign-Aid Programme: Speak Softly and Carry a Blank Cheque," *The Economist,* July 17, 2010: 46.

6 Leticia Linn and Juan Carlos Raffo, "Brasil Acepta Pagar el Precio del Liderazgo Regional," *El Observador* (Montevideo), August 22, 2002: 1. In January 2002, Brazilian Agriculture Minister Marcus Vinicius Pratini de Moraes proposed that BNDES guarantee payments for a set period and up to a specified limit to Brazilian firms for their exports to Argentina, on the understanding that Argentina would later repay Brazil for the financing. "Brazil Minister Eyes Funding Exports to Argentina," *American Journal of Transportation,* January 14, 2002: 1.

7 Mark P. Sullivan, *Latin America and the Caribbean: Key Issues and Actions in the 114th Congress* (Washington, DC: Congressional Research Service, January 4, 2017), 4.

8 Christopher Sabatini, "Will Latin America Miss U.S. Hegemony?" *Journal of International Affairs,* Vol. 66, No. 2 (2013): 2.

9 Institute of the Americas, *Energy Transition in Chile: Progress and the Next Steps* (San Diego: Institute of the Americas, 2017), 1. Available at: www.iamericas.org/documents/energy/reports/Energy_Transitiion_Chile_Report.pdf Chile attracted US$9.2 billion in foreign investment in its energy sector between 2012 and 2016, mostly for large-scale commercial solar-based systems supplying the mining sector in the north of the country.

10 A more pessimistic point of view is offered by Immanuel Wallerstein, who argues that U.S. decline is structural and not merely the result of errors in policy committed by previous U.S. governments. Hence, it cannot be reversed, but only managed intelligently. Immanuel Wallerstein, *The Decline of American Power* (New York: The New Press, 2003), 306.

11 See, e.g., Michael J. Camilleri, "What Does Defeat at OAS Meeting Portend for U.S. Influence in the Americas?" *Latin America Goes Global,* June 23, 2017. Available at: http://latinamericagoesglobal.org/2017/06/defeat-oas-meeting-portend-us-influence-americas/. On June 21, 2017 the OAS General Assembly also failed to elect the highly qualified U.S. candidate to a seat on the Inter-American Commission on Human Rights. The only previous time the American candidate has been passed over was in 2003, when the Bush administration nominated someone with a very weak human rights record (at a time of strong concern throughout the Americas as to whether the U.S. was still committed to robust defense and enforcement of international human rights law).

Bibliography

American Journal of Transportation, "Brazil Minister Eyes Funding Exports to Argentina." January 14, 2002: 1.

Brinkley, Joel. "Iraq Outlook Looks Dim After U.S. Troop Pullout: Some Predict Another Brutal Dictatorship." *Politico,* February 27, 2012: 1.

Camilleri, Michael J. "What Does Defeat at OAS Meeting Portend for U.S. Influence in the Americas?" *Latin America Goes Global,* June 23, 2017. Accessed July 27, 2017: http://latinamericagoesglobal.org/2017/06/defeat-oas-meeting-portend-us-influence-americas/

Heine, Jorge and Brigitte Weiffen. *21st Century Democracy Promotion in the Americas: Standing Up for the Polity.* New York: Routledge, 2015.

Hennigan, W.J. "U.S. Military Escalation, Off the Radar: The Trump Administration has Stopped Disclosing the Number of Troops in Iraq and Syria." *Los Angeles Times,* March 30, 2017: 1.

Institute of the Americas, *Energy Transition in Chile: Progress and the Next Steps.* San Diego: Institute of the Americas, 2017, 1. Accessed August 1, 2017: www.iamericas.org/documents/energy/reports/Energy_Transitiion_Chile_Report.pdf

Linn, Leticia and Juan Carlos Raffo. "Brasil Acepta Pagar el Precio del Liderazgo Regional." *El Observador* (Montevideo), August 22, 2002: 1.

Sabatini, Christopher. "Will Latin America Miss U.S. Hegemony?" *Journal of International Affairs* Vol. 66, No. 2 (2013): 1–14.

Sullivan, Mark P. *Latin America and the Caribbean: Key Issues and Actions in the 114th Congress*. Washington, DC: Congressional Research Service, January 4, 2017.

The Economist, "Brazil's Foreign-Aid Programme: Speak Softly and Carry a Blank Cheque." July 17, 2010: 46.

Toro Hardy, Alfredo. *The World Turned Upside Down: The Complex Partnership between China and Latin America*. Singapore: World Scientific Publishing Company, 2013.

Wallerstein, Immanuel. *The Decline of American Power*. New York: The New Press, 2003.

Index

Made in the USA
Middletown, DE
11 January 2019